Mentalizing the Body

Mentalizing the Body brings together theory and practice with the latest neurobiological and developmental psychological findings to understand the relevance of the body in a wide range of mental disorders, especially personality and somatization disorders.

Ulrich Schultz-Venrath provides insight on individual bodily phenomena within psychotherapeutic treatments – experienced by patients as well as therapists – and focuses on the importance of the intentionality of bodily symptoms and how they can be integrated in the talking cure. *Mentalizing the Body* expands the work of Anthony Bateman and Peter Fonagy, adding the "body mode" in contrast to the popular concept of "embodied mentalizing." Promoting mentalizing in psychotherapy while taking the body into account helps not only patients with somatoform and eating disorders, but also those whose psychological complaints have a missing connection to the body. Schultz-Venrath provides detailed insight on the range of therapies and treatments available, from individual and group psychotherapies to body, art, and music therapy, with clinical case studies and diagrams throughout.

Mentalizing the Body will be of great interest to practitioners and researchers – from psychoanalysts and psychotherapists to psychiatrists and psychologists seeking to understand the mentalization model, and all healthcare professionals working with severe mental disorders.

Ulrich Schultz-Venrath, MD is Professor of Psychosomatic Medicine and Psychotherapy at the Faculty of Health, University of Witten/Herdecke. He is a neurologist (DGN), psychoanalyst (DPV, IPA), and training group analyst (D3G, EFPP, GASI), chair of the Institute of Group Analysis and Mentalizing in Groups (IGAM), and working in private practice in Cologne, Germany.

Mentalizing the Body

Integrating Body and Mind
in Psychotherapy

Ulrich Schultz-Venrath

LONDON AND NEW YORK

Designed cover image: Getty | Klaus Vedfelt

First published in English 2024
by Routledge
4 Park Square, Milton Park, Abingdon, Oxon OX14 4RN

and by Routledge
605 Third Avenue, New York, NY 10158

Routledge is an imprint of the Taylor & Francis Group, an informa business

© 2024 Ulrich Schultz-Venrath

The right of Ulrich Schultz-Venrath to be identified as author of this work has been asserted in accordance with sections 77 and 78 of the Copyright, Designs and Patents Act 1988.

All rights reserved. No part of this book may be reprinted or reproduced or utilised in any form or by any electronic, mechanical, or other means, now known or hereafter invented, including photocopying and recording, or in any information storage or retrieval system, without permission in writing from the publishers.

Trademark notice: Product or corporate names may be trademarks or registered trademarks, and are used only for identification and explanation without intent to infringe.

© 2021 Klett-Cotta – J.G. Cotta'sche Buchhandlung Nachfolger GmbH, Stuttgart

British Library Cataloguing-in-Publication Data
A catalogue record for this book is available from the British Library

ISBN: 978-1-032-38459-7 (hbk)
ISBN: 978-1-032-38486-3 (pbk)
ISBN: 978-1-003-34514-5 (ebk)

DOI: 10.4324/9781003345145

Typeset in Gill Sans Nova
by Apex CoVantage, LLC

Contents

Acknowledgments — vii

1 **Introduction to a Complex Theme** — 1
 1.1 *Affects, Brain, and Body: The Development of An Affective Self* 8
 1.2 *Attachment and the Development of a Mentalizing Self* 21
 1.3 *On the Beginnings of the Mentalization Model* 29
 1.4 *The Role of the Body in the Mentalization Model* 40
 1.5 *Personality Disorders Without a Body?* 45

2 **The Body and Its Relationship With Physicians and Psychotherapists** — 49
 2.1 *Mentalizing in the Medical History, the Initial Interview, and the First Contact* 56
 2.2 *The Disappearing Body in Online Video Therapies* 70

3 **The Discovery of the Body in Early Psychosomatics** — 74
 3.1 *Trauma as a Transdiagnostic Affect-Regulation Disorder* 82
 3.2 *The Paris School of Psychosomatics – The Pioneer of the Mentalization Model* 87
 3.3 *Alexithymia and/or Autism Spectrum Disorder (ASD)?* 90
 3.4 *The Diagnostic Dilemma* 95
 3.5 *Body-Mode as a Mass Phenomenon* 102

4 Bodily or Mental States? On the Development of a Mentalizing Self — 105
4.1 Intersubjective Developmental Conditions for a Body-Self *113*
4.2 Body-Mode or Embodied Mentalizing? *117*
4.3 When the Psychotherapist's Body "Goes on Strike" or "Speaks" *123*
4.4 Dimensions of Mentalizing in Somatoform Stress Disorders *126*

5 Somatizing or Mentalizing? — 129
5.1 Pre-mentalizing Modes *130*

6 Mentalization Enhancement Therapy — 143
6.1 Mentalization in Patients with Somatoform Disorders/ Somatic Symptom Disorders (SSD) *144*
6.2 Interactions That Do Not Promote Mentalization *155*
6.3 Mentalizing in Group Therapies for SSD Patients *156*
6.4 How Do Psychotherapists Learn to Mentalize? *162*

References — *165*
Index — *196*

Acknowledgments

A book such as this one has many "mothers," many "fathers," many "grandparents," and indeed many "children." I could not have written this volume without the many educational and insightful encounters I had with my patients. Nor would it have been possible without the many teachers and mentors I had the pleasure of working under during my time in the Neurology Department of the Free University of Berlin, and without the wonderful colleagues and students I met at the University of Witten/Herdecke. I took particular pleasure in participating in the first Research Summer School Training in 1995 at the University College of London, at the invitation of Peter Fonagy; other participants included Horst Kächele, Erhard Mergenthaler, Folkert Beenen, and Bob Emde, who kindled a fire of interest in more than 400 young psychoanalysts that psychoanalysis can indeed be connected to empirical research. I am especially thankful to Peter Fonagy and Wilma Bucci, the latter of whom mentored my research project at the time about magical thinking, for the many suggestions they sent my way as clinicians.

Every individual is equally part of a learning "organization." As Head Physician of the Clinic of Psychiatry, Psychotherapy, and Psychosomatics at the EVK Bergisch Gladbach, I profited immensely from working with my Senior Physicians Zeynep Atik, Max Aly, Ingmar Niecke, and Gernot Holtz; with the social therapists Beatrix Rey und Ansgar Cordes; and particularly with my concentrative movement (KBT), dance, and breath therapists Ute Oessenich-Lücke, Astrid Fiedler, Regina Hömberg, and Claudia Krüger. I obtained special insights into process and outcome research through working with my research team of Tanja Brand, Dagmar Hecke, Sarah Fuhrländer, Annekatrin Vetter, and Johannes Pries. I am particularly grateful to my long-standing editor, advisor, and supporter of the German series "Mentalisieren in Klinik und Praxis," Heinz Beyer, as well as Oliver Eller, who edited this and other volumes before it.

A special word of thanks to the many critical readers of this manuscript: Peter Döring, Peter Rottländer, Eva Heinle-Schneider, Maria Teresa Diez Grieser, Helga Felsberger, Daniela Fuchs, Ludger M. Hermanns, Edna Baumblatt-Hermanns, and Rolf Haubl. My wife, Dorothee, a concentrative movement therapist (KBT), and my daughters Lenka, Tabea, and Laetitia have, each in their own special way, helped and supported this venture with humor and critical understanding. In an almost literal sense, they had my back in the sense of a *body-mode*.

Last but not least, I would like to thank Joseph Smith very much for the thorough translation of the revised and expanded German version.

Chapter 1

Introduction to a Complex Theme

Nothing is so familiar and simultaneously so unfamiliar as our own body. This is true especially when we lose control over our body and have yet to regain that lost control: Our body speaks to us. You can love your body, hate it, be ashamed of it, be proud of it, nurture it, damage it, abuse it – like an object. The body is where our affects dwell and emerge from; where our basal needs, instincts, and desires are localized; it's the resonance chamber of our selves, our "we," and of all the groups we feel attached to or excluded from. Without our body, with all its affects and emotions, there would be no split-off feeling, no intersubjective life, no communicative exchange – indeed no thoughts at all. Yet the body was not always seen that way apart from a few exceptions.

The Indo-Germanic languages possess several different expressions that refer particularly to somatic experiences, or sometimes to individual organs, to idiomatically describe our emotions, psychosocial phenomena, and strains. For example, "turn a blind eye," "with a heavy heart," "bundle of nerves," "hole in my gut," "gets under my skin," "pain in the neck," "dagger to the heart." Most of these expressions refer to sensual experiences we have all had in life: To "sense" comes from the Latin *sensus*, meaning "sensation, feeling" but also "understanding." A "feeling" is also something we actively do, by directing our attention to our inner workings (Fiedler et al., 2011). To "perceive" something means to "thoroughly grasp," a complex sensual event of transforming what we "sense" into a physical expression. If you listen carefully to what someone is telling you, you will notice a mixture of body language and spoken language, whereby the words stand in for physical processes as well as emotional impulses. We humans can feel and be felt both physically and emotionally – even if it is not always completely clear how that occurs (e.g., "I was touched by your story . . . ," "It really moved me to hear . . . ," "It just gets under my skin when . . .").

If you look at all the words humans use to describe how they "feel," you notice a certain lack of precision: It often remains unclear whether we are dealing with sensual-physical perceptions, with feelings (emotions, affects), with thoughts (projections, wishes), or with behavioral impulses. How the words necessary to describe our subjective bodily perceptions came to be remains one of the mysteries we address later in more detail. Ideally, a patient and their therapist possess a rather well-differentiated vocabulary to characterize such subjective perceptions, affects, and emotions. Using language can help to differentiate our subjective sensations, yet the act of speaking must necessarily consider the "preverbal" state that precedes every word spoken. "The preverbal is called a 'pre,' a 'not-yet,' a 'not-whole' of a signifying process that concludes itself in the word culminative" (Leikert, 2019b, p. 34). Psychotherapists would be well advised to use their own vocabulary to express subtle differences and to attend to and apply these terms critically in therapy, particularly when dealing with emotional and preverbal states. For that is where mentalizing begins and wherever more complex terms and ideas about emotional and physical phenomena are "created" (Plassmann, 2019b, p. 6).

The term "mentalizing" is considered the ability to understand oneself and others regarding inner mental states closely connected to bodily perceptions. Bodily perceptions are situational, intersubjective, and dependent on the person in question; they consist of proprioception, exteroception, and interoception. *Proprioception* describes the perception of one's own location and movement in space, based on the stimuli emerging from our inner body and neuromuscular spindles. *Exteroception* (from the Latin exter "outward" + recipere "to assume") describes external perception, such as what the exterior surface of our body perceives ("haptic perception"). *Interoception* is the perception we have of our own bodily organs.

Fonagy (1991) was the first to define the human ability to perceive both conscious and unconscious mental states in oneself and others – the ability to mentalize. Later, mentalizing came to mean a more or less preconscious, imaginative ability to intentionally exchange so-called terms of mental states (thoughts, feelings, convictions, desires). Only then does the individual truly understand, both implicitly and explicitly, their own actions and those of others as meaningful. The riddle of how exactly the mentalizing of bodily perceptions proceeds, ending in the development of an "embodied" self that can feel and speak "mentalized," is presently not completely understood. Two very opposite models – the simulation theory and the theory-theory – presently dominate the scene: The former assumes that humans can simulate the experiences of other human beings; that they use mirror neurons and common sensory-affective circuitry and shared feelings to develop such an understanding of others (Gallese & Caruana, 2016). The latter has more physical leanings and assumes that we human beings cognitively derive "rules" by observing the social structures around us and use them to construct theoretical convictions and purposes (Baron-Cohen et al., 1985).

Even if it is now accepted that a certain level of mentalizing precedes the development of language, we still don't know whether the way a mother or a father comes to understand the inner workings of their child – how they turn that into a physical experience and communicate it "prelinguistically . . . long before the appearance of the first word" (Bateman & Fonagy, 2019, p. 7) – is a truly "embodied" form of mentalizing.

Historically speaking, the English term "mentalization" was originally mentioned in connection with physical processes. In 1888, the neurologist James

Leonard Corning introduced the term "mentalization" in a paper he wrote on headache and neuralgia, quoting a certain Hammond who had carried out a series of precise urine analyses to discover the composition of urine under "increased mentalization." He reported that an increase in mental effort increased the amount of urine secreted (Corning, 1888 [2018], p. 196). It further surprises that the British dermatologist, psychiatrist, psychoanalyst, and group therapist Dennis Geoffrey Brown (1928–2004), used the term mentalization as early as 1985 – and thus long before the appearance of the mentalization model – in a contribution titled "The Psychosoma and the Group":

> The *meaning* of physical symptoms and expressions needs to be discovered, and at the most primitive ("true" psychosomatic, or protomental) level *created*, for mentalisation to bypass, reverse, or better still, grow out of somatization. As I say sometimes to patients, we need to grow *down* as well as up. This calls for *trust on both sides*, that anxiety, pain, helplessness and rage can be tolerated. Whether in group or individual therapy, we must be able to facilitate communication at deeper, primitive levels, and ultimately translate them into words. We have to dare to go to levels where it is hot, as Foulkes put it.
> (Brown, 1985, 2006b, p. 21)

Affects and emotions play a major role in all mental and psychosomatic disorders. The complaints of patients with so-called somatic symptom disorders or somatization disorders are multifaceted and difficult to decipher. The history of psychosomatics is full of somatoform disorders that have stumped both physicians and psychotherapists. The reason may lie in the fact that symptoms revealed through body language are hard to address using only differential linguistic methods. Yet, this loss of differentiation may sometimes also be traced back to the physicians themselves, who employ wild descriptions to diagnose the broad family of anxiety disorders instead of following sound scientific procedures. They are witness to the breakdown of the intersubjective exchange at a moment when the patient and the therapist should have been busy finding a "new" common language – which is necessary if they are to use their common (!) understanding to enact change, namely, a transformation of the symptoms. Numerous case studies reveal how physicians and psychotherapists, as part of the therapeutic relationship, use empathy, vigilance, challenging interactions, and conscious restraint to influence the course of the disorder – for better or for worse.

Affects and emotions are not only expressed physically but are themselves physiological expressions: Every emotion is accompanied by a physiological change; for example, fear is paired with palpitation, anger with an increased heart rate and blood pressure. Phenomena of this nature have been known since the work of Franz Alexander, one of the earliest pioneers of psychosomatic medicine, and belong to normal human life (Alexander, 1948). They only become disorders when there are too many or too few affects and emotions over a longer time; when they assume a certain dominance or rigidity in the life of the patient, what we now call emotional dysregulation. This is true especially for the negative affects, which presumably stem from our evolutionary survival instincts and have embedded themselves deeply in our memory. Happiness is nice to have, but it contributes precious little to extending our life, much unlike fear and disgust, two affects that warn us of imminent dangers. The confrontation with persistent and "difficult" affects is one of the central challenges to any therapist (Plassmann, 2019a).

This volume was originally titled "Mentalizing Somatic Symptom Disorders." However, while writing I realized that the diagnosis of a somatic symptom disorder is as broad a term as the Grand Canyon. Furthermore, many mental disorders sometimes occur "only" with temporary, more often though with long-term, transdiagnostic somatic symptoms. Medical histories are much like literature genres: Some are short stories, some are long novels. Thus, we can categorize psychosomatic disorders as those with clearly metaphoric/symbolic meaning and those in which cumulative stress has led to a truly functional disorder. Hence, the body is simultaneously the source and the projection screen for all sorts of mentalization disorders – even for organic diseases such as Parkinson's, myasthenia, multiple sclerosis, radicular compression syndrome, and many other syndromes, in which, because of certain transference events, the symptoms suddenly improve or disappear (Kütemeyer & Schultz-Venrath, 1997).

This book feeds off the over 40-year experience gathered with psychosomatic medicine, which began with a group of inquisitive and creative physicians at the Neurological Clinic of the Free University of Berlin, all of whom were devoted to the bio-psycho-social model of the Heidelberg School of Neurology. My own mentor, Dieter Janz, a master at gathering a medical history who amazed and "infected" his students with his methods, was also the Editor of the Collected Works of his mentor, Viktor von Weizsäcker. The latter once said, "We begin not with knowledge but with a question" (von Weizsäcker, 1926). This paved my way much later to the mentalization model of Peter Fonagy and Anthony Bateman. Connecting diagnostic and therapeutic competence with state-of-the-art research results that today are blooming in the mentalization model as a work in progress – that is what this book is about.

Whereas the bio-psycho-social model of psychosomatics presently represents the most comprehensive model of disease with a polypragmatic treatment concept in the absence of an evaluation (Egle et al., 2020), the mentalization model was born out of the lack of effective psychotherapeutic methods to deal with borderline personality disorders (Bateman & Fonagy, 2008). In the meantime, modifications of the MBT concept have been successfully applied to many different mental and psychosomatic disorders. Yet, a true scientific exchange with the bio-psycho-social model and the integration of the two remain elusive and await resolution.

For psychosomatics and even more so for psychiatry in general, the mentalization model represents a future-oriented project that serves to integrate the various disciplines of the neurosciences, cognitive psychology, and the more modern approaches to psychoanalysis under the aegis of treatment. We need both a better understanding and a common and increasingly differentiated vocabulary if we want to understand the complex processes of retreating into the body or persevering in the body. Mentalizing is the magical word, an important code word, since it consists of the ability to properly attribute inner states (feelings, thoughts, intentions, motives) to the behavior of both oneself and others.

Some have tried to differentiate between emotional and cognitive mentalization, whereby the former deals with the body and its sensations, the latter with a form of mentalization oriented toward the cognitive, meaning it can recognize the inner states of others quite well but fails to feel them. We often meet with such phenomena in patients with somatic symptom disorders, depersonalization, borderline, and antisocial personality disorders. Mentalizing as a process (and not mentalization as a noun) has found its way into other psychotherapies and proved to be effective, even when most protagonists of the various techniques didn't plan it that way.

The adage of Edward Weiss from 1947, namely, that psychosomatics does not mean doing less research on the body but rather more research on the psyche, was long the gold standard of the psychosomatics scientific community. Not a few of the exponents of psychosomatic medicine adhered to this postulate and forgot about the body – despite their pretense. More unconsciously than consciously they hitched their wagon to Freud, who was a lifelong skeptic about – if not a declared opponent to – psychoanalytical psychosomatics (Schultz-Venrath, 1995). Once psychosomatic medicine became an established subject, psychosomatic relations were increasingly "psychologized" in psychometric tests, thus becoming less somatic and less clinically relevant. It was easier to gain a medical understanding by emphasizing the "soma" as a biological entity, losing in the process any understanding of the libidinal-erotic, aggressive, or narcissistic body.

When dealing with the body, in addition to a secure attachment, the development of the regulation of affects and emotions plays a central role in the development of one's (physical) self – and survival. A child is not a tabula rasa; rather, like all living beings, it is born with a series of congenital and protomental needs. Today, we like to think that a newborn enters the world with a bundle of intrauterine experiences that have ingrained themselves in their procedural memory as a sort of implicit relationship knowledge and define their postnatal life. The ability of a newborn to differentiate the smell and voice of their mother from that of others (DeCasper & Fiver, 1980), to imitate facial expressions and gestures (Meltzoff & Moore, 1977), and to be soothed by music heard in the womb are all essential proof of prenatal and perinatal learning and relationship processes.

Freud's notion of the three psychosexual developmental steps – "oral," "anal," and "genital" – refers to the dominance of somatic needs in early childhood which serve to organize mental structures. However, in the meantime, the very somatic nature of these terms, which mark the phases of libido, has been lost because of their largely metapsychological application. Modern analytical developmental psychology no longer remembers that the successive nature of Freud's model of erogenous zones served as a model for structuring *affective* bodily experiences. We see in this in a pretty little story Szekely tells (1962, p. 301):

> A child not quite 2 years old is looking out of the window. Outside it is snowing, and a bird is hopping about on the window-sill picking up breadcrumbs. The child watches all this with interest. Suddenly the bird drops something. The child goes over and sees a white speck in the snow. "Birdie do big," calls out the child. There is nothing very remarkable in this. But the question arises: How does the child discover or know what the bird has done?

He wonders how the child knows that the bird has defecated.

> The product, the bird's faeces, resemble snow, since it is white, and not the child's own product, which is brown. Moreover, the child has never seen the act of defecation, and consequently has no visual memory-trace to draw upon. He has only somatic and coenesthetic memory-traces of defecation, for the child has experienced it only as a pleasurable bodily process in himself, and not as a visual event. How, then, did he identify what he saw?

Of course, the analytical observer immediately understands the anal reference as how the child cognitively views the world, although we are in fact dealing with a body–mind organization (cf. Chapter 4).

Similarly, the concept of drives "as a term denoting the border between the mental and the somatic" (Freud, 1915c, p. 214) fails to acknowledge how the body serves as a basis for mental functions in psychoanalysis. Basic emotions are based on instinctive behaviors, which in turn may be traced back to innate action impulses (such as the newborn's search for the mother's nipple). These impulses are employed to fulfill the respective specific needs (such as searching, fleeing, attacking), yet to this day there is no broad agreement about the type and number of such innate needs.

The unloved, hated, pained body of the patient often plays a greater role in the physical countertransference during psychotherapy than the therapist would like to admit, for example, when it "brings tears to my eyes" or "makes me choke up." *How* the therapist listens to the body and its stories (in this we largely follow Alessandra Lemma (2014)) is highly influenced by their own subjectivity, that is, their own generally tabooed experiences with their body, its affects, and emotions as well as the theoretical and technical conclusions and assumptions derived from those experiences. Presumably, that also determines what theory they adhere to as part of their training and how they apply the interventions it foresees. Whether candidates and training analysts truly delve into their own somatic sensations as part of the training analysis and training therapy is at the least questionable in light of the mutual tabooed nature of the matter. This may also be seen in the difficulty of doing research into the supervision of psychotherapeutic training candidates (Grünewald-Zemsch, 2019).

In addition to the continuing separation of body and soul in psychoanalysis (and the methods derived from it), in recent years we have observed a revival of interest in somatic events: The body is being "rediscovered," especially because of the recent profound neuroscientific findings. This is reflected in a series of publications concerning the body that suggest the need for greater inquiry into the embodied olfactory, visual, auditory, and haptic resources. Bodily resonance refers to both how interoceptive signals are experienced as well as to the interaction with the therapist. Mimicry, gestures, postures, prosody, and respiratory motion are all decisive in how the other person is emotionally perceived. Perception and affective assessment have a corporeal component and influence one's counterpart in a sort of circular flow of reciprocal impact, culminating in a mutual physical resonance.

It's worthwhile here to take a more exact philosophical approach: "Resonance" is not just a metaphor for a certain experience of an emotional state; it is also a type of relationship determined by four components: touch (affection – where the affects are active), self-efficacy (feedback), adaptation (transformation), and unavailability (since one cannot willfully establish resonance) (Rosa, 2019, p. 38f.). "A smile on the face of a loved one *may* turn hard and icy, the purring of the cat *may* cease, one's favorite music *may* leave us unmoved, the forest or the ocean *may* deny us any resonance" (Rosa, 2016, p. 295).

From the perspective of the mentalization model, it seems wise for the patient and the therapist to search together for the kind of feeling and meaning of a physical symptom that – inasmuch as it existed at all previously – may go missing along with the resonance. Paying proper, meaningful tribute to a symptom that does not pit the body against language fosters an otherwise sometimes marginal treatment motivation and strengthens the working alliance. This occurs when the therapist, through acceptance and encouragement, directs attention to the symptom. Everyone knows that there's nothing more hurtful – and sometimes more healing – than the spoken word. On the one hand, there is no contradiction between speaking and body (Buchholz, 2014, p. 113). Bodily presence emerges in language, or better said: in speaking and in conversation accompanied by gestures and mimicry. On the other hand, the body constantly sends out messages (e.g., about early traumas) that those affected cannot express themselves in any other way. The SARS-CoV-2 pandemic with its many lockdown-induced online therapy sessions made clear to psychotherapists that video meetings fracture the line between body and speech, ultimately leading to disembodiment (Weinberg & Rolnik, 2020) – while also demonstrating how important physical presence is if therapeutic intervention is to be successful. The psychoanalytic community still fails to reflect that the couch setting is essentially a kind of disembodiment that is primarily focused on listening and associative and imaginative activity. Or as Fonagy (2022, p. 208) says,

> the potentially uncomfortable implication for psychoanalysis of this idea [of MBT, USV] is that the aim of therapy is not deepening specific understandings, but rather the capacity for understanding, almost regardless of the specific unconscious conflicts which may bring a patient into treatment. In other words, the "medium is the message."

1.1 Affects, Brain, and Body: The Development of An Affective Self

> This chapter explores the significance of touch and physical interactions in human development and well-being. It emphasizes the importance of early attachment experiences through touch and sweet sounds, highlighting how newborns rely on physical contact to regulate various bodily functions. It explores various aspects of touch, ranging from early attachment experiences to cultural practices, and emphasizes the interplay between the body and the mind in shaping our experiences and perceptions, developing an affective self.

The initial interactions one has with other human beings occur while still in the womb, and at the latest upon birth, (ideally) through loving touch and sweet sounds. A newborn is rhythmically and melodically caressed and cuddled by its primary caregiver(s), generally the parents, and in recent decades this knowledge has been able to transform even the most sterile forms of obstetrics (Böhme, 2019). Touch is so essential because the newborn can barely see beyond the first 30 cm. Immediately after being born, the newborn stabilizes its breathing, body temperature, pH balance, and even its blood-sugar level exclusively through skin contact (Winberg, 2005). Further, touch during breastfeeding triggers the excretion of oxytocin, a well-known attachment hormone. But mothers, too, profit from the early contact with their babies, which in turn allows them to breastfeed better and longer.

Touch is important throughout life. If a child falls and skins their knee, the parents take the child in their arms, quickly look after the wound, and rub the bruise. If a friend is in mourning, we tend to take their hand, put an arm around their shoulder, or hug them. If we like someone, we want to touch them. Touch between and among humans thus plays a special role: It is not just a tactile affair but is an event controlled by special nerves, the so-called c-fibers, which pass the feeling on to the insula of the brain. Becoming aware of touch takes place not just in the somatosensory cortex, but also in parts of the prefrontal cortex and the posterior parietal lobe, which we now know is the seat of awareness and body perception. Thus, the brain network responsible for the perception of tactile sensations is much more complex than previously thought (Rullmann et al., 2019). In the meantime, Elias and co-workers (2023) found the relevance of special touch neurons, which are required for sexual receptivity and sufficient to induce dopamine release in the brain. Switching off these neurons caused female mice to reject males with whom they would normally have tried to mate. Their findings establish a special skin-to-brain circuit encoding the rewarding quality of social touch.

How a child develops as a subject greatly depends on the quality of the physical interactions they have with their caretaker(s). As adults, children who have been humiliated, beaten, or sexually abused suffer more from major mental disorders or developmental retardation than do their contemporaries who were spared such experiences in their younger years. This leads to the question of what the basic reasons are for such vulnerability and whether they are connected to a modified perception of touch. Tactile sensations influence brain development, provide a sense of one's own body, and serve as well to regulate stress. Put differently, do experiences of violence in early childhood lead to a permanent shift in how social stimuli are perceived and interpreted?

During the recent Covid-19 pandemic, one could observe the effects of social and physical distancing: The desire for intimate contact became ever greater the longer the necessity for social distancing lasted. The problem is not the total amount of supportive touching people remember having experienced during childhood, but rather the individual differences in the type of attachment style they experience: "the more anxiously attached a person is, the more touch was craved during COVID-19 and the more avoidantly attached a person is, the less they craved for touch in this period."[1]

Independent of such occurrences, our Western culture has developed a touching (sub)culture, perhaps as an answer to an ever more digitalized, disembodied world. Proof thereof may be found in the many yoga studios, massage parlors, tantra centers, cuddle parties, and animal-based psychotherapies that have blossomed.

Up to the 20th century, affectionate touch was considered part of the so-called common feeling (*sensus communis*), a familiar part of both the psychological and physiological vocabulary, comprising all sensual perceptions that have their origin within the organism and are not part of the usual five senses. Today, this term has been replaced by more specialized terms such as body scheme, body image, and body self (Fuchs, 1995). Whereas *body scheme* refers to the constitution of the body, *body image* has more to do with the role of the intersubjective context in which the body develops. Body image consists of a "system of perceptions, attitudes and beliefs relating to one's own body" (Gallagher, 2005, p. 24). The mentalization model can make an important contribution to our understanding of the developmental factors and fantasies that accompany the inner representation of the body (= body image) (Lemma, 2014, p. 5), which is distinguished from the innate body schema. If resonance and reciprocity go missing in the early relationship between a baby and their primary caretaker(s), the child develops neither representations nor a stable body image. The consequence: In later years, traumatic experiences lead to resomatization, something Dennis Brown (2006a, p. 52) called "dementalization."

Although we may seem convinced of what we are feeling, it is not unusual that in fact our feelings are not that secure, as they depend on the respective situation or how much stress we are under. Feeling nothing at all, on the other hand, may point to a certain sort of psychopathology – but not necessarily. "The fact that we do not always know what we feel is important, as it is vastly underestimated in contemporary accounts of emotion" (Jurist, 2018, p. 9). One prerequisite for being able to recognize and apply experiences from the earliest years in psychotherapy is the ability to sense somatic sensations that emerge as affects and develop them into emotions as part of a conscious process.

The absence of empathy – in addition to feelings of hate – results from the absence of affect regulation in a teleological mode, a frequent precondition to aggressive impulse breakthroughs, leading at worst to homicide. The ability to empathize demands a sufficient level of development of the basic five senses (hearing, smelling, tasting, seeing, feeling), which are complemented by other sensual competencies, such as temperature (thermoreception), pain (nociception), balance (vestibular sense), depth (proprioception), and several interoceptions (e.g., thirst, hunger, and blood-pressure regulation), which function as detectors or sensors. Without these "senses" – Leikert (2019a) rightly speaks of a sensual self – our perception would be very limited indeed. People whose anxiety symptoms trigger a true catastrophe (such as having a heart attack and the feeling of impending death) cannot suppress the feeling during an acute attack. There is a good cause to conclude that such a situation is based on unstable representation experiences in their procedural memory, formed either from an exaggerated and overwhelmed (or vice versa: completely missing) mirroring of childish emotions caused by early caretakers. This in turn leads to neurobiologically disrupted representational mapping (Fonagy et al., 2002 [2004], p. 34). When representations are absent or fail to be linked together, this emerges as a type of pre-or non-mentalizing mode (cf. Chapter 5.1). Then, only dedicated therapeutic interactions accompanied by congruent mirroring processes can establish a mentalizing and ultimately reflective mode. The body-mode originally put forth by Diez Grieser and Müller (2018) and expanded on by the author is presently not included in the mentalization model. The term "embodied mentalizing" appears for the first time in a chapter on eating disorders by Skarderud and Fonagy (2012, p. 359) and is defined in the glossary as follows: "in which the body is used to fill in moments of mentalizing failure. The term is elaborated to cover mental states related to a person's physical being, including perceptions and cognitions about bodily function and sensorimotor perception" (p. 513). But the term "embodied mentalizing" now in use in the mentalization model does not accurately reflect the phenomena captured in the body-mode: Mentalizing does not (yet) take place in the body-mode or, as Jurist (2022, p. 200) formulates: "The body is not a receptable for unwanted mental life; it informs and supports mental life." Independent of the type of pre-mentalizing mode, certain sensory perceptions cannot be meaningfully applied to interpersonal homeostasis on their own if stable representations are missing to structure sensory experiences.

The development of a body-self cannot proceed without the development of stable neuronal structures in the brain. Living systems consist of open, circular feedback loops in which the system components interact reciprocally – either horizontally or vertically. We already know that the regulation of the immune system, like the regulation of the hormonal and nervous systems, does not occur in isolation but rather in the form of reciprocal influence (Federschmidt, 2017). Immune cells have receptors for both neuropeptides (neurotransmitters) and hormones. Vice versa, the nerve cells have receptors for the transmitters of the immune system, along with the special role played by cytokines. All immunological organs are connected to the fibers of the nervous system. Like the hormones, the transmitters of the nervous system influence the central nervous system and with it our mental health.

Against the background of these bio-psycho-social linkages, the body mirrors the psyche, and the psyche mirrors the body. That is how the hormones in a mother–child dyad interact as well, including their blood-sugar and adrenaline levels, their smiles, their gestures – and their emotions. That is what Winnicott (1952 [1958], p. 99) in his now-famous expression tried to formulate: "There is no such thing as a baby, but only a mother-and-baby unit," which has opened the way to the further understanding that there is no such thing as a mother-and-baby unit extra-context, outside of the triangular context including the father. But it was also Winnicott who attempted to "think of the developing individual, starting at the beginning" *without opposing the mental and the physical*.

> Here is a body, and the psyche and the soma are not to be distinguished except according to the direction from which one is looking. One can look at the developing body or at the developing psyche. I suppose the word psyche here means the imaginative elaboration of somatic parts, feelings, and functions, that is, of physical aliveness.
> (Winnicott, 1949 [2014], p. 244)[2]

Today, the brain is considered an active organ. In the sense of being a predictive brain, it can generate predictions and hypotheses based on sensations (= expectations), which are not limited to reactions to stimuli. It can predict physiological needs, and it can even try to fulfill those needs before the body calls for them (e.g., if your blood pressure were to adapt only after coming to a stop, you would faint). Energetically speaking, that is clearly a more economical solution and serves to adapt to challenges ("allostasis").

Vice versa, individual influences from early childhood ("imprints") and adolescence play a major role in the form of expectations. Participants in experiments report that they experience less pain if the expectation of pain is lower than the actual stimulus. Put differently, if you expect intensive pain, then the subsequent perception is much greater, something that is pronounced especially among anxious people (Paulus & Stein, 2010); also, the side effects of antidepressant medication, such as frequency, intensity, and impairment, over time were more strongly associated with increases in depressive symptoms for patients with panic disorder compared to those without panic disorder (Shankman et al., 2017). It is presumed that this effect stems from a heightened interoceptive awareness of changes in their body, which means such patients are at higher risk than those without an anxiety disorder. Whether interoception is more or less developed appears to depend on the attachment style and the attachment representations. Discrepancies between the expected inner state and the inner state that is actually experienced may precipitate a whole spectrum of maladaptive behaviors that seek to modify the inner milieu to adapt it to the expected state.

When emotional-somatic feedback regarding a secure attachment goes missing over a longer period of time, the results can be dramatic: Romanian orphans who, near the end of the Ceausescu era, were forced to spend their first years of life in extreme emotional deprivation had adult brains that were on average 8.6% smaller than those of comparable British children who had been adopted shortly after birth (Mackes et al., 2020). These effects were found particularly in regions of the brain concerned with functions such as organization, motivation, integration of information, and memory. Interestingly, the right lower temporal lobe of the Romanian children was larger than that of the English children; one interpretation of this phenomenon is that the brain was trying to compensate for the negative effects of deprivation. Romanian children with the largest growth in this area showed low-level ADHD symptoms.

A neuronal and neuroendocrine deficit prevents proper mentalizing by dampening the ability to adaptively calibrate stressors and affects of all types (see Figure 1.1). In addition to impairments in the synaptic and dendritic connections in the brain, we find damage to the so-called stress system – the hypothalamic-pituitary-adrenal (HPA) axis – and to the entire affect control. Further, several neuropeptides are impaired, the best researched being oxytocin. Oxytocin, as it turns out, plays a major role in social belongingness, attachment behavior, social support, maternal behavior, and trust as well as protecting against stress and anxiety. Both emotional and sexual abuse during childhood results in, among other things, a reduced level of oxytocin in the brain fluid of adult women (Heim et al., 2009). All of which relates to problems of social class: Not only are persons with low and medium income exposed to more stressors, which in turn make them vulnerable to all sorts of somatic and psychosomatic disorders (including a propensity toward dissociation),

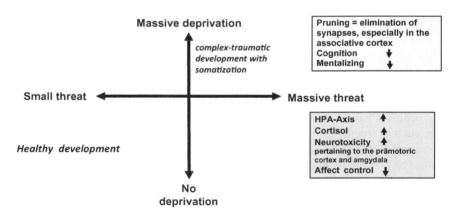

Figure 1.1 Early negative childhood experiences (deprivation and vulnerability) as dimensions of neural development, impaired affect regulation, and mentalization deficits.

Source: Schultz-Venrath 2021; modified acc. to McLaughlin et al. (2014).

their ability to counter their symptoms through mentalization is weakened (Goldstein et al., 2019; Purgato et al., 2018).

In animals, life in a monotonous and socially isolated environment leads to the constrained production of new neurons in their gyrus dentatus, part of the hippocampus. Similar results were found in adults who had spent over 14 months in the Antarctic on their own, including the reduction of the gray substance in the right dorsolateral prefrontal cortex (DLPFC), the left orbitofrontal cortex (OFC), and in the left parahippocampal gyrus of their brain (Stahn et al., 2019). In this respect, impairments of neuronal development due to experiences of deprivation and threat with effects on affect regulation should be properly addressed during psychotherapy as deficits with regard to any limitations of mentalizing (McLaughlin et al., 2014; Sheridan & McLaughlin, 2014).

Only in the new millennium has interest in the importance of affects and emotions for attachment style, the body, and the development of an affective self emerged in the psychotherapeutic scene. Nevertheless, we are "far from having exhaustively researched" the physical and corporeal processes, the role of physical self-awareness in countertransference, and a patient's "integration of somatic perceptions in the chain of associations" (Leikert, 2019b, p. 30). Affects and feelings were long deemed to be of little value in the scientific and clinical world; even as recently as 1987, children were being operated on without the use of anesthesia, on the assumption that they felt no pain (Coates, 2016).

Every newborn, every adult can feel anger – when they receive no response to their interests, when they are ignored, or when their wishes are thwarted. We have all experienced the feeling of being abandoned, of feeling sad. Many of us enjoy playing together with others. These affects are based on nonverbal, physical, and sensomotoric-neurobiological states of our organism in a particular situation. Every affect has its own intentionality, for example, when we spit out something revulsive or toxic or when we take joy in interactions with others. The idea of "intentionality" goes back to Franz Brentano, who suggested this term to describe mental phenomena (such as conviction, desire, perception, intention, etc.). "No physical phenomenon reveals something like that" (Brentano, 1874 [2008], p. 124f.). Independent of the discussion of whether or not affects are inborn, intersubjective, or both, they are quite definitely culturally embedded and change from time to time. For example, during the Middle Ages, it was not unusual to see people shamelessly defecate and urinate in public, wherever they happened to be at the moment. Then came the common public toilets.

Throughout modern European history, we can observe an ever-higher level of the threshold for shame and embarrassment, in correlation with the erection of individual toilets and washing rooms, witnesses to the new physical boundaries that ran parallel to the establishment of modern civilization (Elias, 1939; Gleichmann, 1979). We should recall that Freud's theory of phases (oral, anal, genital) was considerably influenced by these cultural developments. At the turn of the century, the smell of fecal matter in Vienna had reached a level such that it, like many other cities throughout Europe, decided to alleviate its misery by building a sewer system. Whereas earlier the farmers had come to town to haul off the remains and were even willing to pay for them, the city folk now had to pay for its removal. It wasn't much of a stretch for Freud to equate anality with money.

That is a good example of how affects are related to the situation and the person involved (Trevarthen, 1979, 1993), even if we do tend to divide up affects into those that process information (e.g., curiosity), regulate relationships (e.g., anger), or are self-reflexive (Wöller & Kruse, 2018, p. 138). They have two dimensions: one on the level of arousal, one with a "hedonic tone" (Hill, 2015), that is, they are accompanied by either negative or positive states of over-or underexcitation as well as feelings of desire or aversion, pleasure or displeasure. This is reminiscent of concepts from psychoanalysis, namely, that affects that appear later in life may be traced back to neonatal states of contentment or discontent (Krystal, 1978). Later this becomes connected to two very different lines of development: a child's nonverbal affective system and a verbal, desomatisized adult system: "The core of the self is thus nonverbal, unconscious, and embedded in the matrix of affect regulation" (Schore, 2007, p. 43).

The mentalization model rests on the theory of the formation of representations for affects based on the proper attachment to primary caretakers; it tries to integrate several other models that concentrate on the (largely three-part) development of an (affective) self, whether under consideration of findings from developmental psychology or not:

- *Daniel Stern*, who introduced his intersubjective self-concept and dynamic forms of vitality, expressed in terms such as "exploding," "pulsating," or "fading"; these describe more "how" (i.e., the manner) and the style, rather the "what" and "why," of affects. We are, he thought, unable to detect or imagine unseen mental activities such as thoughts, emotions, or even "will" without movement. For Stern, the development of representations or descriptions of an emerging self or "core self" is the central prerequisite for the structuring of a self (Stern, 1985 [1992]; Stern, 2010a). He differentiates between semantic and procedural representations, whereby the former enable symbolization via language and the latter serve as knowledge concerned with, say, *how* to ride a bicycle. Stern was one of the first researchers to declare that interpretations (sensu becoming aware of repressed drives and fantasies) did not suffice to induce change during psychoanalytic treatment (Stern, 2012, p. 52; Stern et al., 2010).
- *Antonio Damasio* presented a neuroscientific concept of four different levels of life regulation. Basal life regulation consists of simple, stereotypical patterns of reaction, among others the regulation of metabolism and reflexes. This forms the basis for emotions (corresponding to the affects) with their complex and stereotypical patterns of reaction, among others the primary (congenital) and secondary (social) emotions (e.g., embarrassment, guilt, pride) as well as background emotions (well-being or discomfort, calmness or tension). These, in turn, spawn feelings as sensory patterns, signaling pain, lust, and emotions, which then turn into ideas and, at the highest level, the higher thought processes (= consciousness) (Damasio, 1994, 1999). He preferred the term "somatic markers for inner

mental states" over "affects," which he thought were acquired through experience but could go missing because of neuronal or cultural damage. They are expressed – among other things – in tension, sighing, or cramping.
- *Jaak Pankse*pp suggested so-called basis affect systems, evolutionarily derived from the animal world, which gave our understanding of the development of a body self a new foundation. These systems stem from the subcortical brain structures of mammals, in the sense of a *primary process* (for which Pankse*pp chose to use the beginning letters of the seven affect systems). The *secondary process* is based on "inbuilt emotional learning mechanisms," and the *tertiary process* is represented by "emotional thoughts and deliberations that are so evident in human experience" (Pankse*pp, 1998; Pankse*pp & Biven, 2012, p. xi). That is where the representations develop that demonstrate a certain level of stability in children aged 3–4 years. But "according to Pankse*pp there are three types of affect: homeostatic and sensory ones (both of which are bodily) and emotional ones (which involve the body but cannot be described as 'bodily' in any simple case" (Solms, 2021, p. 101).
- *Sebastian Leikert* refers to Wilma Bucci, Jörg Scharff, Daniel Stern, and Ulla Volz-Boers. He assumes that the world of representations of the self consists of three different layers: the body self (corporality), imagination, and language, each of which has a different means of organization. As far as treatment is concerned, Stern and Leikert lie very close to the mentalization model, for which a "differentiation of the somatic self-awareness" is suggested for "detoxifying the body self" (Leikert, 2019a, p. 26f.). This largely corresponds to the differentiation of affect experience foreseen by the mentalization model.
- *Mark Solms* reflects on the emergence of consciousness, which is far more primitive than we often assume: It arises in brain regions that humans share with fishes:

The simplest forms of feelings – hunger, thirst, sleepiness, muscle fatigue, nausea, coldness, urinary urgency, the need to defecate, and the like – might not seem like affects, but that is what they are. What distinguishes affective states from other mental states is that they are hedonically *valenced*: they feel "good" or "bad."

(Solms, 2021, p. 96)

The valence registers "the *degree* and *direction* of homeostatic deviations from our biologically viable states" (Solms, 2022, p. 168), giving all affects and emotions a dimensionality. On the other side indicate all affects that they are governed by homeostasis led by the pleasure-unpleasure principle.

To date, the affect and emotion literature has failed to come to a consensus about what exactly affects, emotions, and feelings are – and how a self arises from them. In the cognitive neurosciences, emotion is defined as "free from affect" (LeDoux, 1996). Damasio, however, does not use the term "affect" at all, preferring to speak of the "primordial feelings" of the proto-self, which stores information via the body; this corresponds to the affect system. Damasio sees the prefrontal areas of the brain, home to most secondary feelings, as the decisive neuronal system for obtaining the signal apparatus of the somatic markers acquired by experience (Damasio, 1994). Contrary to those who prefer to differentiate feelings through the affect-labeled mirroring of important others, Damasio imagines a neuronal self with two categories of representations: topographically organized ones and acquired dispositional ones, which are responsible for memorable imaginations within the smaller neuron complexes – and thus form our memory. Although Damasio did not concern himself with findings from developmental psychology, he does defend an intersubjective position: Consciousness "is rooted in the representation of the body" (Damasio, 1999, p. 37) and can only develop "when the organism's representation devices exhibit a specific wordless knowledge – the knowledge that the organism's own state has been changed by an object – and when this knowledge occurs along with the salient representation of an object" (Damasio, 1999, p. 25).

Both in colloquial speech and scientific treatises, affects and emotions are often equally considered unconscious forms of expression, feelings are generally conscious and representations of affects and basal emotions. There have been many attempts to define emotions. In short, one can say: Whenever powerful waves of affects overflow us, we are experiencing an emotion; in turn, if similar, less powerful but still persistent feelings occur, we can speak of a mood (Panksepp, 1998, p. 47). An overwhelming number of emotions is normally accompanied by a disruption of the usual neuronal mechanisms connected to rationality and cognition. At that point, basal, phylogenetic, and ontogenetic older brain stem systems assume the control over our behavior.

As plausible as such a description may be, it fails to do justice to the complexity of how affects and emotions control personal features, personality, and the self – and vice versa, how the autobiographical self influences affects and emotions. It also cannot properly explain how emotions truly function and can trigger an individual's feelings, which are subsequently registered as such. A further conundrum lies in the fact that many terms describing emotions, such as love, shame, and anger, differ from one culture to another and from one language to another, even when translating the exact same terms.

In his monumental work *The Expression of Emotions in Humans and Animals* (Darwin, 1872 [1934]), Charles Darwin assumed that every culture experienced six basic emotions: joy, sadness, fear, anger, surprise, and disgust. Very detailed linguistic-statistical studies have shown that terms for emotion display both cultural variations *and* universal traits (Jackson et al., 2019). For example, people who speak Mwotlap on the island of Vanuatu in the South Pacific have no exactly equivalent expression for the English term *love*; the closest equivalent is the verb *tam*, meaning some form of empathy, largess, and hospitality. That fairly well describes the English idea of *neighborly love*, while failing to include *romantic love* (expressed in that language by a different verb for something like "need" – "I need you") (Matacic, 2019). Even in Western cultures, whose expressions for affects, emotions, and feelings have integrated little from other cultures, there is no clear uniformity. In this sense, affective experiences are highly subject to both the respective experiences and the possibility of dysregulation.

Ekman (2003) presumes there are seven basic affects: anger (rage), fear, sadness, joy, disgust, disdain, and surprise. Mentzos (2009), who studied newborns, also presumes seven affects, albeit not the same ones as Ekman: anger, fear, joy, despair, disgust, surprise, and interest. Such "social emotions" as shame, guilt, pride, and envy were considered complex affects. Panksepp and Biven (2012), in turn, assumed the presence of seven basal emotional systems that go back to the evolutionarily influenced neurobiological instinct systems: SEEKING (a general motivational and exploratory system), PLAY, CARE (loving caretaking behavior), LUST (sexual pleasure), FEAR, PANIC, RAGE[3] (see Table 1.1). Strangely enough, "disgust" is missing from this list.

Even if there is no overall scientific consensus on the makeup of the neurobiological affect systems (whether acquired congenitally or through learning mechanisms), the affect model proposed by Panksepp and Biven (2012) seems to be the best fitted one: In essence, awareness and affective consciousness develop in a stream of feelings from the somatic body-self, "emerging from deep brain functions that generate the physiological changes and instinctual behaviors of emotions." Thus, feeling is conceived of as a process largely shaped by instinct/drive systems that go far back in the evolution of human life. The basis for the human psyche is divided – seen from bottom to top – into primary, secondary, and tertiary processes, and only at the highest, the tertiary level of the human psyche at the top of the brain, "diverse cognitions and thoughts . . . allow us to reflect on what we have learned from our experiences," whereas learning and memory mechanisms can be explained as taking place on the secondary level through conditioning (Panksepp & Biven, 2012, p. 9). The cognitive neurosciences, inasmuch as they have turned their attention to affects at all, are content to deal solely with the

Table 1.1 A taxonomy of the primary affect system (Schultz-Venrath, 2021)

Descartes 1649	Ekman & Friesen 1972	Mertens & Krause 1993	Mentzos 2009	Panksepp & Biven 2012
		Interest	Interest	SEEKING
Astonishment	Surprise	Surprise	Surprise	
Joy	Joy / Happiness	Joy	Joy	PLAY (JOY)
Love				CARE (LOVE)
Desire				LUST (SEXUAL)
	Anxiety	Anxiety	Fear	FEAR
				PANIC (Separation Distress)
Hate	Anger / Rage	Rage	Rage	RAGE
			Disgust	

secondary level. Panksepp and Biven in fact are more interested in studying the lowest level, the "primary processes," which correspond mainly to the definition of the proto-self by Damasio – even though the SEEKING affect, present in every instance of interest and curiosity, highly correlates with Freud's understanding of "libido."

A central task of psychosocial development lies in satisfying our needs. We learn not for the sake of learning, but to establish optimal action plans that can fulfill our needs in the respective environment. That is exactly what Freud meant by "ego development." A baby begins by activating its primary affect-drive system SEEKING (curiosity), a sort of motivational system for various types of goals: the libido of life. That demands enthusiasm and positive vitality toward one's own mental health. Such a system is evolutionarily inborn and generally remains active throughout life and later enables us to seek out our basic survivalist needs, such as water, sustenance, safe accommodation, or a partner. Via the dopamine system, this system corresponds to the basal reward system of our brain. If the SEEKING system is chronically underactive, feelings of depression arise, often expressed as the result of repeated frustrations or in the relinquishment of addictive behavior (e.g., addiction to amphetamines or cocaine).

Because we want to find sexual partners, we indulge in the LUST/PLEASURE drive. PLAY is – despite Winnicott – likely the least-known affect in the psychodynamic world of affects. PLAY is a very primordial activity; preconscious, preverbal, the product of ancient biological structures that existed long before consciousness and the ability to communicate arose (Brown & Vaughan, 2009). It seems to have no real goal, is done voluntarily and solely for its own sake, exerts an intrinsic attractiveness, is accompanied by a diminished level of consciousness of the self, and exhibits a large potential for improvisation and the desire for continuity (in the sense of a "pecking order") by establishing and maintaining limits both within and outside of a group. The repetition of PLAY serves to create structures of the self. If we are to escape dangerous situations, we need FEAR, whereas separation from important others does not create fear but panic, their loss being met with sadness/grief. CARE especially means providing for our offspring as well as looking after (and nurturing) family members and friends. To destroy frustrating objects, we need a portion of RAGE.

Affects are expressed physically through mimicry. Thus, disgust is a signal affect in the mimicry of patients with schizophrenia; contempt is found in narcissistic personality disorders; ostentatious friendliness among patients with anxiety disorders (Krause, 2012, p. 84). That is how the latter attempt to compensate for their separation anxiety rooted in insecure attachment "representations."

By putting so much emphasis on the affect system, early psychodynamic literature necessarily neglected the fact that psychosexuality too must be rooted in sensorimotor-embodied experience (Fonagy, 2008, p. 17). This deficit can be compensated for by viewing the seven basic emotions (including disgust) as drives and assuming the seven basic drives instead of the classical duality (Eros vs. Thanatos). Freud (1905d, p. 67) considered a drive to be "the mental representation of a continuously flowing, innersomatic stimulus source." In that sense, the idea of drive was – and in accordance with our modern knowledge of affects still is – a "borderline concept somewhere between the psychic and the somatic" (Freud, 1915c, p. 214). It is indeed the most psychosomatic of all psychodynamic terms.

The idea of drive is weakened by its being connected primarily to sexuality. Because the latter is largely seen only as a symptom of object relations, it lacks a decisive aspect. Erotic experiences are without a doubt intensely physical, so attaching this aspect (or even physical arousal) solely to a social construction distorts human sexuality by separating it from its roots in physical experience (Budd, 2001). Thus, theories of object relations in their purest form fail to provide a satisfactory theoretical framework of psychosexuality, probably because the separate pieces of the physical and affective self were not properly put together. One missing piece is the ability of one's primary others to mirror unintegrated aspects of a constitutional self-affect state so clearly and coherently that certain affect states of the baby/child are integrated as representations. The child internalizes the reflection of such metabolized affects present on the face of its primary other and regards it as the basis for an embodied representation.

Interestingly enough, mothers are especially poor at mirroring the affect of sexually aroused girls and boys aged 3–6 months – by simply ignoring their arousal or looking away (Fonagy, 2008, p. 12). Fonagy concluded that "brief self-reflection may reveal that while we can fairly confidently say how we might mirror sadness, or even respond to anger, we have no conscious strategies available for mirroring sexual excitement" (Fonagy, 2008, p. 22). This results in an absence of representation – and thus also the "owning" – of sexual arousal; the later adult remains long unsure of their own sexuality and sometimes experiences it as something "foreign." Such a feeling of exclusion "normally indicates mental disorders that in the mentalization theory are denoted by the term 'alien self,' which is the product of improperly mirrored affects" (Rottländer, 2020, p. 176). Thus, "normal" sexuality that is connected to the identity of the core-self actually shows a similarity to "madness or is at least in the borderline spectrum" (Fonagy, 2008, p. 19). Although much research has been done and published on the consequences of violating sexual borderlines and sexual abuse, we still know relatively little about the implications of negative reactions to sexual arousal in children, for example, when caretakers exclaim "Stop that!" and thus reveal their own negative relationship to sexuality (Rottländer, 2020, p. 175).

Further, some aspects pertaining to the development of an affective self remain uncharted: First, when do basic and more complex affects appear that are (relatively) clearly expressed in various parts of the body? And, second, what are their dimensions? Affects and emotions influence our behavior and our physiological states both during life-threatening events and during more pleasant interactions (Nummenmaa et al., 2014). Even though we are often quite aware of feelings such as anger or joy, the mechanisms – the how – that lead to such subjective sensations remain hidden. Yet, various emotional states can be topographically linked, on the one hand, with different cultural and, on the other hand, with universal bodily sensations linked to a large European or East Asian population. Such an experience of affects is important not just for the development of self, but also forms the basis for lifelong conscious and unconscious emotional experiences and behaviors.

To date, affects such as fear are categorized according to their structural level (high, middle, low). Yet, they possess a dimension as well that is expressed in varying conscious or unconscious levels of intensity, a good example being shame (Hadar, 2008; Schultz-Venrath, 2022), which ranges from the unconscious, archaic-malign form of failing to have a right to exist (generally nonverbal but physical and lodged in physical memory); to sexual shame or feeling ashamed; to the cognitive and conscious shame of experiencing a "Freudian slip" of the tongue. The shame that accompanies feelings of attachment uncertainty is expressed in chronic physical "nervous tension" (Figure 1.2).

Interestingly, shame is the first affect explicitly mentioned in the Bible: In Genesis, we read that "In the beginning, there was shame," which was related to the moral emotions of guilt and empathy. Both Adam and his wife, Eve, are naked but

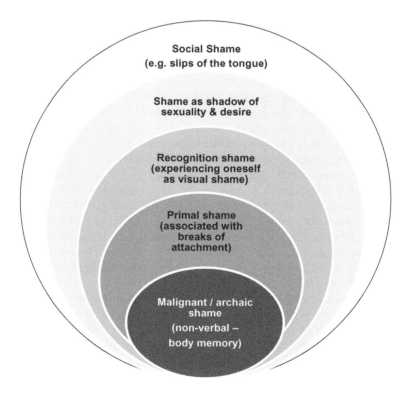

Figure 1.2 Dimensions of shame as an example of the dimensionality of an affect.
Source: Hadar (2008); Schultz-Venrath (2022).

feel no shame – which changes once they have eaten from the forbidden tree of knowledge (!). So, what happens there, what do they *see*? The classical answer says that they look at each other, though now from a different perspective. The essential point about shame is the act of discovering that the other person can see me, that I have no control over *how* they see me, and that I now see and experience the other person in all their physicalness. Precisely because a patient's physical symptoms are accompanied by somatoform disorders – while trying to avoid any psychodynamic connection – do shame and shaming play such major roles in this regard.

1.2 Attachment and the Development of a Mentalizing Self

> The term "mentalization" is traditionally used in psychology and psychotherapy to refer to our cognitive abilities to infer the mental states of ourselves and others. In this chapter, the ability to mentalize is described by the type of attachment and the way the body is perceived as a process by which sensorimotor signals are progressively integrated and built to representations of our embodied signals in given situations. Particular types of affective touch and physical contact and proximal interactions are crucial for mentalizing of the body and the formation of a proto-self or minimal selfhood.

The development of a mentalizing self commences in the womb. The physical wellbeing of a mother has a positive effect on newborns, who are then born with longer telomeres (the protective shields at the ends of the chromosomes) (Verner et al., 2020), which in turn reduces cell aging and elevates the child's resilience and wellbeing. This presumably also affects the ability of the child to bond to their mother.

Paramount to the development of a mentalizing proto-self or minimal selfhood is the original function of a newborn's skin, as long as they cannot differentiate it from other bodily parts. The skin functions primarily as the perimeter for passively experienced, unintegrated inner states, which are sometimes later variously expressed in problems of dependence and separation in the form of detachment intolerance (Bick, 1968). For some, the skin is what produces sensations, which Anzieu (1985 [1995]) used to coin his idea of "Skin-Ego," an interesting approach to self-concept, whereas for others it is smell, the mother's voice, or her nipple in one's mouth. Still others plead more for containment of the child's primary other. In this respect, Winnicott's statement "there is no such thing as a baby" must be extended to the effect: "There is no such thing as a body" (Orbach, 2003) without a primary attachment figure. As important as the loving attachment is between a child and their primary other, which opens the door to the child's psychosomatic development, so little that fact actually determines what goes through the door. Attachment researchers and developmental psychologists have tried to find evidence that affect regulation forms a causal and functional correlation between the quality of early-childhood attachment and the development of mentalization in human beings (Fonagy et al., 2002 [2004]; Gergely & Unoka, 2008a), though they have tended to neglect the role of physical interactions. Ciaunica and Fotopoulou (2017, p. 181) rightly criticize that

> for the most part, scholars of human infancy tend to claim that such effects in humans are mediated by parents' mental states and related higher-order psychological concepts (e.g. theory of mind, attachment style). Even in theories that have stressed embodied aspects of the infant-caregiver relationship, for example, "affect attunements" (Stern, 1985) or "contingent marked mirroring" (Gergely & Watson, 1999 [2014]), these are quickly embedded in more complex mentalistic conceptualizations of the caregivers' mind and therefore the view that infants' minds are first "read out" by mothers and then responded accordingly.

In contrast to Zahavi (2007; Zahavi & Rochat, 2015) they call for a better understanding of the constitutive interdependence between minimal selfhood and we-experiences versus an intersubjectivity that is only directed towards two dynamically interacting persons.

However, it should be remembered that all of these theories depend on the context. For example, the acquisition of an explicit mentalization ability at about 4 years of age (seen in the child's ability to master standardized false-belief tasks; see Section 1.4) was viewed as causally connected with certain developmental factors; these "precursors" of mentalization were considered to go back to the level of security and the quality in the mother–child interactions that take place in the first months and years of the child's life. At the time this research was carried out, the various cultures of physical interactions and their social relevance were largely ignored. For example, the Hungarian researchers Gergely and Unoka (2008a) have a very Eurocentric view of the characteristics of early human interactions between the primary other and the child as one of language, gestures, and visual behavior.

- The interaction between the primary other and the child possesses a unique "proto-conversational" contingency structure, whereby the roles of speaker and listener switch back and forth – something not found in other primates.
- Babies show a specific and innate sensitivity for so-called ostensive cues such as eye contact or contingent reactivity. The primary others use a special prosodic intonation pattern ("motherese") that is specially tailored to the young child.
- From very early on babies react to reference signals in the behavior of others, for example, by shifting their gaze or moving their head, and can thus position their view – but only if these signals are presented in the context of visual communication. (An example would be direct eye contact with the child or a contingent reactivity of others to the child's behavior with alternating communication roles.) At age 1, unlike other primates, babies display a communicative and referential understanding and react with gestures.

- Mother–child interactions are characterized by a relatively rich and sophisticated (and rapidly growing) repertoire of gestures and mimicry of central emotions (such as anger, joy, fear, sadness, disgust, and interest). The regularity and specificity of such basic emotions toward the child's primary others increase throughout the first years of their lives.
- Only in humans do we observe the empathetic affect mirroring of emotional expressions in the parents, which occurs in the affect-regulating, face-to-face interaction with their child; this sometimes also includes contingent mirroring of the child's negative emotional expressions. The patterns of mimicry and vocalization in the affect-mirroring expressions by parents consist of specifically "marked" modifications of stereotypical motoric patterns the parents normally employ to express their "true" inner basic emotions. Apart from the characteristic "attention-grabbing" traits of markedness (e.g., the motoric patterns of expression are executed exaggeratedly, very slowly, schematically, or incompletely), "marked" affect-mirroring expressions are typically related to a specific constellation of graphic-communicative and referential signals, such as direct eye contact, raising the eyebrows, widening/tightening of the eyes, giving "knowing" looks, and a contingent reactivity directed toward the child.
- From birth on, in interactions with their parents, babies are able and motivated to contingently and spontaneously recreate the characteristics of graphic expressions of mimicry and vocalization (e.g., sticking out their tongue, frowning, raising their eyebrows, protruding their lips, opening their mouth, and other components known from basic emotional expressions).

The ability to successfully communicate with other human beings is essential for the everyday life of everyone. Because infants' motor systems are not yet developed and they cannot feed themselves or protect themselves from injury, they have developed an innate social bonding drive and style that is independent of hunger and thermoregulation. However, "this should not obscure the important embodied role of caregivers in regulating the infant's interoceptive states and in turn the foundations of the minimal self" (Ciaunica & Fotopoulou, 2017, p. 185), to which we prefer the term "proto-self."

Like language skills, recognizing vivid emotional expressions depends on the clarity of the acoustic signals as well on what the baby – and later the adult – expect to hear and see. Shai and Belsky (2011, 2017) complemented the list of characteristics that define the development of an affective self and self-esteem. Parental mentalizing capacities are reflected in – and can be assessed by considering – parents' use of the very communicative means that infants employ: the nonverbal kinesthetic mode. It is one of the early experiences of parents that crying babies are easier to calm down if you get up and walk around than if you stay seated. Thus, parental embodied mentalizing (PEM) is the parental capacity to (a) implicitly conceive, comprehend, and extrapolate the infant's mental states (wishes, desires, preferences) from the infant's whole-body kinesthetic expressions, and (b) to adjust one's own kinesthetic patterns accordingly. In their opinion, a decisive element of developing self-esteem may be found in forming feelings of presence, volume, solidity, and mass. Furthermore, the delimitation of the self must be established to set boundaries between external and internal affairs, between me and not-me, between real and imaginary. Thus, one type of touch or movement can express many different meanings or intentions, just as many different types of touch or meaning can produce the same emotional outcome. Only by regarding the interaction of the various kinesthetic qualities[4] at the moment in time of their interplay can we understand the emotional and mentalization-stimulating meaning. This occurs in body-oriented play, for example, the rough-and-tumble play well known in the animal world. Although such play used to be seen as putting boys at risk for developing aggressive behavior, more recently it is assumed that it not only furthers social competencies but also stimulates the development of mental representations in the parts of the brain responsible for inhibiting behaviors (Panksepp & Scott, 2012).

Against this background, we may observe a series of physical symptoms during early development that reveals that "failed" affect regulation – and thus also the concomitant need for self-assurance – results from neglect; this, in turn, belongs to the pre-mentalizing body-mode (cf. Chapter 5.1), for example, the stereotypical head-banging and head-bobbing found in young children; the persistent, hyperkinetic, repetitive movements known in children on the autism spectrum; or nightly enuresis, which can sometimes continue to adolescence and beyond (Collins, 1965; de Lissovoy, 1963; MacLean et al., 2023).

Psychodynamically speaking, so-called jactations are considered transitional phenomena or predecessors to transitional phenomena (Gaddini & Gaddini, 1970; Winnicott, 1971). They serve to help the infant cope with fears and the absence of the primary other. When the primary other is missing, the child dips into atavistic systems to overcome fear, often couched in fight/flight or freeze reactions. Such atavistic affect regulation may also be found, for example, in the earlier descriptions of psychogenic seizures as "hyperkinesia" or "playing dead reflex" (Schultz-Venrath & Masuhr, 1993), which in infant research is also described as "frozen fear." It is assumed that rhythmic swaying movements, such as head-bobbing and head-banging, help to stimulate the evolutionarily young system of stress reaction and to maintain the inhibition of phylogenetically older systems should important others not be available, and the child cannot revert to representations for basal affects (Collins, 1965). Thomas Ogden (1989, p. 129f.) already formulated it similarly, that "the rhythmic component of the head banging and motion of the crib can be viewed as an effort at self-soothing through the use of an autistic shape." Gergely and Watson (1996, p. 1190) observed within the framework of a "normal" development a form of social biofeedback (understood as the process whereby the child interactively gets to know their own inner states by marked mirroring through the primary other(s); during the first 3 months of their life babies are inherently interested in experiencing perfect reaction-stimulus contingencies (if, then . . .). After 3 months, however, they turn their attention to more imperfect social contingencies (in a so-called contingency switch), that is, by concluding that everything that is not perfectly contingent with their own actions does not belong to them (Gergely, 2005; Gergely & Watson, 2014). Such imperfect social contingencies mean, among other things, that the mirroring need not be 100% exact to be accepted. This in turn opens the child up to the social world around them, where the mirroring of persons other than their primary other(s) can productively take place and be accepted.

Should, however, no mentalizing primary other(s) be available at all, then the new preference cannot be consolidated: The baby receives no social biofeedback and experiences no successful affect regulation, which if recurrent can result in the absence of stable representations. In situations in which interactive fear regulation is missing, the infant may revert to trying to placate themselves through body movements. In this regard, the well-known phenomena of thumb-sucking (found even in the womb), head-banging, and head-bobbing appear to be means of compensating for insufficient interactive affect regulation. From a scientific perspective, it is undisputed that the quality of early parental embodied mentalizing (PEM) is decisive both for whether the child is sickly or healthy and whether the child subsequently leads a life of fulfillment or alienation. PEM is a recently validated video-measure used to capture the parental mentalizing ability to understand the infant's kinesthetically manifested mental states and adjust their own kinesthetics accordingly, with no consideration of the verbal or vocal exchanges (i.e., volume is turned off when coding) (Shai & Belsky, 2017). It seems that high-mentalizing parents often use ostensive cues (examples include making eye contact; accurate turn-taking; appropriate and contingent reactivity in time, tone, and content; and frequent use of a special communicational tone that addresses the child's experiential world), "which signal to the infant that they are being perceived and treated as unique subjective beings. By doing so, parents foster epistemic trust in their infants, allowing the infant to use the parents a reliable source of knowledge to learn from" (Shai et al., 2022). Presumably, the influence of early childhood attachment relations determines whether later behavior includes psychosocial competence and the tendency to adopt democratic structures – or, in contrast, a susceptibility toward populistic and/or authoritarian-aggressive structures, with even the potential of showing violent behavior.

An infant has a high sensibility for "contingent relations between its proprioception (intentional movements) and the outside world" (Fonagy et al., 2002 [2004], p. 24). The authors, who refer to Gergely and Watson (1996), mean the following: The infant can identify contingent relations between its own physical actions and the resulting stimuli; and the infant can calculate – and maximize – the probabilities of these contingent relations. Against this background, Gergely and Watson (1996) attribute to the infant an inborn module to discover contingencies that cause them to explore how often and under what conditions a particular action might lead to a certain stimulus.

Developmentally, we may assume that infants do not yet possess stable representations for their emotional states, which is why we differentiate between the establishment and the development of such representations as well as the "online" regulation of affects. The contingency of the mother's reaction to the "online" regulation of affects plays a special role: Infants have the innate ability to perceive contingency relations; they move rhythmically together with the babytalk – the sing-song of their primary other(s) – which can even be detected as rhythmicity in the EEG during breastfeeding (Lehtonen, 2006). The synchronization of these rhythms leads to moments of intense contact. The repeated occurrence of events gives the newborn from day one the ability to *expect* something, which newborns use to differentiate between the marked affect-mirroring of their primary other(s) and their own diffuse, emotional-physical state. Thus, from the very beginning, the infant disposes of a self as a "physical actor." The embodied self is recognized as a distinct "object" that can carry out actions and thus also act causally. An infant's movements are not involuntary flounderings but subject to the child's (relative) control: They create perfectly contingent sensory repercussions. Infants do a lot of exploration regarding such contingency relations during the first 2–3 years of life, and they work to take control over their bodies (posture and movement), which was considerably impeded after birth because of gravity.

Furthermore, touching one's own body and experiences with one's own body point to a reflexive structure. When a child uses a finger to touch their body, two complementary sensations incur: the skin that touches and the skin being touched. In this model of reflexive touching, further reflexive sensations (such as hearing one's own voice, smelling one's own smell, seeing oneself in the mirror) ensue, even reflexive thinking (Anzieu, 2016) as a precursor to reflective thinking (Ensink et al., 2015). The proprioceptive feedback – which by the way is not limited to the infant phase in life – allows the child to differentiate between own and other activities as well as creates space for the development of self- and object representations.

Case vignette: A severely deprived patient with a borderline personality disorder said the following: "As a child, I was always on the lookout for the odor from the armpit of my (often absent) father, which provided me with at least a semblance of familiarity and security."

Actions initiated by oneself or by others are always experienced as physical sensations. Certain self-initiated actions produce physical feedback not found in the actions of others. When the infant discovers their own affects in the primary attachment relationship, they come to "understand" themselves as a mental (= emotional) actor. Based on his studies, Daniel Stern (Stern, 1985 [1992]) said that the self-perception of an infant is organized like a preverbal subjectivity; this includes preverbal experiences of propriety, physical cohesion, and temporal continuity. The origin of a mental space lies in a child's earliest somatic experiences, much as all affects are originally total-body sensations that stem primarily from experiences of touch. According to Anzieu (2016), via internalization these form a mental shell containing the mental contents. This skin-shell, which is then complemented by a smell-shell, corresponds down the road to the somatopsychic (i.e., not just mental!) space, a receptacle or network that captures and then externalizes (proto-mental) thoughts.

The mechanism through which such a receptacle or network is created around the time of birth was previously more or less unknown. Now, however, the importance of early sensory stimuli in the development of more elaborate means of communication has been decoded (Gretenkord et al., 2019). Except for the olfactory system, the sensory system is immature in the early phase of life. At birth, the olfactory system cements the interactions between the mother and her child and ensures the child's survival. It appears that the communication that goes on between the bulbus olfactorius and the lateral entorhinal cortex – the gatekeeper of the limbic circuit – is especially relevant during early development because the olfactory stimuli activate the entorhinal cortex, which in turn act as a gatekeeper to control the cognitively relevant neuronal networks. A blockage or overstimulation of the sense of smell within the bulbus olfactorius during early development of the brain may trigger faulty communication between the various brain areas. That points to the importance of sensory experiences during early childhood for the development of attention and memory faculties, including the development of representations in the adult. In some patients, particularly those with functional body complaints, precisely such connections of these representations (or parts thereof) seem to be missing or interrupted, preventing their enjoying a stable self.

Resonating significant others are imperative for the development of such infantile representational networks. The nascent ability of the infant

> in understanding the self as a psychological (emotional) agent begins with infants' discovery of their own affects through their primary attachment relationships. Infants' budding capacities to experience their emotions as *feelings* are based on internalizing the caregiver's contingently responsive marked emotional expressions. The caregiver's mental representations of the infant's emotional states are exemplified in her behavior; intuitively, she *presents* these expressions to the infant. In turn, the infant begins to develop a mental representation of his or her own emotional state as feeling – an emerging form of emotional self-awareness. These representations gradually form the basis for *mentalizing emotion* and thereby for affect regulation and impulse control: feelings become recognizable; they do not have to be acted out; and they can be shared.
> (Allen et al., 2008, p. 81)

Today we know that the inclination of primary other(s) to treat their newborn as a sort of psychological "agent" is very conducive to the development of a secure attachment in children.

Since the 1980s, a question has been central to developmental psychology: To what extent need one not share these feelings? That is, at what point in time can children understand other people using attributions of convictions and desires they simultaneously see as representational states? The discovery of this skill using so-called false-belief tests (cf. Section 1.2) formed the basis for the "theory of mind" (TOM) of cognitive psychology (Wimmer & Perner, 1983). The easiest way to imagine the development of mental "representations" is to view them as dynamic neuronal networks that are intricately connected with each other via fluid excitation curves and are layered on top of each other.

Even before birth, the embryo develops a primitive tactile-proprioceptive perception system that manifests itself in the impressive and well-known intersubjective, visible, and palpable kick against the inner wall of the womb. Because the breast-seeking reflex is innate (= already present), one cannot speak of a "re-presence" (which is why Bion deliberately calls it a "preconcept"). Only later do affect-oriented perceptions (in the form of perceptive and iconic object representation) develop via repeated affect regulation in identical situations. These perceptions in turn leave behind marks on the child's inner self and traces of self-perception, whether of primary attachment objects and interactions with them or of the internalization of entire scenes containing images of the self, of the object, of the circumstances, and the respective affects (the latter in the form of conceptual and/or symbolic self-object-representations).

Despite the infant's desire for independence, during the first year of life they in fact develop a double dependence, namely, physical and emotional. Then, at about one year of age, the child can "keep alive the idea of one's mother and her usual care for a certain time, 10 minutes, 1 hour or longer" (Winnicott, 1958, p. 230). This points indirectly to the fact that the child has developed an initial form of object representation, something the older toddler can use on the iconic level. More than half a century ago, Winnicott described in clear terms a series of maternal activities and attitudes necessary to the establishment of such a mentally and physically equipped child who can then go on to experience something like "integration," which then – though not without setbacks – emerges from the previous state of "unintegration" (Winnicott, 1958, p. 231). The latter need not necessarily be considered a threat – as long as the child gets a feeling of security from the mother. This "integration work" is closely tied to defined emotional or affective experiences, such as anger or feeding stimuli. If this complex process of integration is successful, then the child's psyche and soma remain connected through a continual exchange; if it is unsuccessful, then the body is often painfully overwhelmed and becomes an "intermediate buffer for unbearable affective charge, which cannot complete its integration into the ego. At the same time this charge cannot be formulated into communication with the outer world" (Hartung & Steinbrecher, 2018, p. 99).

The formation of representation may be disturbed or interrupted, for example, if parents delegate or project their own needs and affairs onto their children, often described by the modern term of "helicopter parents." Here, children assume aspects of an ideal self, such as "giftedness," or a negative self, such as "scapegoat." Particularly, the separation anxiety of parents who remain glued to this role for too long is one of the main factors behind such behavior, which can impair the development of the bodily self and identity of (adult) children. In the opinion of Seiffge-Krenke (2014), the role of the concept of lifespan for the development of an affective and corporeal self has recently changed: Childhood has become shorter, adolescence speeded up via secular acceleration tendencies and extended job training, and a completely new phase has been introduced between adolescence and adulthood: *emerging adulthood*, between the years of 18 and 25(–30). To date, we have little research concerning what these changes may mean for the development of an affective-sensual self or the body-self.

1.3 On the Beginnings of the Mentalization Model

> This chapter will look at the similarities and differences in French, British, and German history regarding the importance of the mentalization model. While the body was in focus in the theorizing of psychoanalytic psychosomatics by the Paris group around Pierre Marty, it was largely lost to the British group around Peter Fonagy and Anthony Bateman through the confrontation with the cognitive representatives of the theory of mind in the 1990s, as it was in the preceding attachment theory of John Bowlby.

The mentalization model of the group of scholars around Peter Fonagy is a work in progress that integrates new empirical findings from attachment and affect research, cognitive developmental psychology as well as trauma research and the neurosciences. In this sense, it can be seen as an extension of the basic concept of psychoanalysis and psychosomatics that influences psychotherapeutic treatment. Thus, for patients with somatic symptom disorders, it is also a work in progress. Although the idea of mentalization does not specially emphasize the body, neither does mentalization represent a wholly mental process. Like the drive model, the preliminary stages of mentalization lie at the border between soma and psyche, as does the ability to mentalize, which results from the process of regulating earlier bodily and affect experiences. Mentalizing is impossible without the body!

Mentalizing commences with the body and is experienced only through the body, which is already well captured in the term "parental embodied mentalizing" (Shai & Belsky, 2017; Shai et al., 2022). In this sense, the mentalization model revives the integration of body and mind, of body and soul (even though the English terms "mind" and "mental" do not expressly include the body). These linguistic and historical differences surrounding the role of the body which have developed over time in France, Germany, and the Anglo-Saxon world led to small but sometimes subtle differences in the interpretation of theories and concepts of mentalization – which then influence the means of treatment.

The model of conflict specificity by Franz Alexander was long predominant in the world of psychosomatic medicine. Alexander saw conflicts as the most important stimuli for the vegetative nervous system – replacing physiological stimuli (Alexander, 1934). Later, Alexander (1948) tried to methodically underpin this model by using semiverbatim records of patients with gastrointestinal complaints, leading to the formulation of his select seven psychosomatoses – his "holy seven."

Yet, the new, expanded specificity model, containing personality profiles, was in danger of slipping into the symbolic interpretation of bodily symptoms, causing it to be rejected by many psychosomatics (Hoff et al., 1958). Even Pierre Marty, the founder of the Paris Psychosomatics School, whose volume *Psychosomatique et Mentalization* (Marty, 1991) had created quite a sensation (albeit primarily in France), rejected Alexander's specificity concept – with one exception: allergy patients who, in his opinion, suffered from an "allergic object relationship." Such patients, he said, were characterized by their inability to "set boundaries that differentiate them from real objects, to separate them and keep them away" (Marty, 1958, p. 422). Here, Marty spoke of being fused with the "guest and host object," although – because of the experienced equality – one could not differentiate between the two. Every failed attempt at achieving proximity causes an allergic reaction (asthma, eczema, urticaria, etc.) that ensues from regression to a level of archaic fixation on which the subject and the object were not clearly separated from one another. The pre-mentalizing design of the "equivalence mode" later developed by Fonagy and his workgroup is clearly present here on the physical level.

In contrast to the specificity model, Marty and colleagues (Marty et al., 1963) found especially among "patients with psychosomatoses" a special way of thinking, something they called "operative thinking" (*pensée opératoire*). They understood this as "conscious thinking" that appeared to "(1) have no inner relationship with an accessible imaginative activity," and that "(2) reproduced the action like a copy" (Marty & de M'Uzan, 1963 [1978], p. 974). Thus, from their standpoint, somatization was the result of a failure of mentalization: What occurred mentally was interpreted as a physical event. Karen Gubb (2013, p. 117) put it differently (and better): "This mind cannot express itself as a mind because it is all body." Here, "somatization" is used as a rather unspecific term that incorporates the entire spectrum of physically determined, psychogenetic, and functionally somatic syndromes such as irritable bowel syndrome and fibromyalgia syndrome. Bouchard and Lecours (2008, p. 110f.) expanded this operative thinking to include the idea of what they called "tangential associations," which are distinguished by words duplicating actions, the expressions of which are stereotypical, clichéd, and conformist, the thoughts and memories uncoupled from the present framework. This is why the context is not used for mentalization. The only thing that occurs is an empty or "white relationship" that is missing any connection to any other living object.

The French working group used the term "psychosomatosis," by the way, to describe a personality disorder that "in a conflict situation largely chooses the somatic outlet because of its disposition" – something also observed in "character neuroses" (according to the diagnostic taxonomy of the time). They describe the act of thinking and speaking that is oriented toward the factual and the present instead of the libidinous and the relational. Both are separated from the object and the imaginative activity and thus also from the body. Marty and M'Uzan's school was consistent in presenting a series of neologisms, an example being "dementalization," which describes the lack of mental functions, the paucity of dialog with the psychotherapist, and the absence of a mental expression of both internal and external objects (Jaeger, 2019, p. 754). What we don't know is the extent to which this observation also goes back to the inability of the therapist to perceive and act on even the smallest of affect expressions to make them resonate. Only recently has research been done on physicians and psychotherapists who themselves suffer from a disorder on the autism spectrum (Moore et al., 2020).

"Dementalization" occurs parallel to so-called empty relationships, where the "link to an inner and truly vibrant object" is missing and the patient presents a dearth of associations, dreams, and free associations. In light of such massive deficits in identifying means on the part of the patient, the analyst or psychotherapist may themselves become "confused." "Anyone who is not used to dealing with such patients will have their own identification difficulties and be hesitant about how to carry on the psychotherapeutic treatment" (Marty & de M´Uzan, 1963 [1978], p. 975).

Both in the cultural history of France and the more than 100-year history of psychosomatics in Germany, there would appear to be a closer affinity to the body, more so than, say, in the British culture, which has no independent field of psychosomatics. In Germany, psychosomatics has formed its own field of study since 1992 and has its own national association, the German Society for Psychosomatic Medicine (DGPM). In the Anglo-Saxon world, as a subdiscipline of psychiatry, psychosomatics has more or less atrophied and is intensively practiced only by a psychodynamic group within child and adolescent psychiatry. That may be the reason behind the cultural differences – and why the mentalization model in France was created to treat patients with so-called psychosomatic disorders, whereas in Great Britain it is advocated for the treatment of patients with borderline personality disorders.

One result of this lack of intercultural exchange may be seen in the attachment model devised by the pediatrician John Bowlby and his pupils Mary Main and Mary Ainsworth (Ainsworth et al., 1978; Bowlby, 1958, 1969 [1982], 1978; Main & Goldwyn, 1994), which found little echo in the German scientific psychiatric literature and treatment methods. This was particularly the case for the so-called internal working model (IWM), which played a major conceptual role in the representation theory. In this view, under favorable conditions, a maturing child develops an IWM with their most important other(s), meaning a largely cognitive means of embracing mental representations to understand the world, oneself, and others. The child uses memories of earlier social interactions to control future social and emotional behavior, resulting in relatively stable attachment styles up to about the age of 25 (Bretherton, 1999; Grossmann et al., 2006). IWMs are associated with various forms of attachment styles in young children. Depending on the stability of the primary other, this results in a secure, an insecure-avoidant, an insecure-ambivalent, or an unresolved-disorganized style of attachment (Main & Solomon, 1986).

Although the IWM is central to attachment theory, it contains several problems regarding its scientific and theoretical background: First, we know too little about the neuronal principles, in particular about changes that take place during aging; second, meta-analyses have shown that the IWM of attachment, which presume long-lasting and stable personality factors, in fact have only a limited stability and predictability (Fraley et al., 2013). Thus, it remains unclear whether we are dealing here with a state or a trait parameter; that may also be the reason why very different mental representations and memories of social interactions are applied throughout development to control the social-emotional response capacity – something that has been demonstrated in both children and adolescents (Debbane et al., 2017). Finally, attachment style and attachment representations are often combined.

A secure attachment to one's primary other(s) is a central part of the mentalization model. Based on the present empirical evidence, however, the attachment model can apply experiences with relationships to organize emotional reactions and to act as a catalyst for the increasing level of understanding of one's own behavior and the behavior of others, based on the emergence of both self- and object representations. The quality of early attachment relationships is decisive for the development of neurocognitive, embodied, and social competencies. The concept of mentalization embodied through the parents represents the attempt to account for nonverbal, parental competencies that play a meaningful and influential role in the child–parent(s) interaction – and that relate to the whole body (i.e., not just the head or the face). This type of mentalization plays an active role in the communication between parents and their children regarding psychophysical states.

The development of stable self- and object representations depends on the presence of consistent emotional reactions by the primary other(s) during the early stages of life: eye contact, accurate turn-taking, proper contingent reactivity (e.g., regarding time, prosody, and content), repeated use of special communicative sounds (baby-talk), adapted to the child's world. Just how important such communication is may be seen in the development of face representations: When primates fail to see a face immediately postpartum, they remain unable to develop face representations (domains) despite their having normal retino-optical organization (Arcaro et al., 2017). Early visual deprivation thus precipitates a highly selective cortical developmental deficit in the inferior temporal cortex, so that primates then fail to follow faces in their field of vision. Clearly, looking into a face is thus not just an innate but also an acquired ability. The environment influences how a child sees the world, which in turn leads to the development of neuronal activity, and neuronal activity creates the representation of faces.

Insecure children 1 year of age taking the Strange Situation Test suffer from a higher level of tachycardia than secure children as well as from a greater rise in their cortisol level after only 15–30 minutes (Spangler & Grossmann, 1993). Animal models confirmed this finding: Rats that had been intensively licked and groomed by their mothers proved to be more resilient under acute stress conditions and less anxious toward new things in their environment; they also displayed less defense behavior when faced with dangerous stimuli. The offspring of rat mothers displaying less grooming behavior, on the other hand, reacted more intensely to adversities than those whose mothers provided a high level of grooming (Menard & Hakvoort, 2007).

From the vantage point of developmental psychology, insecure attachment and the resulting insufficient development of "representations" would thus appear to be – at least in Europe – the missing link needed to explain somatic symptom stress disorders. An insecure attachment accompanying deficient mentalization efforts on the part of the primary other(s) may express itself at every level in the form of "somatization" or self-destructive behavior. More recent findings, however, argue for a more critical and less deterministic approach to the attachment model (Keller, 2017; Otto & Keller, 2014 [2018]), especially since even insecure children may possess some secondary resilience factors (e.g., positive experiences in nursery school or well-meaning teachers) that allow them to remain "healthy" or at least stable. Toddlers also seem to have fairly good adaptation abilities regarding their attachment behavior; they allow themselves to be influenced and formed by others. Strikingly, to date, attachment research has studied almost exclusively the dyadic relationship to the child's primary other; other relationships, such as the nuclear or extended family in which the mother (as part of the reciprocal affect regulation) has the role of group "speaker" have been largely ignored. Further, studies dealing with attachment styles and attachment representations among patients with somatoform disorders are rare. Even though the few existing studies employed a broad range of measurement tools, one thing they do agree on is that for the most part patients with somatoform disorders possess anxious attachment strategies (Riem et al., 2018). Deficits in maternal sensitivity exhibited toward a child at 18 months promote somatization at age 5, whereas maternal deficits in sensitivity toward a child of 6 months do not produce later somatization (Maunder et al., 2017). The authors of this prospective study presume that maternal behavior does not affect future somatization at this early age because the behavior has yet to be internalized, that is, the child has not yet formed a stable "internal working model of caregivers and self, an internalized scheme of the world that forms a basis for emergent personality organization" (Maunder et al., 2017, p. 511). Attachment insecurity among adults correlates highly significantly with somatization expressed primarily in health and attachment anxieties.

In the meantime, we know a little bit more about other factors that may influence attachment style and the development of attachment representations, for example, differences in temperament and epigenetics. Meaney and Szyf (2005) show in their classic study on mother rats licking their pups that increased levels of pup licking/grooming by rat mothers in the first week of life alter DNA structure at a glucocorticoid receptor gene promoter in the hippocampus of the offspring. This correlated with differences in the DNA methylation pattern between the offspring of high- and low-licking/grooming mothers emerged over the first week of life. These findings "help us to embed attachment more firmly in the realm of the physical: sensitive responsiveness and attentive caregiving are not simply the manifestation of internal working symbolic processes, they also involve costly effort and physical investment" (Fonagy & Campbell, 2017, p. 40). This could specifically mean in the case of attachment figures: we relate in the way we touch.

Differences in temperament would seem to greatly influence which type of attachment style develops independently of existing environmental impacts. More optimistic and even-tempered people can deal with new events, even negative ones, quite well; more reserved and anxious people, on the other hand, react with less confidence and are more easily unsettled by radical changes in their life circumstances. The largely epigenetically determined differences in temperament should not be confused with the environmentally determined (i.e., care-oriented) differences that occur. Parents who have more than one child quickly notice that, from the very beginning, infants differ in temperament and behavior; their emotionality is different in the form of sensitivity, reactivity, anxiety, calming capacity, and bashfulness. Some are very relaxed, uncomplicated, deal flexibly with changes; others have more pronounced reactions, place greater demands on their environment, and adapt less well to changes in routines. Temperament seems to be a biological, genetically impacted condition that plays a role in how susceptible someone is to anxiety. In this sense, the intensity of variable inborn timidity determines how quickly, how often, and how intensely the attachment system is activated. These natural differences also affect the significant other(s) and the sensitivity of their caregiving.

Traditionally, attachment scholars have focused on maternal sensitivity as a key factor in the development of attachment security as well as how it affects developmental results. A decisive parental competence that influences the child's development is mentalization, that is, the ability to see – and treat – one's child as a psychological protagonist motivated by inner states. A high level of parental mentalization results in better socioemotional development, including well-adapted social behavior, minimal psychopathological symptoms, and epistemic trust (Fonagy & Nolte, 2023; Fonagy et al., 1995; Katz & Windecker-Nelson, 2004; Luyten et al., 2020) (Figure 1.3). Paraphrasing a quote from Patrick Luyten and

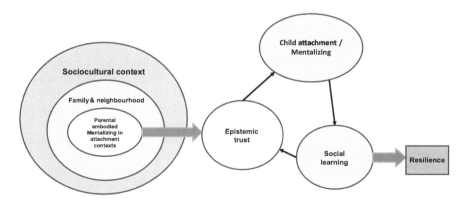

Figure 1.3 Social-evolutionary communicative model of the role of mentalizing in development.
Source: Staun & Schultz-Venrath (2023); modified acc. to Luyten (2020)

colleagues (2020, p. 300) is the capacity for parental "embodied" mentalizing the capacity to understand one's child as motivated by internal bodily (more than mental!) states. This is embedded within a broader set of factors influencing child development, including family and neighborhood, and the general sociocultural context. The development of the self is a group one. Nevertheless, it is surprising to discover that – but for one exception (Shai, Dollberg et al., 2017; Shai, Laor Black et al., 2022) – nearly all previous psychometric techniques for assessing mentalization are based solely on the semantic contents of verbalizations – even in the case of infants (Luyten et al., 2019)!

The various attachment styles and representations are accompanied by various behaviors (see Table 1.2), which in turn are expressed in various competencies of affect perception and affect regulation as well as various means of psychophysiological regulation; via various paths, these behaviors may lead to somatic symptom disorders (see Figure 1.3). For example, an uncertain-anxious attachment style creates a greater awareness of all signs of being unable to "reach" someone, known in psychospeak as "clinging." This triggers relationships that display an increasing need for social coregulation. Insecure-avoidant attachment styles, on the other hand, are characterized by a retreat in the form of detachment: Others are deemed categorically inaccessible; this leads to demonstrating one's own independence as pseudo-independence and to a less pronounced need for social coregulation. A relatively secure adult attachment style emerges when a person accepts help when truly needed, for example, in stressful times or emergencies.

The American author Paul Auster describes such an active but insecure attachment style very precisely in a somatic symptom disorder stemming from a reaction to a missing father (or rather, from a failed triangulation). By localizing the mentalization background as the cause of his symptoms, the figure in the novel *The Invention of Solitude* (Auster, 1982, pp. 20–21) points to a later (successful) therapy:

> Earliest memory: his absence. For the first years of my life he would leave for work early in the morning, before I was awake, and come home long after I had been put to bed. I was my mother's boy, and I lived in her orbit. I was a little moon circling her gigantic earth, a mote in the sphere of her gravity, and

Table 1.2 Attachment styles and behaviors

Insecure-anxious	Insecure-avoidant	Secure
Hyperactivation strategies	Deactivation strategies	Proximity seeking under stress/when in need
Growing need for social (co-)regulation	Decreasing need for social(co-)regulation	(Co-)regulation of stress through social interaction
Increase dependence	Increase independence	Others are accessible
Heightened salience for signs of others' unavailability	Others are generally unreachable	The self can seek help when needed

I controlled the tides, the weather, the forces of feeling. His refrain to her was: Don't fuss so much, you'll spoil him. But my health was not good, and she used this to justify the attention she lavished on me. We spent a lot of time together, she in her loneliness and I in my cramps, waiting patiently in doctors' offices for someone to quell the insurrection that continually raged in my stomach. Even then, I would cling to these doctors in a desperate sort of way, wanting them to hold me. From the very beginning, it seems, I was looking for my father, looking frantically for anyone who resembled him. Psychotherapists of all schools cherish the (justified) hope that the various different attachment styles and representations can remain a life-long part of human life, but that they can also be manipulated and are mutable. Some psychotherapists who do not adhere to the attachment model are well aware of the changes that symptoms undergo over time: When anxiety, distress, unacknowledged rage, terror, or unusual excitement are *somatized* instead of being recognized and processed mentally, the individual is submerged in a primitive form of thinking in which the signifiers are preverbal. In other words, there is a regression to infantile methods of dealing with affective experiences. A baby can only react somatically to either physical or mental stress, when this stress is not metabolized by the mother's handling and care. Somatizations might be conceptualized as forms of preverbal or protosymbolic functioning which, therefore, constitute a "protolanguage."

(McDougall, 1995, p. 155)

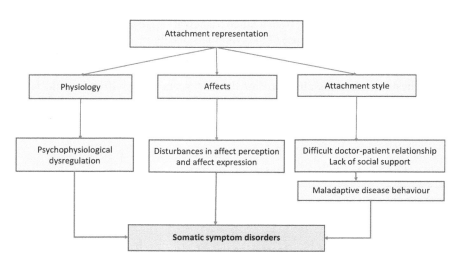

Figure 1.4 Attachment representation and attachment style as a vulnerability model for somatic symptoms disorders.

Source: Modified according to Waller and Scheidt (2002).

One general weakness in the attachment theory of Bowlby and his followers lies in the lack of attention they pay to the drive concept – although the desire for attachment may also be seen as a drive. Furthermore, they propound neither different types of culturally contingent affect regulation nor a relationship between the culturally contingent attachment style and the body and its incorporation in a group of humans with varying attachment styles. However, transcultural differences in stress and affect regulation would seem to influence the development of different affect and emotion representations (Otto, 2014 [2018]). There's a well-known African saying to the effect that "It takes an entire village to raise a child," and this is practically realized. African cultures do not extol the mother–child dyad quite as highly as the extended family, in the sense of "multiple motherings" (and thus a multitude of bodies), where the child grows up. Although the African approach is less oriented toward the birth mother (very early on the child is cared for by so-called alloparenting methods), regulation between the caretakers and the children occurs primarily through body contact and body stimulation, i.e., the skin: The mother and the child "talk" to each other via the skin; the child's needs as well as their level of satiety and comfort are communicated via the skin; the child's responses, too. Greek and German parents, on the other hand, handle these situations predominantly via eye contact. Keller (2014 [2018], p. 4) criticized the fact that the "conception of maternal sensitivity, as well as later embodiments of 'optimal parenting' (e.g., mind-mindedness), rests on an assumption of Western, middle-class psychology that does not apply to much of the world." This mainstream developmental psychology in general has been described as WEIRD (**w**hite, **e**ducated, **i**ndustrialized, **r**ich, **d**emocratic) psychology (Henrich, 2020; Henrich et al., 2010).

Children raised in the Western world develop a hierarchy of attachment relationships, although someone else in the family, such as the father, grandparents, or some other adult in the household may well become the primary attachment figure (Bowlby, 1969 [1982]). Thus, we are dealing with culturally contingent parental behavior with the respective varying affect regulation and resonance. Because of the group socialization tendencies and the individual's experience of always being "carried" by the group, fewer anxieties arise, as Otto (2014 [2018]) noted among the Nso in Cameroon.

Early stable attachment experiences and especially the quality of the relationship to their primary others generally determine how healthy the psychosocial and psychosomatic development proceeds (Maunder & Hunter, 2001; Maunder & Hunter, 2008). How closely the mother's and the child's affective expressions overlap is not decisive for the quality of their interactions but rather their capacity for interactive mending, i.e., their ability to flexibly switch back and forth between concordant and non-concordant affect states (Tronick, 1982; Tronick & Cohn, 1989). The specificity of sensitive responsiveness found in Western culture is based on face-to-face interaction, whereby the perspective and view of the infant (directed toward the primary other) are just as important as any verbal and vocal exchanges. These dyadic, reciprocal, largely undramatic interactions lend support to the (Western) cultural ideal of infants as "agents" in their own stead, who are sensitized to apply their personal qualities and attributes as the primary reference point of their actions. An infant recognizing the projection of their primary other as central agent functions as a true "kicker" in the epistemic game.

The (much larger) non-Western world, on the other hand, emphasizes physical caretaking and views the infant attached to their primary other differently: The infant looks out into the world and sees the world as the primary other(s) see(s) it. This enables the child to perceive the perspective of others. The primary other(s) have the role of instructing, leading, and guiding the child as a sort of "apprentice"; further, children and their primary other(s) take part in multiple, parallel developing activities. This, in turn, underpins the child's cultural ideal as an agent who is sensitized to attend to the needs and interests of others – and then to use them as a reference for their own actions. The infant recognizes the other(s) as an example of a generically different attribute of the community. This, again, gives the epistemic game a kick from I-mode and me-mode toward "we-ness" or a "we-mode" for joint action (Wu et al., 2020). The infant learns about themselves only secondarily (i.e., object-oriented). Of course, these ethnological-culture anthropological observations are based mostly on the comments of white (Western) observers. Yet, in both of the aforementioned attachment scenarios, mentalizing is not understood statically (as mentalization) but as a process.

Independent of cultural dependence and the multitude of possible mental and psychosomatic disorders, the early relationship between the relatively helpless child and the primary others (we purposefully use the plural here), which is largely concerned with keeping the child alive, is nevertheless paradigmatic for the development of a stable self and for the proper functioning of all later (intimate) relationships – and above all for the body awareness in later life. The relationship between an infant and their primary others is characterized by bodily interactions. When a mother nurses her child, this occurs through the suckling and the special attention a mother directs toward the child, coupled with certain skin sensations and rhythmic EEG patterns – an intensive corporal interaction that also serves to satisfy the child's innate existential needs. Such early experiences provide the foundation for the development of a child's body-self with respect toward their primary other(s).

For this reason, Lehtonen (2006, p. 420) suggested that we should view the early development of the body-self as a sort of matrix-like structure that connects the internal with the external stimuli as well as the resulting reactions, and that thus regulates the entire mental state of the organism. This means that the body-self originally could be seen as a matrix-like network. Perhaps the feeding conditions (breastfeeding vs. bottle-feeding) with their typical rhythmic neurophysiological processes formed the prototype behind the emergence of early mental organization. This early mental matrix, Lehtonen said, is derived from two sources: the needs and bodily sensations of the infant and their interaction with their primary other(s) who willfully recognize those needs and react accordingly.

Insecure and/or unstable attachment experiences during early childhood, on the other hand, generally tend to promote mental and/or psychosomatic disorders because of mental and/or physical neglect, negligence, or numerous changes in the child's important others (Neumann et al., 2015); such disorders are also often coupled with a certain overall rigidity and anxiety. Yet, modern stress research seems to be less interested in studying individual stressors (such as abuse, neglect, or experiences of loss) and more interested in looking at the mechanisms that lead to hyperactivity in the neurotoxic cortisol system of children, which is then designated as "early life stress." In the presence of multiple stressors during early attachment phases, these effects are indeed exponentiated and ultimately lead to a cumulative stress effect on the child's health, a phenomenon known as "allostatic load" (Sturge-Apple et al., 2011). This term is part of the regulatory model of allostasis, where the predictive regulation or stabilization of internal sensations in response to stimuli is ascribed to the brain (Sterling, 2012), because homeostasis cannot be only the primary mechanism for regulation. Predictive regulation refers to the body's and brain's ability to anticipate needs and prepare to fulfill them before they arise, e.g., if the blood pressure or glucose release has to be regulated even before the actual action (fight or flight) takes place (Figure 1.5). Allostatic load describes the price of adaptation, e.g., the consequences of prolonged activation of the neuroendocrine "stress axes," which can lead to diseases in the medium and long term (Henningsen, 2021, p. 28).

Physical availability and proximity, such as bodily contact and stimulation without verbal elaboration and mentalization, are now considered central to providing sufficient and loving care to a child (Fonagy & Campbell, 2017; Lancy, 2008; Otto & Keller, 2014 [2018]). Nevertheless, for the complete development of a body-self, there is still the need for an eroticization of the body surface. John Bowlby, on the other hand, with all due British sobriety, coined the term

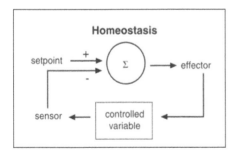 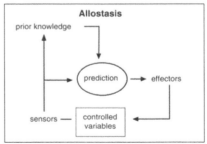

Figure 1.5 Homeostasis and allostasis as important further developments of the stress concept.

Source: Sterling (2012).

"environment of evolutionary adaptability" (Bowlby, 1969 [1982], p. 39), which in his opinion likely lies behind psychological adaptations, including social relationships and parenting styles.

Regardless of these two contradictory approaches, Fotopoulou and Tsakiris (2017, p. 3) ask whether "our mental life is initially and primarily shaped by embodied dimensions of the individual or by interpersonal relations is debated in many fields, including psychology, philosophy, psychoanalysis, and more recently, cognitive neuroscience." In their opinion, even minimal

> aspects of selfhood, namely, the feeling qualities associated with being an embodied subject, are fundamentally shaped by embodied interactions with other people in early infancy and beyond. Such embodied interactions allow the developing organism to mentalize its homeostatic regulation. In other words, embodied interactions contribute directly to the building of mental models of the infant's physiological states, given the need to maintain such states within a given dynamic range despite internal or external perturbations.
>
> (Fotopoulou & Tsakiris, 2017, p. 3)

1.4 The Role of the Body in the Mentalization Model

> This chapter explores the significance of incorporating the physical aspect into psychotherapy and mentalization models. However, the chapter questions whether this principle is being followed in contemporary psychotherapy practices. It emphasizes the importance of the therapist's physical presence in establishing a therapeutic relationship, particularly in group therapy settings. The chapter also discusses the evolving understanding of mentalization, which traditionally focused on the cognitive aspect but now recognizes the role of the body in mentalizing processes. Additionally, the chapter explores the cultural significance of the body and the implications of bodily symptoms in social dynamics. It discusses the differentiation between the subjective and physiological aspects of the body and their relevance in psychoanalysis and psychosomatics. The chapter concludes with a plea for a more comprehensive approach to include bodily experiences as access to mental states in the sense of promoting mentalizing.

Nearly 100 years ago, Felix Deutsch (1926, p. 493) wrote that "every analysis contains some element of the physical – indeed it must if the analysis is to be a proper one"; again and again "a certain group of organs manifests itself in the analysis, and this group is somehow predestined to do so . . . and through its symptoms accompanies all complexes that rise to the conscious level." This quote could be valid even today for every psychotherapy, but the question is whether it is being adhered to. The physical presence of a psychotherapist guarantees in no way a both complex and tenuous fine-tuning of the "therapeutic dyad on the level of kinesthetic processes" – although every therapist is involved in the treatment process, whether consciously or unconsciously (Leikert, 2016, p. 31). Fonagy and Campbell (2017, p. 39) have already realized through the aforementioned work of Fotopoulou and Tsakiris that "the theory of mentalizing as indicated by its name (mental in opposition to physical) risks implying a similar kind of abstraction." The situation is even more complex for group therapists. The rather philosophical concern of whether we *have* a body or *are* a body when it comes to our feelings has now been solved in the assumption that, depending on the situation and the level of development, both are true. The literature exhibits much less interest concerning what happens to the psychotherapist's body during psychotherapy with so-called difficult patients. Thus, it comes as no surprise that the body of the individual and group therapist expresses itself in the form of coughing, throat-clearing, or hesitant speech, displaying an emotional involvement during case histories, seminars, as well as at meetings and congresses.

In the mentalization model, Bowlby's attachment concept mentions the word "body" only in passing, in the form of "embodied mentalizing," as a sort of incarnate mentalization (Fonagy & Target, 2007). The latest edition of the *Handbook of Mentalizing* admits that mentalization precedes speech development because the maternal understanding of the child's inner state is communicated physically (or at least preverbally) long before the child's first words (Bateman & Fonagy, 2019, p. 7). This represents a major modification of the previous theory of mentalization, in which the ability to mentalize was presumed – as stated in the theory of mind (ToM) – to occur from about age 4 onward with the emergence of the (mental) false-belief paradigm, without the body having assumed a meaning.

In such situations, children must be able to predict someone's behavior based on the false belief of that person, while ignoring their own (true) beliefs. For example, a child is confronted with a situation in which another child ("John") puts a toy on a shelf and then goes away. During John's absence, the toy is placed somewhere else (e.g., in a basket). Typically, 3-year-olds predict that John will first look in the basket and not on the shelf after returning since they already know that the toy is no longer on the shelf. That is, 3-year-olds ignore that John cannot possibly know that the toy is now in the basket and still (falsely) believes that the toy is on the shelf. In contrast, older children (and adults) account for John's false belief and predict that he will first search on the shelf. These insights led to the argument that ToM demands complex thought processes and thus appears rather late in a child's development. Upon reaching the ToM stage for the first time, usually designated by the term "mentalization ability," the child comes to understand false beliefs, lies, fraud, deception, and gaffes. Further, ToM enables the child to leave the realm of concrete thinking (equivalent mode) and proceed to irony, sarcasm, and metaphors. Newer studies, on the other hand, using simpler test designs, assume that the ability to retain the convictions, goals, and intentions of others as alternative descriptions of the world can be seen as early as 7 months of age (Kovacs et al., 2010). At the latest at 24 months, beyond directing their visual attention, toddlers can imagine what "others see, hear, and know . . . particularly in operative contexts" (Tomasello, 2019). From age 3 onward, children can develop a sort of collective intentionality, that is, they can participate in a group based on common principles, norms, and conventions (Tomasello, 2018). The aforementioned Hungarian workgroup assumes that early on there is a specifically human "social sense" that depends on the developmental stage of the infant's brain.

The brain may have two different structures that mature at different speeds and lend us the ability to empathize with others. The supramarginal gyrus, for example, responsible for the nonverbal perspective, develops earlier than the temporoparietal transition and the precuneus, through which we understand how others *think* – and not just how they feel, see, or will act. The workgroup around Grosse Wiesmann (2020) showed 3- and 4-year-olds a videoclip in which a cat observes a mouse disappearing into a box. Then, the cat turns its back on the box for just a second, so that the mouse can scurry over to another box. When the cat turns around once again to see where its prey is, it goes to the first box. Using eye-tracking methods, the workgroup followed the eye movements of the young test participants. The result: Both 3- and 4-year-olds were able to predict where the cat would first look. They recognized that the cat still thought the mouse was in the first box and would thus search there first – even though they know that the mouse was somewhere else. However, when the researchers explicitly asked the children where the cat would search for the mouse, they gave the wrong answer. Their eye movements thus properly predicted where the cat would look, but they failed to confirm this in their verbal answers. Only the 4-year-olds were able to supply the correct answer. According to this workgroup, this is proof that we are dealing with two different decision-making processes with respectively different brain structures: a nonverbal variant communicated through their eye movements and a verbal variant revealed in their answers.

These results suggest that "embodied" (implicit) mentalization is different from cognitive (explicit) mentalization as the integrative capacity of the various pre-mentalizing modes, since, according to the classic definition, mentalizing is impossible on the preverbal level. A further innovation lies in the recognition that the body must be seen as part of a cultural system:

> in cultures where the body is experienced as the seat of the self, the family consists of a number of "selfs." In other cultures, the central unit is not the body or "self" of the individual, but the community and especially the family – a quasi "common body" or "family self."
>
> (Asen et al., 2019, p. 233)

Thus, bodily symptoms signal disharmony in the social order, which is expressed in groups through various disturbances to interpersonal relationships (Friedman, 2007). Nevertheless, in the mentalization model, the word "body" remains hardly more than an eye-catcher. For example, the terms "somatization" and "body" rarely even pop up in the standard works by Bateman and Fonagy (2016; 2019) – although particularly therapists of patients with personality disorders are confronted first and foremost (and sometimes exclusively) with bodily symptoms (a good example being eating disorders) that express the existential distress the patients are experiencing.

Both psychoanalysis and psychosomatics fail to "precisely differentiate between the body, the body-self, and the phantasmatic drive-body" (Kobylinska-Dehe, 2019). But how are we to differentiate "the body-self" from the "body" from the "phantasmatic drive-body" when all the English language has available is the simple term "body"? In both German and French, the corporal experience is divided into the subjectively experienced body (*corps propre*) and the body as a physiological entity: Kobylinska-Dehe's statement (2019, p. 526): "We are an animated body and have a physical body." While the body is equally the link to sensorimotor interactions in the social and natural environment, conscious "experience . . . is therefore not only tied to the physiological body [*Körper*] as its biological basis, but also to the subjective body [*Leib*]" (Fuchs, 2017a, p. 97). Therefore, in phenomenological philosophy, the body [*Leib*] is considered the site of a "basal feeling of life: of diffuse comfort or discomfort, of vitality, freshness, or fatigue, of pain, hunger, and thirst" as well as a "resonant space for all the moods and feelings we experience" (Fuchs, 2017a, p. 97). The emphasis placed on the dual aspect of the body [*Körper vs. Leib*] is aimed at the Cartesian dualism that recurs in neurobiological reductionism and manifests itself in the intersubjective relationship. This relationship – at least in prepandemic times – resulted in the handshake, which was not only a symbolized convention of a bodily movement but for therapists is sometimes so indicative that a (too strong or too weak) handshake serves as a diagnostic hint – and among the more experienced ones even as a preliminary diagnosis. Thus, a sweaty palm suggests a generalized anxiety disorder, while patients with disc-related back pain or heart problems maintain a firm, sometimes almost painful handshake (in the sense of a "pressured pattern"), which has been assigned to "Type A behavior." The latter is considered a risk factor in coronary heart disease because such individuals are characterized by extreme ambition, restlessness, competitive drive, anger, and hostility (Friedman & Rosenman, 1971). A toneless, limp handshake, on the other hand, might suggest suicidality.

In this respect, it is worthwhile to take a brief look back in history. Kobylinska-Dehe (2019) noted that, apparently, Sigmund Freud, who published *The Interpretation of Dreams* in 1900, and Edmund Husserl, who published *Logical Investigations* (Husserl, 1900 [1922]) in Vienna in the same year, knew nothing of each other. Both had sat as young students in the same university hall and listened to the lectures of Franz Brentano, the father of the concept of "intentionality" who enriched conventional psychology with this important aspect (Brentano, 1874 [2008]). The philosopher of science Daniel C. Dennett took up this concept and gave it a central meaning in his definition of mentalization (Dennett, 1987). By pointing out the intentional directionality of mental processes toward something in the world and by providing a processual version of the soul, Brentano opened up a whole new dimension of phenomena that differed from both mere physiologically conditioned sensations and mental constructs. While Brentano remained trapped in conscious actions, his student Edmund Husserl used this concept to expose a layer of the original experience of the world and the self, something he later called the "lifeworld" [*Lebenswelt*]. This concept – today we would likely speak of the "bodyworld" – is understood in phenomenological philosophy as the foundation of prereflexive experience, as the functioning/functional intentionality that precedes every act, whereby the animated body [*Leib*] represents a transition point between inside and outside. Thus, Husserl (1973, p. 110) coined the phrase: "The body [*Körper*], the living body [*Körper*] of the Other, is the first intersubjective thing." This formulation forms a bridge to the "vitality forms" propagated by Daniel Stern, who focuses more precisely on the dynamic properties of experience, "especially on the fluctuation profile of excitation, interest, and liveliness" (Stern, 2010b, p. 57). The phenomenological tradition of the German idealists distinguished between the animated, "lived body" (Leib) that is experienced first personally and the physical, material, objective body (Körper), which is subject to the laws of physics, causality, gravity, and so on (Moran, 2017, p. 28). It is an interesting finding that Husserl emphasized that touch and self-movement is constitutive for the development of a bodily self. But that the eye cannot see itself, so it is excluded from the circularity involved in the touching relation (Moran, 2017, p. 34). In the end, it was Husserl's student Maurice Merleau-Ponty (1945 [2012]) who laid the foundation for the mentalization model in the sense of *intercorporeality*, applying the bodily, affective, intersubjective, and implicit character of intentionality. The phenomenological approaches to empathic perception may be seen as resulting from a dyadic process of embodied interaction (here the group is theoretically ignored), whereas today the dominant theories of social cognition, such as ToM, are based on the assumption of internal simulations or inferences through which we gain access to the hidden feelings and intentions of others (Fuchs, 2018b).

Against this background, the term "body" might seem to be perhaps a bit too broad at first; it would be more modest to first deal with the gestures that form the origin of human language development and at the same time reinforce speech via gestural expressions of the hands and face, though without causing a break between the levels of expression (Küchenhoff, 2012, p. 86). In contrast to their closest relatives in the animal kingdom, humans are characterized by the ability to perceive representatives of their species as intentional beings endowed with mental states (Tomasello, 2001). This act of "mind-reading" we humans practice seems to be missing in apes and with it also our practice of inserting ourselves into the perspective of the perceptions and actions of our own kind. But exactly this orientation toward intentions and mental states as the "hidden" causes of bodily movements is necessary to train techniques to maneuver the attention of others. These techniques, as observations of infants interacting with adults have shown, quite clearly form the basis for language acquisition. Yet, the view that humans are unique in this respect cannot be sustained. Clever experiments show that great apes can indeed grasp the intentions and perceptual situations of their conspecifics (de Waal & Suchak, 2010): The intentions, perspectives, and knowledge of the other group members are taken into account to enable action control especially when it comes to food and hierarchy; they just cannot tell anyone uninvolved about it.

The integration of the body into the mentalization model also means extending the previous definition of mentalizing, described as "a particular facet of the human imagination: an individual's awareness of mental states in himself or herself and in other people, particularly in explaining their actions. It involves perceiving and interpreting the feelings, thoughts, beliefs, and wishes that explain what people do" (Fonagy & Bateman, 2019, p. 2). By integrating the body, mentalizing becomes an imaginative capacity to intentionally exchange terms of mental states (thoughts, feelings, beliefs, desires) and terms of bodily states and perceptions of oneself and others (e.g., in the group). In this way, an individual or a group implicitly and/or explicitly understands the actions of themselves and others as meaningful. Without a better term at our disposal, however, it must be conceded that the word "mental" is then no longer entirely correct.

1.5 Personality Disorders Without a Body?

> The mentalization model, initially developed for the treatment of personality disorders, neglects the significance of the body and bodily symptoms in theory and therapy with the exception of eating disorders. In this respect, it is also understandable that pre-mentalizing affect regulations, which are physical, are only assigned to the teleological mode, which is primarily object related, or to the equivalent mode in somatic symptom disorders. However, patients with personality disorders not infrequently express physical symptoms that primarily relate to the self, to feeling existential in the face of the inner object void. The integration of the body into the mentalization model is suggested to expand the understanding of mentalization as an imaginative capacity to exchange terms of mental and bodily states, both implicitly and explicitly.

The concept of mentalization was originally developed by the research group around Bateman and Fonagy for the psychotherapeutic treatment of patients with borderline and/or antisocial personality disorders (Bateman & Fonagy, 2004; Fonagy et al., 2002 [2004]). Subsequently, it became apparent that it could also be helpful with other mental and psychosomatic disorders, to focus on whether and how such patients mentalize – or whether and how their mentalizing is disturbed. Unfortunately, even in the second edition of their *Handbook of Mentalizing in Mental Health Practice* (Bateman & Fonagy, 2019), they largely ignored aspects of the body and bodily states, except for the chapter on eating disorders (Robinson et al., 2018; Robinson & Skarderud, 2019) and the reference to the cultural embeddedness of the body of both patients and therapists (Asen et al., 2019). This is surprising because patients with a personality disorder are quite prone to a wide variety of somatizations and functional body complaints. And physically ill patients are also in need of mentalization-based treatment concepts.

After some time, a 20-year-old female patient admitted that she had repeatedly attacked and abused her body because, she said, it was not an object of love for her. She noted: "At the time, I felt comfortable in this emptiness. In reality, I was so blinded by myself that eventually I just wanted to disappear completely so that I would no longer feel the pain. And whose body is this anyway? I didn't need it. But I did need it!"

A meta-analysis of 64 studies involving 275,183 adolescents and young adults confirmed that "self-injurers" reported higher levels of body dissatisfaction, body disownership, and deficits in experiencing and evaluating body sensations than those who did not engage in self-injurious behavior (Hielscher et al., 2019). In this context, disturbed bodily sensations appeared to facilitate a propensity toward self-injury more than dissatisfaction with one's body.

Such patients attempt to compensate for a disturbed sense of self-worth as well as a lack of social acceptance by enacting changes to the body, for example, through tattoos, piercings, or other types of self-injury, the goal being to feel that they belong to a different group. In this respect, body designs should be viewed not just from the perspective of the individual, but also from the social perspective. Like the decorated, colorful skin of indigenous peoples from all continents, body art ingeniously expresses the respective cultural idiosyncrasies of a community, which is why fellow human beings react approvingly or disapprovingly when they "compare their own conceptions of body design with those customary in other cultures" (Reichel-Dolmatoff, 1997 [2001], p.15).

Regardless of the different cultural significance, however, the phenomena of bodybuilding, the "adornment" of the body with tattoos as well as piercings, and the aggressive physical accentuations of so-called skinheads signify more than just body art in the Western world. All of these skin-based phenomena can also be seen as attempts to experience oneself concretely by forming a "second skin," as both a protective and a delimiting object, accompanied by painful injury and a pictorial expression (the tattoo) (Bick, 1968). One of my male patients, who had grown up under very deprived circumstances, had his entire body – impressively and skillfully – tattooed as a crocodile, thereby expressing simultaneously his unintegrated aggression. In this sense, plastic surgeons also form a professional group that resembles tattoo artists: They are among the first people patients approach who want to adapt their bodily boundaries to some body ideal, usually originating from a social body ideal, for example, through breast enhancement, nose straightening, liposuction, or labia reduction.

From the perspective of the extended mentalization model, these body ornaments or manipulations represent a variation of the pre-mentalizing body-mode (cf. Chapter 5.1). They usually refer to an early disorder with a deficient representational development of the body-self. This deficiency sometimes appears as such an unbearable (traumatic) emptiness that only self-ornamentation or even self-injury can rectify. They are a kind of "prostheses" with which the person attempts to compensate for the traumatized imperfection. During their search for identity, adolescents – now no longer children but also not yet adults and feeling isolated – see in the body-mode their chance to literally engrave the dramatic changes to their existence into their flesh for all eternity (or to injure themselves). The body markings, resulting from a lack of affect marking in childhood, may also constitute an attempt to confirm themselves.

Whenever mentalization is understood exclusively as a psychological and not also as a physical, that is, as a psychosomatic function, we use constantly to explain human behavior based on internal states, then effectively we are maintaining the Cartesian split between body and soul. Mentalizing asks: What are the feelings, motives, thoughts, or intentions underlying a particular action – in oneself and in others?

> Why exactly did I act like that? What is going on inside that person that they were so short-tempered yesterday?

Yet we often take mentalization for granted, making it difficult to describe and understand what exactly it means. The recent descriptions of mentalization as a special facet of the human imagination imply that

> any act of mentalization is by its very nature uncertain; internal states are opaque, changeable, and quite often difficult to pin down, even in the individual's own mind. This means that any attempt to make sense of mental states is vulnerable to error or inaccuracy.
> (Bateman & Fonagy, 2019, p. 3)

Indeed, it is easier to describe *disorders* of mentalization. Failure to mentalize is expressed in others seeming to be incomprehensible, in unclear inner states, in ruminative thought patterns. But fears may also come to dominate, and a stronger need for control, even rigidity and feelings of anger are possible. Mentalization disorders are furthermore expressed in different pre-mentalizing modes, which represent early childhood experiences and are accompanied by physical phenomena (Chapter 5.1).

There are sufficiently well-documented scientific reasons to believe that declines or prolonged deficits in mentalizing play a central role in the transition from mental health to mental and psychosomatic illness – and vice versa (Katznelson, 2014; Schwarzer et al., 2021). Mentalization deficits or collapses in mentalizing are associated with poorer mental and physical health, as evidenced by patients with personality disorders, autism spectrum, eating disorders, psychosis, and with somatic symptom disorders (Ballespí, Vives, Alonso et al., 2019; Ballespí, Vives, Debbané et al., 2018; Weir et al., 2020).

Mentalization is a higher-order cognitive ability that allows individuals to make sense of what is going on in their own psyche and in the psyches of others (Bateman & Fonagy, 2016). Furthermore, mentalization is a multidimensional skill that conceptually overlaps with the social cognition model, social neuroscience, ToM, insight, and metacognition: the ability to sense what is going on in one's own body and in the body of the Other.

Notes

1 Fotopoulou, A.: *Social versus Physical Distancing: Experiences and Desires of Social Touch During COVID-19 and in Psychotherapy,* retrieved on 11 July 2020, Neuropsychoanalysis Around the World. https://npsa-association.org/event-details/neuropsychoanalysis-around-the-world-abstracts/
2 Original emphasis.
3 Panksepp wrote his names for the basic emotions in capital letters to distinguish them from their everyday language meaning. He wanted to indicate that he meant whole brain functions and not just feelings.
4 Kinesthesia = the sensation of movement.

Chapter 2

The Body and Its Relationship With Physicians and Psychotherapists

As a young resident, I met an approximately 50-year-old woman in a neurological outpatient clinic. Shortly after I had greeted her, she managed to talk for more than 30 minutes on end about how she had unsuccessfully consulted with more than 20 doctors in the last months because of her diffuse body pains. Every attempt on my part to take a deeper, biographical anamnesis was brushed aside with an even more intense urge to talk, so that I hardly intervened at all. As an act of impotent helplessness – trying to somehow stop this torrent of talk – I finally exclaimed: "You're getting on my nerves!" To my surprise, the patient, a true Berliner, interrupted her flow of speech and uttered, "Well, after all, but you are a neurologist!" – whereupon we both had a hearty laugh.

Today, knowing what I know about the mentalization model, I understand this exchange to be the patient, with her sharp Berlin tongue, "mentalizing" me within a split second – at least following my own utterance. I, however, had fallen into a prementalizing state, which in the mentalization model is called the equivalence mode. To my further surprise, following this interaction, the conversation continued as a rather normal dialogue, which can also be understood as an "acting out of countertransference." So, finally, I was able to take her medical history.

The famous German comedian from Munich Karl Valentin (1882–1948) had a rather anorectic appearance, which promoted his landlord, who had provided him with a stage to perform on in Munich, to call him "Skelettgiggerl" (approximately ribbed caspar). It is said that he introduced himself to a general practitioner with the words:

"Doctor, my stomach hurts, my liver is swollen, my feet are killing me, the headaches won't stop, and, if I may say a word about myself: I don't feel well either."

A family physician once commented:

"And, then, if the patient comes to my practice for the fifth time, I am annoyed . . . it seems to me as if some patients actually wish they had a horrible disease . . . and that makes me angry. They should be happy that they don't have anything. . . . At some point, I end up lacking compassion. . . . It's very exhausting!"

DOI: 10.4324/9781003345145-2

Many patients express disappointment at their diagnosis: "My doctor found nothing wrong with me!" Patients with somatic symptom disorders are experienced as "difficult" because of their conviction that there is some organic cause to their woes, which is often accompanied by unrealistic treatment expectations ("You must do something! You are my last hope!"), despite or because of the chronification (Roenneberg & Henningsen, 2016).

The concept of somatosensory reinforcement developed by Arthur Barsky (1992) might be helpful for patients with such dynamics. Somatosensory reinforcement describes a characteristic way individuals observe signals from within and on the surface of the body and how they evaluate such perceptions. The response of such patients to interoceptive signals, manifested in a marked tendency toward somatosensory reinforcement, goes back to an insecure-avoidant attachment style in early childhood (Waller & Scheidt, 2006; Waller & Scheidt, 2008). This attachment style, in turn, is accompanied by altered psychophysiology and affect perception and is characterized by at least the following four features:

- a tendency to preferentially experience physical sensations as intense, harmful, and impairing;
- a tendency to pay special attention solely to unpleasant sensations;
- a tendency to see unpleasant bodily sensations as something pathological rather than normal;
- a total reluctance to associate unpleasant bodily sensations with mental states.

More unconsciously than consciously, in an act of congruent countertransference, physicians tend to focus on somatic causes because they fear overlooking a physical illness. The reason lies in the peculiar concern physicians have of becoming entangled in legal disputes, whereby they have far less fear of making the medical error of overlooking a psychogenic or psychosomatic disorder or participating in its possible chronicity. Medical uncertainty leads to unnecessary apparative examinations to exclude all possible somatic causes; the repetition of such apparative examinations, which usually also have an economic background, can be seen as a "relationship disorder" in the healthcare system.

One of the best-known problems of patients with somatic symptom disorders, referred to in the literature as modern afflictions (Shorter, 1992), is their firm conviction that psychotherapy is of no use to them because in fact they "know" that their illness is biologically rooted. For example, in the context of inpatient treatment, one patient told a music therapist, "This therapy doesn't do anything for me, I'm made of concrete and steel!" Such statements, belonging to the teleological mode (Chapter 5.2), leave even experienced therapists helpless and put them under great pressure. Such dysfunctional illness behavior makes physicians and psychotherapists alike feel insecure when dealing with such patients and creates stressful interactions for both sides. It often begins with the patient idealizing the therapist even before therapy begins, for example, because they have heard positive things about the therapist from social media, friends, or other sources. The patient's expectations in turn correspond with the ideal the practitioner has carried with them since choosing the profession. This not only causes the therapist to accept the patient's expectations (feeling, at least initially, flattered), it also opens the door to overt or covert promises that ultimately cannot be kept. This in turn leads the patient to repeated disappointment, devaluation, and finally massive criticism of the practitioner, who not infrequently reacts by sending the patient to another colleague, sometimes even to one they hold in less esteem. This precipitates a kind of mentalization failure on both ends (see Figure 2.1).

Although the relationship is experienced by both sides equally as "difficult," such patients keep seeking out (other) physicians despite their dissatisfaction. Out of disappointment at not having fulfilled their helper ethos, the latter react with stigmatizing terms, such as "luminary killer syndrome" or "doctor-(s)hopping." In the face of such a failed doctor/therapist–patient relationship, unconscious dynamics on both sides come to play a central, intertwined role: Not only does the patient find themselves in a prementalizing mode with their complaints, but the doctor or the psychotherapist does so, too.

It is unclear whether it is specifically these patients who rob the physician/psychotherapist of their empathic ability, or whether this phenomenon is being fostered by a more general societal decline in the ability to empathize. Other considerations suggest that people in the helping professions, especially physicians, develop an empathy deficit or even an empathy blockade because of overwork and exhaustion. In light of an (unspecified) feeling of endangerment as well as a simultaneous inability to communicate their stress, one can indeed conceive of such an empathy deficit as a relational defense, so that patients feel increasingly less understood. Physicians who have difficulty identifying their emotions and regulating their negative feelings experience emotional exhaustion more quickly, must

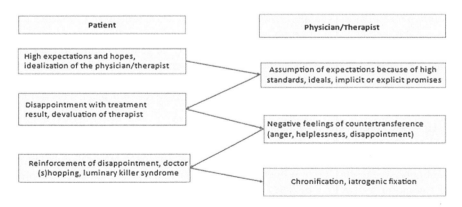

Figure 2.1 A physician–patient interaction cascade for somatic symptom disorders.
Source: Roenneberg and Henningsen (2016).

distance themselves from patients, and exhibit a diminished perception of their performance, including simple boredom (Gleichgerrcht & Decety, 2013).

A failure of medical mentalizing may be assumed when a patient's complaints are diagnosed (too) quickly as "psychological," without this assessment having been sufficiently secured during the conversation. Then it may happen that an important examination or treatment option is omitted. A classic example is the misdiagnosis of hyperthyroidism as an anxiety disorder (Janneck & Krenz, 2018). In this sense, making a correct diagnosis is also a physician's mentalization performance.

The influence of the settings in the organization of outpatient and inpatient clinics that promote or inhibit mentalizing should not be underestimated in the treatment not only of this patient group (Bales et al., 2017). Much less visible, but no less influential, are the management and administration of such institutions, which can support or defeat relationship-oriented therapy concepts. In this context, the profit orientation of the healthcare system in which these institutions are embedded also plays a considerable role, favoring apparatus-based medicine over conversational medicine for economic reasons.

Interestingly, even the location of the encounter with such patients plays a role in the symptomatology. For example, as a young neurology resident, I noticed that anxiety patients recovered more quickly from the physical symptoms of their panic attacks in the surgical department in the presence of much surgical equipment than in the neurology-internist emergency department. My hypothesis at the time was that the surgical equipment seemed to ensure a greater sense of security than a mere "consultation" with a physician.

Even if no reliable research data are available for such observations, it can be assumed that non-mentalizing treatment teams also negatively influence the course of treatment and the treatment outcome by choosing inappropriate therapy strategies. Unfortunately, this is true not only for patients with functional physical complaints but for almost all patient groups as well.

Somatically insufficiently explored, so-called nonspecific functional bodily complaints (in short: somatic symptom disorders) are frequent and multifaceted physical phenomena that turn up in both medical and psychotherapeutic practice. In a study on the prevalence of bodily complaints in the general population in Germany, 82% of the participants surveyed reported complaints that had affected them at least "slightly" within the previous week; 22% of the respondents reported at least one complaint that had "severely" affected them in the past seven days (Hiller et al., 2006).

However, prevalence estimates of somatoform symptoms are subject to wide variation regarding the definition, diagnostic criteria, and populations studied. A review of 23 epidemiological studies on the European general population (Wittchen & Jacobi, 2005; Wittchen et al., 2011) found a 12-month prevalence of somatoform disorders of 6.3%. In Austrian general medical practices, 17.1% of patients were found to have somatoform disorders, with high comorbidity observed with depression (48.1%) and anxiety (42.6%) (Jank et al., 2017). The

German S3 guideline "Functional Body Complaints" assumes that about 10% of the general population and about one-third of adult patients from clinical populations have functional body complaints which not only affect the quality of life and performance but are also costly (Roenneberg et al., 2019). From a diagnostic perspective, like mental disorders, somatic symptom disorders are constructs, more descriptive than explanatory. That is why they are helpful for communication and treatment planning but, unlike clearly somatic disorders, do not usually establish causality.

General practitioners and even specialists find it difficult to classify patients with functional body complaints, despite their frequency. Thus, such patients tend to receive inadequate care, not only in the German-speaking countries but in all European healthcare systems. On average, it takes three to five years until a clinically relevant functional body complaint or somatoform disorder is recognized and a specific treatment appropriate to the clinical picture is initiated (Wittchen et al., 2011). Unnecessary, often expensive diagnostic measures lead to irrelevant secondary findings that have no explanatory value for the presented illness. Indeed, they may harm rather than help the patient: In addition to promoting chronicity, repeated apparative and laboratory examinations facilitate expensive (incorrect) treatments, sometimes even producing complications that require their own treatment. Patients – and not infrequently their relatives as well – are often both frustrated and insecure, since they are truly suffering from their physical complaints, sometimes considerably, and yet have no satisfactory explanation for their suffering or access to successful treatment. Untreated somatoform disorders usually tend to take a chronic course.

Successful psychotherapies of individual cases show, however, that it is possible to extract oneself from this deficit shared with patients, if some common element is discovered. André Green saw the solution to the problem in analysts and their patients suddenly discovering something in common above and beyond the conventional analytic paths:

> I remember reports from psychosomatic cases (Marilia Aisenstein) in which free association seemed to be blocked and which, thanks to the inventiveness of the psychotherapist, resulted in new ideas that also touched on analytic material; this occurred following conversations departing from the analytic style, often about topics that happened to arise, among other things, from the fact that both partners had read the same book or watched the same movie.
> (Green, 2017, p. 114)

This observation could also be understood as filling an "empty relationship" with a common third element, which enables the patient to dock onto the therapist and vice versa.

The difficulties in the doctor/therapist–patient relationship leave their mark not only on the diagnostic process, but also on the theoretical understanding of the body and somatic symptom disorders. At the latest, they became apparent with the appearance of war neuroses in World War I in two very different tendencies:

> a strongly physiologically and experimentally oriented direction . . . and a tendency apparently opposed to it, which Henry Ey condemned in the field of psychiatry as the "insanity of sense" . . . and which could be regarded as a kind of reign of terror of the symbol.
> (Marty et al., 1979, p. 899)

This found its diagnostic expression in 20th-century psychosomatics in the form of conversion vs. organ neuroses (Fenichel, 1945) or conversion vs. vegetative neuroses (Alexander & French, 1948).

The term "conversion disorder," however, raises questions: What does the diseased body want to express that language cannot? Does not the varied symptomatology *always* express a different individual, conflictual unconscious? How an illness is expressed characterizes only the effect it has on an observer impressed by it. Thus, it is hasty to infer disgust in chronic vomiting (formerly called "vomiting neurosis"); it could just as easily be defiant anger. "Determining what is being expressed through the body and what the symptom is trying to say is . . . difficult, uncertain, and likely only an approximation, because a biological process cannot simply be translated into its meaning" (Küchenhoff, 2019, p. 769).

With the emergence of psychosomatic medicine as a discipline all its own and different from psychiatry, with its unique development in Germany (Geisthövel & Hitzer, 2019; Janssen, 2017; Zipfel, 2018), its theories oscillated between holism (or "panpsychism," as Georg Groddeck called it, where every somatic symptom was related to a specific repressed psychological event: "illness as symbol") and a science-oriented man–machine model. Both models proved to be unsuitable to providing successful therapeutic treatment for the interpersonal problems of patients with somatic symptom disorders, including their specific illness behavior, because both models are accompanied by a mentalization deficit in the patient–doctor interaction. In such an interaction, it is not unusual for a subgroup of patients with somatoform stress disorders or functional body complaints to attribute their complaints solely to an organic cause in the sense of the teleological and/or body-mode (see Chapter 5.2). An example would be to presume a viral etiology in the case of fibromyalgia syndrome (FMS) or Lyme disease, even though all – usually repeated – medical examinations speak against such an assumption up to now. Negative findings, however, fail to reassure such patients; rather, they are convinced that only clearly observable, material causes apply to their affliction, causing them to continually press for proof of (so-called) objective facts regarding their disease or to cite supposed "evidence" that sometimes turns out to be simple laboratory errors. Thus, it is not surprising that a qualified conversation that promotes mentalizing is impossible with a large proportion of these patients, who cannot fathom possible psychological causes of their physical complaints. They prefer to practice a subtype of magical thinking, which in turn may be regarded as a special form of the teleological mode. In this mode, the patients organized in the German Lyme Disease Society and the German Association of Lyme Disease and Tick-Borne Encephalitis have used all means to fight against anyone who thought otherwise. For example, in 2018, they took legal action to try to force their view of the matter into the guidelines of the German Society for Neurology (https://idw-online.de/de/news691101) – but eventually failed.

Magical thinking (= overmentalizing) corresponds to a distorted (i.e., unwarranted) cognitive belief, for example, when patients are firmly convinced that the cause of their complaints is radiation from their smartphones or other electrotechnical sources ("electrosmog"). In magical thinking, patients – and sometimes also clinicians – know exactly what the possible causes of their complaints are and sometimes even how they can best be controlled, without letting themselves be bothered by medical reasoning or alternatives. Such convictions existed long before the fantasies against mRNA vaccination as they appeared vis-à-vis the Covid-19 pandemic. In contrast to disease-related rumination, magical thinking manifests as the misinterpretation of a correlation as a cause. For example, belief in paranormal, telepathic, or clairvoyant – and thus generally unacknowledged – attributions of cause assumes that one can influence the external world by use of words, formulas, and spells, and thoughts or the internal world by magically connoted "natural remedies." While magical thinking is known to be a precursor to psychotic phenomena, such "preoperational thinking" (Piaget) has only recently been discovered in somatic symptom disorders as well as in organic diseases with unpredictable courses (Hausteiner-Wiehle & Sokollu, 2011; te Wildt & Schultz-Venrath, 2004). Nowadays, magical thinking may also be found as equivalence mode in so-called conspiracy theories/conspiracy beliefs from the perspective of the mentalization model (Chapter 5.1, Pre-mentalizing Modes). Campbell and colleagues (2021) found a correlation between mistrust and credulity – both of which are thought to favor magical thinking – with adverse childhood experiences and higher scores on the Global Psychopathology Severity Index. Both factors partially mediated the link between early adversity and mental health symptoms. Mistrust and credulity were positively associated in their study with difficulties in understanding mental states and insecure attachment styles.

Where the encounter takes place likely also plays a decisive role in the ability of patients with somatization disorders to gain a perspective different from an exclusively medical one. Since many of these patients currently do not receive adequate treatment from specialists or psychotherapists but often exclusively visit their family doctor, a care concept that commences directly in the family doctor's office and is open to psychosomatic disorders may reduce this barrier. At its core, such a model offers not only an on-site consultation by a specialist for psychosomatic medicine and psychotherapy but could also prevent the humiliation patients experience at being turned away (Hartmann et al., 2018). This model enjoys high acceptance not only among patients but from all parties involved.

2.1 Mentalizing in the Medical History, the Initial Interview, and the First Contact

> This chapter emphasizes the importance of the initial interview and the first contact in building a successful therapeutic relationship. Due to the lack of time in healthcare, physical complaints often convey both physical and psychological perspectives, and the history should focus on the contextual nature of somatization to understand the underlying background. The author presents a house-building model of mentalizing interactions that includes attentional regulation, affect regulation, and explicit mentalizing. The quality of mentalization depends on the level of stress and attachment style, for which reasons therapists should adopt an inquisitive stance and value empathic the patient's subjective experiences. The chapter includes clinical examples and emphasizes the need for continuous learning and understanding of mental states in order to build effective therapeutic relationships on the ground of epistemic trust that needs to be developed.

The medical history, initial interview, and the first contact are highly significant to whether "bonding" succeeds or fails. People decide very quickly (within 100 ms), based only on looking into another person's face, whether that person is trustworthy or not (Willis & Todorov, 2006). Patients are equally quick to make judgments about the therapist's clothing, the arrangement and decoration of the room (e.g., diplomas on the wall), and other features of the therapeutic environment.

Because of economic pressures in the healthcare system, hospitals afford each patient only about four minutes per day and general medical practices only eight minutes per day (Becker et al., 2010). This circumstance often causes the dual meaning contained in bodily complaints to be overheard, including both the physical and the mental perspective: for example, when "fatigue" stands for resignation, loss of appetite for dislike of life, and nausea for an aversion toward a person or an intolerable situation. Therefore, any medical history should focus on disturbed body sensations resulting from sleep disturbance, loss of appetite, or digestive problems as "door openers" into the background of somatization. A bodyache may indicate the loss of a beloved object; dizziness and weakness may contain a moral component: I am lying, fooling others; I am too weak to speak my mind. Lamentations reflect accusations and are one way to publicize and eliminate suffering: Wailing walls and dirges provide space for grief. In this respect, it is always worthwhile to listen to the dual meaning of words with medically attuned ears (Kütemeyer & Masuhr, 2013).

Patients with numerous bodily afflictions to complain about often go to a psychotherapist for quite different reasons than because of their bodily symptoms. If a patient comes to a psychotherapist and argues that they have come because they are suffering from gastric ulcers, an initial mentalizing question might be, "Could it be that you are confusing me with a gastroenterologist?" The patient probably responds, "Well, my doctor told me quite emphatically that it's all psychosomatic." This might be followed up by the question of what exactly the patient means by "psychosomatic" or "mental." To some psychoanalysts, psychosomatic symptoms alone do not yet represent a real need for therapy, whereas according to the mentalization model, this should trigger a differentiated cascade of questions to elicit, layer by layer, the conscious and unconscious wishes the patient harbors toward the therapist and the therapy. In this way, patients may begin to take a greater interest in the cause and solution to their suffering.

Discoveries from early-childhood developmental stages of mentalization can be used to promote mentalizing interactions during the anamnesis. These consist of interactions that conduce an awareness of affects and emotions via the three stages of attention regulation, affect regulation, and explicit mentalization, analogous to a house-building model developed by Maria Teresa Diez Grieser and Roland Müller (2018) (see Table 2.1).

Functional body complaints or somatic symptom disorders are context-dependent, which is why they occur in all cultures, albeit with very different manifestations. Numerous therapists have impressively documented their experiences of treating refugee asylum-seekers in recent years (Joksimovic et al., 2019), where they had to deal with a wide variety of pre-mentalizing modes, in particular with the body-mode in persons with an insecure residence status. To promote mentalizing, it is worthwhile orienting oneself to the different dimensions (see Figure 4.1)

Table 2.1 First interactions regarding mentalization of the body (mod. according to Diez Grieser & Müller, 2018, p. 174)

Attention regulation ("basement"): Stimulate listening and waiting, help to calm down; provide supportive and empathic interventions; affect focus: cautiously, reservedly, but positively bring feelings into play; arouse or strengthen positive feelings, use respectful humor; make and keep clear agreements (e.g., in the case of excessive contact requests); quickly stop and de-escalate any emerging disturbances or risky actions.

Affect regulation ("ground floor"): Identify, name, distinguish, and explore the feelings of all participants (including a partner who is not present); provide support by inquiring and clarifying ("reading") the affective states of oneself and others, by discussing events, behavioral sequences, and facts, etc.; apply a kind of "slow-motion technique"; accept and validate subjective experiences; carefully externalize emotion-oriented parts of self; help to adjust the "operating temperature" to a moderate level; (possibly) give simple psychoeducation on feelings, empathy, and mentalization.

Explicit mentalizing ("1st floor"): Apply basic techniques; confront, challenge (especially in the pretend mode), using humor and "disturbing" ideas (Columbo attitude); use metaphors; stimulate thinking about one's own self parts and about the parts of others as well as about the relationships among them.

that are organized along different polarities (Luyten & Fonagy, 2015). The quality of such mentalizing depends on two essential factors:

- on the stress or arousal level
- on the quality of the individual attachment history, which includes that of the therapist as well.

To design a mentalization-based medical history such that, in the end, patients with physical complaints feel seen and understood is a lifelong project for both physicians and psychotherapists. It also offers the opportunity to shore up missing epistemic trust: Every case history – like every treatment, by the way – is unique, so even experienced therapists never stop learning. Surprisingly, the therapist's attachment style and attachment representations do not differ that much from those of their patients (Schauenburg et al., 2006). Insecure-ambivalent or insecure-avoidant attached individual and group psychotherapists are therefore more likely to intervene according to some theory and/or manual than more securely attached ones. Even though it would seem to be self-evident, video analyses show that displaying a friendly interest right from the beginning regarding the patient's origin (and possibly also name and dialect) is in fact surprisingly rare.

First and foremost, a curious "not-knowing" stance belongs to every mentalization-promoting approach. Yet therapists, who have studied medicine for six years and trained for another five years to become a specialist – or a similar length of time after their psychology degree to become psychological psychotherapists – find adopting such a stance particularly difficult. In the context of a mentalization-promoting medical history, however, it has proven very useful to adopt such a not-knowing, and consequently ever-questioning, attitude toward all patient statements, affectively free of all reproach and with friendly comportment. Even if, to validate certain affective states, it may seem beneficial to express understanding, adopting a more differentiated understanding of mental states, depending on the phase of the conversation, tends to promote greater curiosity in patients to expand their exploration.

It is not primarily a matter of convincing patients to participate in therapeutic or psychosomatic treatment, but rather to establish a relationship that promotes mentalization, the centerpiece of which is a "now moment" formed by the empathic "validation"[5] of the complaints. Doctors and psychotherapists succeed best if they not only speak and understand a "generic language," but if they also attune their ears and speech to "unfamiliar" language games. Empathic validation means putting oneself in the patient's shoes as if one were experiencing the pain, grief, or loss oneself, and expressing this to the patient in a marked way. It corresponds to the marked mirroring of the infant by the primary attachment figure. This means exploring the patient's physical discomfort, such as pain or dizziness, such that the patient develops the feeling of being present *in* the therapist.

Here's an example of intervention for empathic validation: "Such a headache must be just terrible!" (And after a short pause) "But perhaps could you describe to me again exactly what I would have to feel or how I would feel the pain if it were mine?" Such a strategy promotes trust, maybe even epistemic trust in the treatment relationship.

A bigger problem arises when patients absolutely do not want any contact with a psychosomatic therapist or a psychotherapist, under any circumstances, but such contact is desired by third parties. For example, more than 30 years ago I was called as a consultant by a senior physician of an orthopedic university clinic to a patient who had been describing severe back pain for almost 14 days. A peculiarity of this young patient's back pain was that it was accompanied by a long-lasting and sudden occurrence of an acute forward tilt to the trunk, which disappeared during sleep. Phenomenologically, this is a so-called camptocormia, clinically well known as a form of mass neurosis that occurred during World War I. The physical symptomatology expresses equally shame and submission to military authority along with the simultaneous inability to pick up a rifle or perform any other military functions. Reports also described camptocormia sufferers as frequently speaking with a falsetto voice. Furthermore, the symptomatology proved to be very resistant to treatment.

I must admit I entered the ward with a particular expectation, since to my knowledge this was the first case of female camptocormia to date.

I greeted the patient and introduced myself, mentioning in passing that I was a consultant from the Department of Psychosomatic Medicine. The patient, facing me, asked surprisingly gruffly, "*Where* are you from?" I repeated, somewhat intimidated and perhaps even with a slight stutter, "Fffrom the Psychosomatics Department," to which the patient replied, "Then I don't want to speak a word to you!" Up until then, I had never experienced so much rejection within such a short time, but I took heart and asked the patient, "But how are you going to get well without me?" to which she replied, "You'll see!" Within the next two to three days, the patient had abandoned her symptomatology completely. The attending physician's history revealed that a recent wedding had involved rape on the part of the husband, to which the patient had responded with this symptomatology.

This vignette is a cautious indication that even relatively brief contacts can sometimes be therapeutically quite helpful, through an interaction technique now called "challenging." This proved to be the case even though the cause of the patient's painful deformity very likely remained unconscious to her, meaning the risk of renewed psychogenic body complaints may be assumed to have persisted. This is likely true above all for short-term psychogenic body complaints that have yet to experience any secondary gains.

However, the fear of a new experience stemming from an offer of psychotherapy may be expressed in coming late to the initial consultation, despite an agreement between patient and therapist. In such situations, psychotherapists should consider such a "miss" as a joint enactment of a (later-to-be-worked-out) message of an attachment disorder. Today, we know that psychotherapists are not neutral regarding their relationship with their patients but always remain actively involved and cannot ignore their own role. In our opinion, the authentic, bodily-affective reactions of the therapist are just as important for the formation of representations of affects and emotions as, for example, voice, speech, and the common understanding of possible "slips."

Physicians have an important advantage over psychological psychotherapists: They can take the patient's history during the physical examination, for example, scars ("How did this happen?" "How did you get this?" "What were you doing there?") or body postures can be discussed "incidentally." The goal is to discover more about the body's "memory traces" in a curious, casual manner – with a "not-knowing" attitude.

Giving greater consideration to subjective physical complaints, so-called body complaints, would improve diagnostics overall and better delineate the classification of underrepresented clinical phenomena (Kütemeyer & Masuhr, 2013). A more systematic consideration of the patient's sensations promotes a receptive attitude toward the physician, which in turn is helpful for differential diagnosis. An example are the physical phenomena that accompany anxiety disorders: In half of the cases, they express themselves polysymptomatically (physically) without a conscious experience of anxiety, for example, in essential hypertension, unclear dizziness with nausea, visual disturbances, tinnitus capitis (i.e., of the head rather than the of the ear), seizure-like weakness, fatigue, exhaustion with paralysis, itching seizures, tingling and other paresthesias, balance disturbance with unsteadiness of gait, distension, tightness, hot flash, ravenous hunger – but especially characteristic are fits and starts of ever-changing multilocal pain, especially in the evening and at night.

Employing an anamnesis technique that promotes mentalizing is also helpful in the presence of somatoform (psychogenic) pain, which presents almost identically to neurogenic pain and can often be differentiated only after a precise neurological examination. In cases of somatoform pain with a psychogenic cause, patients often describe their complaints using culturally dependent metaphors:

Pain travels through the body "like a lightning bolt"; pain in the face feels "like a hot knife" cutting from the lower jaw across the cheek and forehead (across all trigeminal borders); lower back pain "radiates" into the neck or forward on one side and into the groin (like a finger pointing toward sexual assault); patients say it's "as if someone is breaking my back," "chiseling away at me with a hammer and pick," "pulling off my skin." Dissociative pain is usually distinctive: It is often excessive and peracute, like the trauma itself; the invasive metaphors are undigested, omnipresent condensed narratives of violent scenes suffered ("as if someone . . ."); the nonanatomical radiation of pain often refers to the site of denied or repressed injuries. For example, when a patient opens the conversation by stating their diagnosis: "I have lumbago," the doctor can cheekily ask, "Who did that to you?" which allows an underlying pain of separation to surface more easily.

Metaphors are particularly useful for capturing the dual meaning of physical discomfort. For example, some patients answer the inquiry into how they are feeling by saying "dead to the world," "completely drained," or "put through the wringer." That is how they unconsciously narrate their past or present traumatic history – by addressing such affect-oriented questioning with casual, flippant retorts. Yet: The more they can describe their pain through metaphors, the easier it is to access biographical narratives.

Persistent somatic symptom disorders may be understood as resulting from early traumatic experiences that, because of their origin in the still immature cortex, are stored primarily in implicit memory structures. Neuroscientific data presume that this period starts during the prenatal development of the brain and ends at around the age of 18 months; only then does the hippocampus seem to become fully functional so that increasingly long-term memory is possible, representations can occur, and the increasing ability to reflect enables mentalizing. In the presence of sufficiently secure attachment experiences, patients can integrate nontraumatic early experiences into further self-development via this maturation process, whereas early traumatizations and extreme prenatal experiences remain implicitly at a sensorimotor level, where they express themselves as posttraumatic processing patterns in the form of somatizations. Pre- and perinatal traumatizations express themselves largely physically so that they are very difficult, if not impossible, to process in the classical, conversational psychotherapeutic context. These implicit matrices are hardly accessible to active memories via thought-associative processes and can thus be integrated only with great difficulty.

Nevertheless, the symptoms of somatic symptom disorders differ according to the type of complaint, explanatory model, attribution of meaning, and means of expression, including the existence of "culture-bound syndromes" that occur only within circumscribed cultures (Hausteiner-Wiehle et al., 2013). Independent of the transcultural aspects of somatic symptom disorders, a problem arises when taking the patient's history, something Freud (1905 [1953], pp. 15–16), far ahead of his time, pointed out:

> I begin the treatment, indeed, by asking the patient to give me the whole story of his life and illness, but even so the information I receive is never enough to let me see my way about the case. This first account may be compared to an unnavigable river whose stream is at one moment choked by masses of rock and at another divided and lost among shallows and sandbanks. I cannot help wondering how it is that the authorities can produce such smooth and precise histories in cases of hysteria. As a matter of fact the patients are incapable of giving such reports about themselves. They can, indeed, give the physician plenty of coherent information about this or that period of their lives; but it is sure to be followed by another period as to which their communications run dry, leaving gaps unfilled, and riddles unanswered; and then again will come yet another period which will remain totally obscure and un-illuminated by even a single piece of serviceable information. The connections – even the ostensible ones – are for the most part incoherent, and the sequence of different events is uncertain. Even during the course of their story patients will repeatedly correct a particular or a date, and then perhaps, after wavering for some time, return to their first version. The patients' inability to give an ordered history of their life in

so far as it coincides with the history of their illness is not merely characteristic of the neurosis. It also possesses great theoretical significance.

This precise description of the difficulties of taking a case history is true for a large proportion of patients with somatic symptom disorders. However, knowledge of these difficulties can also be helpful when diagnosing somatic disorders, as Freud wrote:

Another physician once sent his sister to me for psychotherapeutic treatment, telling me that she had for years been treated without success for hysteria (pains and defective gait). The short account which he gave me seemed quite consistent with the diagnosis. In my first hour with the patient I got her to tell me her history herself. When the story came out perfectly clearly and connectedly in spite of the remarkable events it dealt with, I told myself that the case could not be one of hysteria, and immediately instituted a careful physical examination. This led to the diagnosis of a not very advanced stage of tabes.
(Freud, 1905 [1953], p. 15)

Freud appropriated from Charcot the integration of a physical examination and the precise, almost photographic, clinically exact nosography of psychogenic bodily phenomena:

The hysterical phenomena have primarily an excessive character: The patient describes their hysterical pain as one of the highest degree; their anesthesia or paralysis easily becomes absolute; their hysterical contracture depicts the utmost in shortening a muscle is capable of.
(Freud, 1888b, p. 79)

At the time, of course, the theoretical understanding of these phenomena had not yet been developed.

Almost every modern clinical medical textbook contains a reference to the fact that an anamnesis is extremely important for both diagnosis and therapy. But how to structure the anamnesis, the complex interplay between the linguistic and non-linguistic intentions of a patient, and the professional demands made on a physician/psychotherapist to embark on a fruitful exchange by using techniques of stimulation and listening are unfortunately rarely mentioned. A recent exception is an anthology on medical communication that proposes the so-called NURSE scheme for history-taking (see Table 2.2: Naming, Understanding, Respect, Support, Emotion), which differs slightly from the mentalization model (Waller, 2018).

Largely forgotten is the clinical interview designed by Felix Deutsch and William F. Murphy, who called their technique "associative anamnesis" and first published detailed tape-transcribed anamneses in the 1950s (Deutsch & Murphy, 1955 [1964]-a, 1955 [1964]-b). This interview technique was aimed at patients with "psychosomatic" and neurological disorders (e.g., bronchial asthma, psychogenic pain syndromes) using the concept of free association in the initial interview. Here, not only what patients say is important, but how they reveal that information. The authors had noticed that patients with somatic symptom disorder speak a sort of double language – a somatic and a verbal one (Deutsch & Murphy, 1955 [1964]-a, p. 19). They argue that the somatic language is as comprehensible to clinically experienced psychotherapists as the sign language of the deaf and mute is to initiates. Physical phenomena are the first signs of an unconscious mental content, which can be expressed verbally only much later. The aim of this anamnesis technique is that patients establish a connection between unconscious mental and somatic processes, between illness and conflict, on their own, a thesis also represented by the mentalization model. Positive transference and identification with the ego-strengthening parts of the parent figures should help the patient to associatively clarify the underlying infantile structured relationship conflicts via key figures and keywords.

This approach is given additional weight if one considers that patients with somatic symptom disorders (this applies incidentally analogously to people with

Table 2.2 Similarities and differences between the NURSE scheme and mentalization-oriented anamnesis

NURSE schema	Mentalization-based anamnesis technique
Naming an emotion (". . . Mrs. M., you seem so depressed . . .")	Initiating the anamnesis by asking about emotions ("How do you feel?")
Demonstrating *Understanding* (". . . I can well understand how this is stressing you.")	Questioning emotions and use of metaphor language ("I haven't quite understood that yet, can you please describe it to me again in more detail?" "What do you mean by . . . exactly?"). In this context, it seems to be advantageous if the physician uses gestures to ask questions, touching the part of their own body the patient is describing as painful.
Offering *Respect* (". . . I'm impressed with how you keep trying to maintain all the relevant aspects in view as best you can.")	Showing respect, perhaps even lavishing praise if the patient can make a connection between their emotions and their symptom(s) ("That makes a lot of sense to me" or possibly just "I'm impressed!")
Expressing *Support* (". . . What could we do to ease this feeling?")	Opening up about oneself ("If it were me, I'm sure I would feel [such and such]")
Exploring the *Emotion*	Marks the beginning of a mentalization-based anamnesis ("What would your pain feel like to me?")

autism spectrum disorders [ASD] and traumatic experiences) have language problems. Not only do they display a deficiency in attributing feelings to more complex concepts, but they also often express a literal-concrete understanding of spoken language (Tebartz van Elst, 2016). While spoken language is usually full of ambiguity, and metaphorical idioms and allusions must be intuitively inferred from the situation, this can cause particular problems for both patient groups, making "small talk" with them possible only to a very limited extent, if at all.

Thus, from the point of view of the mentalization model, it makes sense to focus on facial expressions and voice, a kind of microtracking that aims at a piecemeal reconstruction of existing emotionally stressful experiences. Repeating the patient's keywords seems to be helpful by bringing up repetitions from the patient's life history stemming from negatively connotated memories. Unfortunately, that the therapist's and the patient's voice can serve as a seismograph of the respective state of mind, as it were a medium for communicating the inner state to the outside world, has been little studied so far, let alone addressed in supervision. This also applies to the messages therapists leave on their answering machines, which usually sound rather monotonous if not depressive and thus presumably negatively dampen the callers' expectations. Seen positively, of course, this may also determine the patient–therapist pairing procedure.

Taking a patient's history therefore represents the – sometimes quite impossible – attempt to achieve a certain level of mentalization via speech and communication, in particular using an affect-focused inquiry into the patient's symptomatology. A mentalization-based anamnesis serves not only the therapeutic relationship – by giving a patient the feeling of being understood in their subjectivity, when they feel they are being taken seriously – but also the chance to change our perception of our self as well as of the social world. For a long time, psychoanalysis was thought a discipline that consisted of nothing more than – apparently passive – *listening*, considered a sufficiently differentiated activity to initiate processes of change. A mentalization-based anamnesis, however, is characterized by both active *and* passionate listening and observation. This was also well known to the pioneers of psychoanalysis: Psychotherapists should "learn how one speaks to the other without words" (Reik, 1976 [1948], p. 165). Because of the couch as a means of treatment, psychoanalysts should "learn to listen with the 'third ear'," which from today's point of view of implicit communication is a little too short-sighted. Physical sensations and symptoms should be granted at least the same importance as the patient's biographical background, current life circumstances, and the psychodynamic context. In the meantime, there is a multitude of empirical findings that take a closer look at every conceivable sensory experience, such as smelling, seeing, feeling, and hearing, under the term "embodied communication."

This fits quite well Freud's rather hands-on approach to therapy as described by Cremerius (1981) and May (2019). Today, the principles of empathic and embodied communication using actor-patients are now applied in the training of physicians at some universities. Yet, too little attention is still paid to nonverbal interactions as expressions of unconscious symptomatology, expressed, for example, in hand and foot movements in the form of nervous restlessness, rocking, nesting, fumbling, nibbling, playing with one's fingers, fidgeting. Possibly as an unconscious defense against such interactions, in their everyday practice physicians have proved to interrupt their patients in the initial interview for the first time after only about 19 seconds (Koerfer et al., 1994). Given the increasing bureaucratization of healthcare and the observation that quite a few physicians now type the medical history directly into their PC during the interview, this time window has probably shortened even more over the last 25 years. Henningsen (2003) therefore rightly asked whether such an interrupted speech flow should be regarded as an iatrogenic form of interaction that ultimately costs even more time than it claims to save.

Clinicians orientated toward language theory have proposed the idea that human speech is *always* able to express the inner processes, depending on the explicit knowledge of the speaker. The reason for this is that "language represents a complicated medium of its own, which in and of itself seems to be able to represent a hitherto unknown wealth of processes of the most diverse nature" (Argelander, 1991, p. 7). However, a language-oriented anamnesis technique requires modifying the physician's self-conception: It must become less about active exploration than about enabling the patient to speak freely through discretion on the part of the investigator, who can then better observe and analyze the patient's emerging discourse behavior. In doing so, the interviewer does more than just "receive," as Freud's metaphor might suggest; the therapist must also apply "means of prioritizing attentiveness directed toward the patient" (Schöndienst, 2017, p. 296). To do so, the clinician/therapist must facilitate a conversational framework that provides sufficient space for patients to "dock" onto.

In mother–child dyads, the equivalent to this anamnesis technique is called *joint attention* and *joint intentionality*, which generally enable "epistemic trust." Epistemic trust is accompanied by an openness toward new information and the ability to learn from that information (Fonagy et al., 2019; Shai et al., 2022). For patients, such attention is established using vivid cues (or ostensive cues) in the form of certain physical and vocal signals, e.g., eye contact, a patient-appropriate choice of words, or a certain prosody. Such body-related signals make it clear to the patient that they are important, and that, without their intentionality, there can be no understanding of the problem. Meanwhile, there is also scientific interest in mostly unconscious body signals and postures. They seem to be associated with improved self-disclosure when they take place synchronously (Vacharkulksemsuk & Fredrickson, 2012).

Based on history-taking interviews conducted using this technique and subsequently transcribed, Martin Schöndienst worked out the differences in the individual linguistic characteristics of patients with dissociative seizures, focal epilepsies, or seizure-like anxiety disorders. Thus, in contrast to those patients with epilepsies, patients with dissociative seizures made different statements:

> The patients themselves – whether before, during, or after their seizures – usually discuss only their experiences in a few keywords. Attempts by the therapist

to focus on the subjective semiology of the seizures often remain unproductive. Accordingly, there was a regular lack of the varied formulations characteristic of patients with epileptic auras, which characterize their often-puzzling aura experiences.

(Schöndienst, 2017, p. 297)

Patients with dissociative seizures rarely reported what they had tried to do to interrupt the seizure, whereas those with epilepsies very often spontaneously addressed some measure that had occasionally worked for them to interrupt or abort an approaching seizure (Schöndienst, 2002). Furthermore, there was a lack of coherence in the narratives, which is also true for other dissociative disorders, for somatoform pain disorders, or functional body complaints.

Marilia Aisenstein and Claude Smadja – students of Pierre Marty – called for a special technique to address so-called psychosomatic patients:

To interest such a patient in the thinking process, one must think with him and involve him in the process. We would even go so far as to talk of a kind of 'seduction' that tries to help the patient recognize that nobody has 'nothing to say', no life is without its story, and that no story is without its words, its wealth, and its sorrows. Everything should be done to support and stimulate preconscious work and thereby help patients to discover and share in the pleasure of constructing emotional experience through speech.

(Aisenstein & Smadja, 2010, p. 629)

Thus, a first "seductive," and at the same time mentalizing, question directed toward these patients at the beginning of anamnesis is: "How do you feel?" This question immediately moves the conversation away from the conventional and characteristic everyday approach of "How are you?" or "What brought you here?" and into the realm of a *relationship*. Either the patient immediately begins to speak about themselves, or they ask, "What do you mean – now or ever?" The mentalizing art of the practitioner lies in responding to the patient that they can choose what to talk about.

It cannot be emphasized enough that every taking of a case history can proceed in a manner that promotes or inhibits mentalizing, depending on the therapist's level of training and their interest in the patient. The prerequisite for a mentalization-promoting technique is posing primarily open questions, such as:

- "What were the circumstances when the symptoms first occurred?"
- "What was going through your mind *before* the panic attack set in?"
- "What exactly happened before the vomiting? Could you describe the situation to me once again?"
- "What do you think might be the source of the pain?" (question about the subjective theory of illness)

- "Could you please describe it to me again in more detail, I haven't understood it yet." (in the sense of "Columbo")[1]
- "How would the pain/symptoms feel to me if I had them?" "Where are they exactly, where do they radiate to?"

By employing such an "art of questioning," the therapist encourages patients to express their feelings and emotions, which the therapist should then empathically support by saying, for example, "Yes, I can relate to that," possibly supported by an unreserved formulation: "I think I would have felt similarly in such a situation." One can also reinforce the patient's experience of resonance by underlining questions with fitting gestures, in the sense of a synchronous movement, for example, by touching one's head when the patient talks about headaches or one's back when the patient talks about back pain. In addition to increasing the patient's attention, such gestures serve to counteract any fears in the patients that their body is not being properly perceived. Since bodily sensations are particularly suitable for differentiating between neurological, psychotic, and psychogenic disorders as well as for discriminating psychogenic disorders from one another, the physician/therapist can apply the anamnestic peculiarity that bodily sensations can only be grasped communicatively, namely, by listening carefully to the patient's narrative. However, good listening must be trained and developed.

Closed questions (yes/no), on the other hand, are not conducive to mentalizing:

- "Are you depressed?"
- "Was your mother kind to you?"
- "On a scale of 0 to 100, can you tell me how much this hurt you?"

Therapists pose more closed-ended and intrusive questions than they realize. It is not conducive to mentalizing to ask questions arbitrarily and technically in the sense of "fact-checking," which produces a situation more like an interrogation that puts patients under pressure and induces fear. For the therapist, such an approach has the role of *preventing* the activation of attachment patterns. Rather, the therapist should proceed to inquire in a friendly-empathetic, sometimes even provocative-confrontational way (in the sense of challenging), but with a not-knowing stance. The decisive thing is the motive: If the goal is to get the patient to mentalize, then the path is quite different from letting oneself be guided by one's affective reactions in the therapeutic relationship.

That this endeavor is not always successful was revealed in the documentation published by the Munich association "Ethics in Psychotherapy": Of the 540 reports lodged in the period from 2006 to 2015, "empathy failure" on the part of therapists was the most frequently mentioned complaint, with violations of social boundaries being the second most frequently reported complaint, both of which point to a mentalization failure on the part of the therapist (Franke et al., 2016). Even if one can only speculate about the reliability of the data (statements from the "accused" side were unfortunately missing), "empathy failure" should nevertheless be taken very seriously as an indication of the need to improve psychotherapeutic training. Violations of social boundaries also suggest mentalization deficits or irruptions among therapists. Questioning the patient in the initial interview as well as during the subsequent therapy in a curious and interested manner that promotes mentalization is certainly no guarantee of empathy, but without empathic questioning efforts, physicians and psychotherapists remain forever stuck in "technical neutrality" – which patients may perceive as a failure of empathy, especially if the therapist fails to provide resonance for action- and solution-oriented attitudes.

In a sense, patients with somatoform disorders may appear to be "depersonalized." We can better understand the phenomenon of empathic failure if we view empathy as a process of cooperative dialog that starts from body perceptions. When these patients trigger specific, sometimes even negatively connotated physical countertransference reactions, doctors and therapists are often overwhelmed by a mountain of examination results that are supposed to prove the somatic etiology of the complaints.

For example, a patient with a somatization disorder handed me two file folders with over 1,000 pages of laboratory findings that were presumed to prove his "Lyme disease." Parallel, the doctor/psychosomatics specialist/psychotherapist is criticized with the words: "Haven't you read the documents I sent you?"

Patients with somatoform disorders (and their suffering) are often overlooked because they function so very well in everyday life and are often very well adjusted ("high functioning"). However, such seemingly "well-adapted" patients force the therapist to be even more attentive to keep the initial interview and even more so a therapy alive. It is not uncommon at intervision meetings to hear psychotherapists say that they hope such initial interviews or therapy sessions would go away or would at least pass as quickly as possible. This sometimes is nothing but an expression of the therapist's exhaustion. Therapists must often tap their energy reserves to creatively fill an "empty relationship."

Of course, doctors/therapists too can experience "depersonalization" because of the constant density of therapeutic work, especially in inpatient and day-clinic settings. The argument often heard is that there is not enough time to take a good history, supported by the observation that therapists now spend more than half of their time on indirect stationary care, such as documentation, writing reports, general service meetings, or other internal organizational tasks (Wolff et al., 2017), instead of focusing their efforts on actually treating patients and discussing their cases in team meetings.

In our view, in the end, one likely *saves* time by taking a thorough history that promotes mentalizing. Fewer instrument-based examinations are then required, which also results in fewer incorrect treatments and incorrect referrals. The (justified) complaint that physicians take too little time for their patients could be countered by the fact that they are not trained to use their limited time effectively. Instead of concentrating on the essential problem, they tend to address several problems at the same time. However, the better the (mentalization-promoting) communication and the better the ensuing resonance between doctor and patient, the higher compliance will be regarding treatment, which tends to be rather low in patients with chronic somatoform disorders.

There are several "homemade" conversational disorders on the part of the practitioner that do not promote mentalizing: monologizing (talking a lot and incessantly), generalizing ("always," "never"), dogmatizing (postulating inviolable doctrines), overtaxing the patient (too much information, too many topics). Taking a mentalization-promoting case history, on the other hand, resembles the concept of motivational interviewing, characterized by the following (Miller & Rollnick, 2015 [2013]):

- *engaging* – relating to someone,
- *focusing* – narrowing down, elaborating concerns,
- *evoking* – eliciting willingness to change, awakening, working with ambivalence,
- *planning* – developing a concrete change plan.

The authors assume that almost everyone has the potential for change within them. Patients are generally not without motivation, they are just ambivalent: They see both the arguments in favor of change and the reasons for leaving everything as it is; they want to change, while at the same time they do not want to change. Wherever they are allowed to interject their ambivalence into the relationship increases their willingness to change. However, many patients with somatic symptom disorders should – at least in the eyes of others (spouses, parents, etc.) – change something, even though they themselves see little reason to do so. This can be relatively quickly elucidated by asking what mentalization-based therapy calls "challenging questions":

- "Have you ever tried to change something in the past and then given up?"
- "Is it possible that you don't want to change anything at all?"
- "What benefit might the symptom have (for you)?"

For this group of patients, developing an ambivalence would be considered progress! The solution for change lies equally within the patient and within the therapist, something the latter should signal by trusting the patient's competencies. Yet, regardless of the respective pre-mentalizing state, engaging in arguments and confrontations usually only serves to create resistance and hinders the change process.

Patients with narcissistic traits are particularly difficult to reach via conversation. Patients with narcissistic personality disorder are characterized by an increased interest in the self and an excessive need for admiration. They generally think they are much better informed than doctors/therapists, something they apply to control their narcissistic injuries stemming, for example, from a threat to their self-image after interpersonal ruptures. Thus, their fears often revolve around physical health or bodily integrity (as if one's physical self might actually "fall apart"). This led to the question of whether severe narcissistic pathologies tend toward hypochondriacal or somatoform disorders. Yet pathological narcissism does not directly correlate with somatic symptoms; it "only" facilitates them indirectly, through somatosensory enhancement: Physical hypersensitivity and hypervigilance influences the perception of somatic distress (Kealy et al., 2018).

Initial medical consultations usually end with a summary of all findings and suggestions for further procedures. However, when all medical examinations fail to provide evidence for a somatic etiology, this can be quite distressing for patients. In this case, it may be advantageous to take an approach that promotes mentalizing and ask the patient what *they* think the cause might be, that is, to obtain the patient's subjective theory of their ailment. If the patient's and the physician's ideas lie far apart, orientating oneself to the following six criteria has proved useful for establishing a basis for further therapeutic collaboration. Burton and colleagues (2015, p. 87) proposed six criteria for the rational explanation. These are based on the constructive normalization type of explanation, the common-sense model, and the principle of personal relevance:

- It is plausible (to both doctor and patient).
- It does not imply weakness or fault on the part of the patient.
- It promotes therapeutic partnership or action.
- It applies a descriptive label (which need not be a specific diagnosis).
- It addresses causation, although this may be through perpetuating mechanisms rather than root cause. It is created through dialogue between doctor and patient.

For the subsequent therapeutic procedure, it is important not to reinforce implicit processes – neither associatively, regressively, nor even psychodynamically – as is possible with nontraumatic experiences; rather, patients should be encouraged to have a presence experience, which, if a joint discovery, can further develop into an initial object representation. After such an initial interview, patients sometimes say: "Nobody has ever asked me that before."

2.2 The Disappearing Body in Online Video Therapies

> This chapter explores the impact of global digitalization on our relationship with the body, particularly in the context of psychotherapy and therapeutic relationships. It discusses the challenges posed by the use of online video psychotherapy, exacerbated by the COVID-19 pandemic, where the patient's body is largely absent from the therapeutic gaze and the therapist's body is limited to a two-dimensional representation on a screen. The chapter highlights the importance of creating a safe space for patients, where the therapist's body is considered part of the therapeutic setting. It delves into the

> stress experienced by therapists during online sessions, the impact of self-mirroring on attention and observation, and the need for active engagement to establish trust and security. The chapter also addresses the concept of disembodiment in virtual communication, the challenges of the holding function in telephone therapy, and the varying experiences of different patient groups, such as individuals with autism spectrum disorder (ASD) and alexithymic patients. Additionally, it raises questions about the development of identity in virtual spaces and the influence of online interactions on the body-self and sexual identity.

The current global digitalization hype is changing how we interact with the body. In influential media, it is also pushing the phenomenon of overlooking the body, something critical social psychologists describe as a "culture of forgetting" (Turkle, 2018). Turkle criticizes our emotional engagement with so-called empathy machines that undermine the notion of empathy because they offer no space for embodied experiences. In 2019, no one could foresee that the SARS-CoV-2 pandemic would drastically exacerbate the already difficult situation. Physical distancing, mask-wearing, and the steadily increasing use of online video psychotherapy in both individual and group settings – whether as an initial interview or as a long-term treatment – largely removed the patient's body from the therapeutic gaze and the therapist's body from the patients' sight. The screen shows only one body part, usually the head or at most the upper body, two-dimensionally, as well as (maybe) an unobscured backdrop, which invites various speculations, fantasies, and sometimes questions. This picture may be disturbed by a television running in the background or when the therapist's library or a patient's kitchen furnishings (including exhaust hood) are on full display. All of this complicates and changes the traditional therapeutic relationship. Under such circumstances, one may draw only indirect conclusions about the true emotions and affects of one's counterpart. In addition to the task of ensuring a safe space on both sides of the camera (including guaranteeing privacy and discretion – is some family member listening behind the door?), there is a significant change in "intercorporeality" or an impairment of sensory presence.

A safe setting exists when a space is created in which patients can "use" their psychotherapists as containers/vessels (Winnicott, 1971), where the body of the psychotherapist is part of the setting. For Winnicott, such a space is an extension of the patient's body – from a modern standpoint one must add: of the therapist's as well. Faced with difficult patients, therapists struggle to remain "in the game." This is a particular challenge in video-online therapies.

Most psychotherapists experience video-online sessions as stressful. One factor behind this phenomenon, among others, is the fact that both patients and therapists see themselves on the screen, in the sense of self-mirroring, and are thus constantly distracted from observing the other person because they may be preoccupied with their own facial expressions:

A 50-year-old female patient felt suddenly disturbed by her screen self and her "frozen smile," although she did not feel like smiling at all.

An alexithymic (!) 45-year-old patient experienced his first video-online group therapy as an irritating and alienating "pilot experience." He felt "no or only few emotions at this form of communication technology," especially since he already found it very difficult to establish "closeness" and trust with others. As soon as a "live" group session is once again possible, he would like to be part of it. After sharing this opinion with the group in one of the next sessions and learning that the others felt the same way, he was able to continue participating in the online sessions.

In addition to the pandemic, the buggy technology inherent to online sessions increases the anxiety level on both sides. This makes it imperative that online therapists maintain an active attitude, as is already the case in mentalization-based online therapy: The greater the anxiety, the more important it is to conduct sessions regularly at the same time and same place, in order to induce a continuous feeling of security, normality, and perseverance. Where the patient makes online contact with the therapist must be a safe place. Since digital technology is involved in the process as a more or less "scary" or "trusted" third party (Dettbarn, 2019), the therapist should be thoroughly familiar with the technology and be able to advise their patients on how best to establish reasonably trustworthy safety standards. Despite reservations toward new technology, only digital literacy can enable mentalization-enhancing interactions: the creation and dynamic administration of an adequate "container" to promote the flow of communication. Yet, in doing so, psychotherapists should not be only a container but "a resonance box for the patient's kinetics, . . . and on a prerepresentational level. These are thus not inner images but an organized psychophysiology" – think: body-mode (Chapter 5.2) – "that can be correlated with a specific world of experience" (Krause, 2016, p. 70). This succeeds when therapists actively strive to establish presence, introduce empathy into the space by asking what is going on behind facial expressions, establish trust and confidentiality, and radiate a sense of security and stability, all of which serve to reduce acting-out in the classical sense.

To date, online initial interviews and psychotherapies, as part of both individual and group psychotherapies, are just being scientifically researched and are still something quite new (Weinberg, 2021). We are not talking just about defense mechanisms; the very establishment of contact too must be understood as an entirely bodily process. In a lively face-to-face group, intentionality is vastly more visible and perceptible, at least for some participants: who wiggles in their seat, sighs, laughs, cries, and crosses or uncrosses their legs.

Weinberg and Rolnik (2020) used the term *disembodiment* for this entirely new form of "connectedness." I prefer *dysembodiment* because the body is already visible, albeit only in a two-dimensional context and affected by the medium on both ends. Thus, virtual body-to-body communication occurs in an altered setting-frame.

Yet, the loss of control, of no longer being master of the setting, can unsettle therapists. Being bodiless – for example, in telephone therapy – provokes for some the question of how a *holding function* (Winnicott, 1971) might occur at all. Is the voice of the therapist enough for this?

The holding function is still primarily used to symbolically describe real parental hands embracing and enclosing a baby. How can this be enabled solely by the therapist's voice, which may be altered, if not sometimes distorted, by the microphone? Certain patients, on the other hand, find the connection of mouth and ear on the phone more enriching and intimate than the traditional consultation encounter. While more highly structured patients may be less comfortable with online-video individual and group psychotherapies, people with ASD or alexithymic patients seem to benefit from the new relationship: Shaking hands was always rather awkward for them, so keeping one's distance and refraining from hugs actually accommodate the tactile aversions of these people (Nashef, 2020). ASD patients tend to welcome online-video therapies, with the argument of being able to connect from a safe place and appear particularly relaxed; they seemed to be more communicative, particularly in online group psychotherapies. This led one of my ASD patients to suddenly say that he did not like online video because the group was not physical enough!

The rapid development of virtual communication technologies raises the question of how an identity can develop under these conditions. What effect does the virtual world have on the body-self, on the body-mode, especially regarding so-called online identities? How does easily accessible pornography affect the sexual identity of adolescents? What does it mean when, in a project on online identities ("Future of Identity"), one of the key observations was that some individuals expressed a sense of having "achieved their 'true' identity for the first time only online" and of having been "perceived by others as a 'normal' person" (Beddington, 2013, p. 10)?

Note

1 Lieutenant Columbo, played by Peter Falk, was a famous police officer from the American crime series of the same name, who stacks the deck rather deeply, often appears slightly obtuse, and always nonchalantly asks the most important question while standing at the door, shortly before the end of a conversation. Unlike him, however, the MBT therapist really does know nothing.

Chapter 3

The Discovery of the Body in Early Psychosomatics

In his understanding of the body and mental development some 100 years ago, Sigmund Freud knew very little of "embodied interactions." Rather, his theory took its starting point from the individual, from the ego, without reverting to intersubjective, developmental, and group references. Witness his famous formulation, which upon closer inspection is not easy to understand: "the ego is first and foremost a bodily ego; it is not merely a surface entity but is itself the projection of a surface" (Freud, 1923, p. 25). Leikert (2019a, p. 13) rightly wondered: But if the ego is not the body but rather (only) a projection that "*represents* the body, what access do we have to the body? What then is the body itself? What would the self be if the self were a body? Is the self a body-self?" With the concept of the surface, Freud borrowed his vocabulary from the cortical-based *homunculus* already known at that time, the so-called brain-man:

> If we wish to find an anatomical analogy for it we can best identify it with the "cortical homunculus" of the anatomists, which stands on its head in the cortex, sticks up its heels, faces backwards and, as we know, has its speech-area on the left-hand side.
>
> (Freud, 1923, p. 25)

This image of a representation brought the body to the center of psychoanalytic-psychosomatic theorizing for the first time, albeit in a rather neuroanatomical and static sense, even if Freud writes "above all" to mean "first and foremost":

> A person's own body, and above all its surface, is a place from which both external and internal perceptions may spring. It is *seen* like any other object, but to the *touch* it yields two kinds of sensations, one of which may be equivalent to an internal perception.
>
> (Freud, 1923, p. 24)

Here, Freud not only distinguishes the body as subject and object, but he also concedes the possibility that objects in the social world can be explored with one's own body. Thus, the image one makes of oneself or one's self-representation has its

DOI: 10.4324/9781003345145-3

origin in perceived bodily sensations and in reflection on one's body image – and less so in embodied interactions. In a lesser-known footnote, Freud added to the English translation in the Standard Edition, he expressed the following:

> The ego is ultimately derived from bodily sensations, chiefly from those springing from the surface of the body. It may thus be regarded as a mental projection of the surface of the body, besides, as we have seen above, representing the superficies of the mental apparatus.
>
> (Freud, 1923, p. 25)[1]

In his graphic depiction of the id, ego, and preconscious, Freud attached a small rectangular box with the label "akust." (acoustic) which sits on top of the latter two (Freud, 1923, p. 23). Apparently, in the course of things, Freud had neglected to denote what was heard as an acoustic-sensory interaction experience – and one of the possible "sensations" – so that further explanations of the "bodily sensations" remained hidden, much like the interior of the body itself.

In the first two decades of the 20th century, some colleagues and students, quite sympathetic to Freud, had become very interested in the diseased body and had ventured so far as to support psychosomatic standpoints, among them Franz Alexander, Felix Deutsch, Georg Groddeck, Sándor Ferenczi, and Ernst Simmel (Schultz-Venrath, 1992 [1995]). Quite a few of them, in fact, through their enthusiasm for psychoanalysis, even went so far as to explain *all* organic disorders, whether organic diseases or so-called organ neuroses, in psychodynamic terms. Every organic disease was "after all a neurosis in miniature," because organ diseases arise from the same "psychic sources" as the "psychic symptoms of a neurosis, namely, as a consequence of libido disturbances, repressed unconscious desires, fixations, regressions, and disturbances in the balance of the sexual and ego drives" (Deutsch, 1922, p. 291f.).

In contrast to numerous students, however, Freud remained skeptical of psychosomatic concepts throughout his entire life:

1. Because of its primary focus on the psyche, psychoanalytic theory was unable to resolve the Cartesian body-soul and drive dualism – and at its margins even promoted a "panpsychism."
2. The theory of psychoanalysis and Freud's actual practice did not coincide: For Freud, and this may surprise many, the focus was not on "the relationship to the patient, healing the patient, or the therapeutic act, but on finding, working out, guessing, and (re)constructing unconscious infantile experiences and fantasies and discovering the further fate of these psychic factors up to their contribution to current suffering" (May, 2019, p. 97).
3. Finally, Freud's rejection of psychosomatic relationships could also be based on the fact that he himself had been a "psychosomatic patient," prone to hypochondria and other somatizations (Kollbrunner, 2001). Between 1880 and 1900, for example, Freud repeatedly suffered from sciatica, rheumatic muscular calluses,

migraine attacks, and painful cardiac sensations that, in the context of his fear of death, could be considered cardiac anxiety neurosis. Between 1906 and 1912, Freud also suffered three fainting spells (Schur, 1972) that were closely tied to the father–son death-wish theme. Above all, however, he struggled with "Konrad," a series of physical, especially intestinal, complaints. Not unlike a "psychosomatic" patient, Freud was incapable of considering a psychological etiology for his complaints; rather, influenced by his friend and ENT physician Wilhelm Fliess, he allowed cauterizations and minor surgical procedures to be performed on his nose.

In 1923, Freud received the diagnosis of a carcinomatous disease in the oral cavity, which gave rise to numerous surgical interventions, without his ever becoming completely pain-free. In the same year, he assigned a special significance to pain in the development of a body-self:

Pain, too, seems to play a part in the process, and the way in which we gain new knowledge of our organs. *A painful illness is perhaps exemplary of how one comes to conceive of one's own body in the first place.*[2]

(Freud, 1923, p. 24)

In the absence of pain, Freud argues, one's own body, which is hardly consciously perceived by the ego, behaves like an inconspicuous companion, a kind of silent, background presence. Only through pain or some other unpleasant state does it come to the forefront and receive greater attention, now perceived as something separate from the ego, indeed as an object of the ego. However, the paradox remains that, despite the great importance of pain in his own life as well as in the lives of his patients with hysteria, Freud did not develop a "pain neurosis" analogous to his anxiety neurosis (Kütemeyer & Schultz, 1989).

Freud's reservation toward a deeper understanding of bodily processes was expressed, among other things, by his failure to establish a theoretical foundation for anxiety neurosis, which clearly lagged in quality compared to his work on hysteria and compulsion. He summarily attributed the three so-called actual neuroses juxtaposed to conversion, namely, anxiety neurosis, neurasthenia, and hypochondria, to an "accumulation of excitement" that permitted "no psychic dissipation" (Freud, 1895b). Interestingly, the disorders Freud himself suffered most intensively from received much less theoretical consideration than the bodily symptoms that accompany hysteria. It is also reasonable to assume that Freud preferred a psychophysiological theory of anxiety not only because of the influence of his physiologically oriented friend Wilhelm Fliess, but also because of his own disposition toward anxiety neurosis. Freud's understanding of body and ego (the self is rarely found in his work) and the influence it had led to psychodynamic psychosomatics being reflected in two opposing models throughout the 20th century (from which only few students deviated): the model of conversion, with a symbolization of the body, and the model of actual neuroses, without symbolic representation.

Central to both models is the drive model, with its reciprocal "interactions" between psyche and body, with priority always being given to the rather mechanistic notion of the "mental apparatus." Although the mental apparatus is formed only through interaction with the body, it has the primary task of dealing with the excitation quantities created by the biologically constituted drives. This contradiction – that the mental apparatus is formed from body/drive experiences – has yet to be truly resolved. Some authors, such as Loewald (1980), tried to solve the dilemma by positing the interesting thesis that, for Freud, the drive and the life of the body are one and the same; they become separated only when we begin to distinguish between soma and psyche. Nevertheless, the drive concept remains controversial to this day, especially the question of "whether or not a comprehensive psychoanalytic theory should place drives at the center of its theoretical structure and how best to conceptualize how many drives to posit, which particular motivations are most explanatory, and the relation of these motivations to the body and to biology" (Aron, 1998 [2015], pp. XXI–XXII). If we take this thought of Lewis Aron, a prominent representative of relational psychoanalysis, further and equate the notion of "motivations" as expressions of drive with primary affects and their intentionality, we arrive at an interesting solution to the problem of drive theory: Drives and affects share being living entities that come and go and move, that appear and rise and subside. They are accompanied by specific bodily feelings and the corresponding images; they are no different than "afficere" – lat.: to endow, provide, equip, affect, fulfill, treat, put into a state.

Freud understood psychosomatic phenomena to be transitions from the mental to the physical: For him, conversion was the mechanism of "rendering an incompatible idea harmless," so that its "sum of excitation is being transformed into something somatic" (Freud, 1894, p. 48). Physical symptoms arise when a strong, "incompatible idea" is transformed into a weak, compatible one that is then put to another use. In this way, the extent of affect originally present in the imagination and then in repression can be torn away from the psyche and applied to the soma in its place. The further development depends on the respective mental disorder. In the case of hysteria, conversion ensues, in the case of anxiety neurosis, projection. The different means of dealing with the repressed affect the symptomatology: In hysteria, the symptom represents an experience – a "memory symbol" – that has been repressed into the unconscious: an unbearable psychological conflict expressed through body language and thus no longer consciously experienced; in anxiety neurosis, the symptom represents merely the equivalent of a mental state; and actual neuroses, which primarily appear physically, cannot be derived psychologically (according to Freud):

> the symptoms of the 'actual' neuroses – intracranial pressure, sensations of pain, a state of irritation in an organ, weakening or inhibition of a function – have no 'sense', no psychical meaning. They are not only manifested predominantly in

the body (as are hysterical symptoms, for instance, as well), but they are also themselves entirely somatic processes, in the generating of which all the complicated mental mechanisms we have come to know are absent.

(Freud, 1917, p. 386)

Actual neuroses, functional body complaints, and somatic symptom disorders all represent a historically interesting example of the early observation of mentalization disorders using other terminology. On the other hand, it was obviously difficult to formulate a theoretical framework comprising all of these observations. The psychoanalytic world long overlooked the fact that many of Freud's patients complained of *physical* symptoms (Breuer & Freud, 1956; Freud, 1955). It would seem that the variety of these symptoms led him to be the first to establish a diagnostic taxonomy of mental and psychosomatic illnesses.

Remarkably, however, the concept of somatization is missing completely in Freud's works. This is astonishing because neurasthenia and anxiety neurosis are characterized by numerous physical phenomena – more than 20 symptoms for anxiety disorder alone (Freud, 1894; Kütemeyer & Schultz-Venrath, 1996, p. 1083). They alone would justify a diagnosis of "somatophilia" (e.g., essential hypertension), whereas an anxiety disorder fails to be perceived by about half of the patients and is often denied by patient and physician alike (Figure 3.1). The multitude of physical expressions of an anxiety disorder also explains why it is so difficult to differentiate anxiety-related physical symptoms from a somatoform disorder.

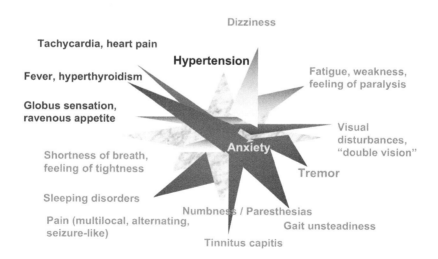

Figure 3.1 Some physical (black) or pseudo-neurological (gray) complaints in anxiety disorders described by Freud (1894).

Source: Modified acc. Kütemeyer and Schultz-Venrath (1997, p. 720).

Freud saw the cause of anxiety-related symptoms as something physical rather than psychological, thereby – a well-kept secret – a little bit plagiarizing the psychiatrist Ewald Hecker from Wiesbaden, who had discovered shortly before him, "that the character of the feeling dominating [the patient] does not always come to consciousness as fear [!] but is interpreted differently by him until enlightenment is obtained," e.g., as "asthma" or "vertigo" or "ravenous hunger" (Hecker, 1893). Such wonderful descriptions of a misperception are unfortunately no longer found in today's textbooks of psychiatry and psychosomatics. Freud did not assign hypochondria, nowadays a special form of somatic symptom disorders, to the actual neuroses until many years later – 1914 (cf. Figure 3.2).

Outside the psychosomatic, psychiatric, and psychoanalytic "community," the term "actual neuroses" – in contrast to conversion – has probably been largely forgotten. In his historically significant differentiation of anxiety neurosis and neurasthenia, Freud (1895b) offered as a commonality a biochemical etiology rather than early conflict or even insecure attachment styles as an explanation: Any libido quantities (sexual substance quantities) not discharged in an adequate orgasm remain in the body and have a toxic effect on the organs.

Freud, who later preferred to deny his neurobiological origins, understood the body and the psyche as a functional continuum, "the key element of which is a process of differentiation of mental functions that progresses from the body to the psyche, but one that psychoanalysis investigates by going backward, from the psyche to the body" (Gaddini, 1981a, 1981b [1998], p. 21). Here we find a boundary

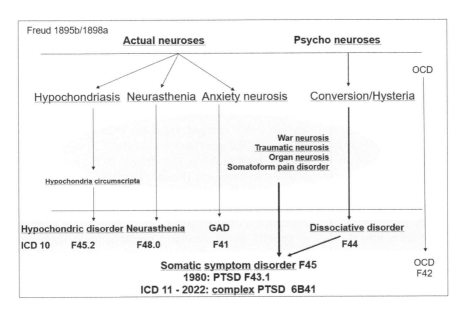

Figure 3.2 The historical taxonomy of somatoform diagnoses since Freud; classification from ICD-10; GAD: Generalized Anxiety Disorder.

Freud was very well aware of, since the reverse path seemed impossible at the time for lack of methodological concepts: "Psycho-analysts never forget that the mental is based on the organic, although their work can only carry them as far as this basis and not beyond it" (Freud, 1910, p. 216).

At the turn of the century, the following were considered neurasthenic symptoms:

> Faintness, absence of nervous capability, dyspepsia, spastic constipation, headache, and spinal pain. More often, however, one finds among the so-called neurasthenics another type, which stands out glaringly and is characterized by overstimulation, agitation, restlessness, acoustic irritability, anxiety in all forms, anxiety with acute and chronic course, anxiety accompanied by paresthesia, accompanied by heart acceleration, sleep disturbances, convulsions. It is important in individual cases to reveal the masked anxiety [!]. . ... This allows one to distinguish neurosis from neurasthenia.
>
> (Freud, 1894)

What Freud means is anxiety neurosis, which here received its first diagnostic terminology. The concept of actual neuroses is still used today, because this term leads directly to modern conceptions of psychosomatic affections. As to the genesis of neurotic and psychosomatic symptoms, Freud had in mind both the nonsatisfaction of sexual drives and the suppression of aggressiveness. Despite his ambivalent attitude toward his psychosomatically oriented disciples, it should not be forgotten that Freud subtly observed "how the body has its say, for example, when Dora plays with her handbag, when a patient clears their throat, or when flatus happens on the couch" (Buchholz, 2014, p. 110).

The term "somatization" (and the verb "to somatize") first appears in the 1920s in the work of one of Freud's first analytic patients and later Viennese colleague – and rival – Wilhelm Stekel (Stekel, 1924, p. 341). Nikos Kazantzakis, a Greek patient who later became famous as a philosopher and author of, among other things, *Alexis Zorbas*, had sought out Stekel because of a sudden and massive facial eczema following an erotically charged rejection (Kazantzakis, 1965, p. 353f.). Kroll (1932) in turn adopted the term from Stekel and infused the physical symptom with an unconscious death problem. Forerunners to the term "somatization" were the concepts of organ language (Stekel, 1908) and organ jargon (Adler, 1927), which denoted the symbolism of psychologically determined physical symptoms.

Stekel understood the development of a symptom as the "conversion of emotional states into physical symptoms" in the sense of a symbolic organ language, i.e., the transformation of more or less differentiated affects into a physical symptom. With this definition, he saw in somatization the equivalent of the conversion mechanism and thus expanded Freud's concept of conversion, which he had explained with the epoch-making sentence "in hysteria, the incompatible idea is rendered innocuous by its sum of excitation being transformed into something somatic. For this I should like to propose the name of conversion" (Freud, 1894, p. 49).[3] Such "incompatible ideas" were, namely, those that had been suppressed by moral or social taboos ("solely and exclusively sexual life" (Freud, 1897, p. 248)) or could be expressed only by means of conversion. In contrast to Stekel, many analysts continued to loyally adhere to Freud's concept of actual neurosis and distinguish between hysterical conversion symptoms and somatic symptoms caused by other mechanisms. Franz Alexander (1948), for example, dispensed with the concept of somatization altogether and instead maintained the basic idea that organic diseases were under the control or chronic aberrant innervation of the sympathetic or parasympathetic autonomic nervous system, for which he introduced the term "vegetative neuroses" (Hoffmann & Eckhardt-Henn, 2017). If anything, psychological conflicts accompanied the somatic symptoms by influencing physiological functions, though they were not the cause of the conversion mechanism. According to Alexander, for example, elevated blood pressure did not occur instead of an affect or a (repressed) idea but was the physiological phenomenon that accompanied anger in the sense of an affect equivalent.

Freud's call to distinguish between conversion hysteria and those somatic disorders that resembled actual neuroses was supported by Edward Glover, Joyce McDougall, and John E. Gedo, among others. Others, such as Felix Deutsch, Georg Groddeck, George Engel, Angel Garma, Leo Rangell, and Melitta Sperling, followed more closely Stekel's approach of transferring the conversion concept from the hysteria concept and applying it to visceral organs and other parts of the body innervated by the autonomic nervous system. Fenichel (1945) took a middle position and made an important distinction between conversion symptoms and somatic symptoms associated with "organ neuroses." Although he viewed conversion symptoms as the translations of specific fantasies into "body language," he now understood somatizations to be bodily in nature – either as affect equivalents or as the consequences of drive needs that affected physiological functioning. He expanded Freud's concept of conversion to include a group of symptoms that expressed pregenital conflicts via conversion symptoms. Max Schur (1955) represented a more modern concept, namely, the idea of desomatization and resomatization, by assuming that mental and physical development had separated somewhere during development: Experiencing became increasingly "desomatized." Physical experience was relegated to the level of preconscious perception and was generally no longer perceived as such – only in the form of the associated affect (e.g., fear). Under psychological pressure, this process could be reversed in the sense of ego-regression and "resomatization," yielding a developmental psychological model of affect regulation. Nevertheless, to this day the question has remained unanswered whether actual neuroses and psychoneuroses truly differ from one another or whether somatization can be viewed as a psychosomatic process analogous to conversion (Taylor, 2003).

3.1 Trauma as a Transdiagnostic Affect-Regulation Disorder

> This chapter discusses various concepts and perspectives related to traumatic relational experiences and their impact on individuals. It highlights the role of physical, procedural memory in storing traumatic memories that cannot be consciously recalled or expressed in words. The passage also discusses the phenomenon of somatoform pain disorders and their connection to conversion or dissociation disorders.
>
> The passage emphasizes the difficulties trauma patients face in verbalizing their experiences and the role of the right hemisphere in trauma-related flashbacks. It explains that trauma can interfere with self-perception and bodily experience, leading to challenges in understanding and expressing physical sensations and emotions. The importance of integrating fragmented elements of trauma into the narrative of one's life will be discussed to restore the differentiating between past and present experiences.

Traumatic relational experiences are stored primarily in physical, procedural memory and therefore cannot be consciously recalled or consciously remembered or even expressed in words (at best after marked mirroring!). A phenomenon little noticed in today's pain therapy is that somatoform pain disorders occupy a dominant place in the case studies of conversion or dissociation disorders described by Freud and Breuer (Freud, 1955; Freud & Breuer, 1895d). In particular, the conversion pain described by Freud using clinical phenomenological terms represents four psychodynamic concepts:

- neutralization of a conflict;
- pain in identification;
- conversion pain as an expression of an organic pain;
- pain as a psychophysical response to a traumatic separation.

Pierre Janet, on the other hand, offered a concept of dissociation that focused on the altered state of consciousness as a disturbed integration of mental functions. Such a disorder includes so-called compartment mentalization symptoms (Scalabrini et al., 2020), which can manifest as amnesia, distancing symptoms (detachment), depersonalization, derealization, or out of body experiences, but also as a structural dissociation of the personality accompanied by changes in self-concept. The symptoms correspond to three nonintegrated neuronal levels. Thus, interruptions in the temporal-spatial structure of brain activity lead to nonintegrated experiences. In dissociation, the right anterior insula plays a decisive role in abnormal intero-exteroceptive integration, although the autonomic nervous system, which is affected by a wide variety of traumatizations just like other brain regions, is equally significant. In addition, traumatized people are severely limited in their bodily experience and in everyday life via an increased release of stress hormones, which permanently alters their perception. The tendency of traumatized people to project their trauma onto everything in their environment largely corresponds to the pre-mentalizing equivalence mode, with its loss of mental flexibility. The consequence is that memories are repeatedly "overwritten" by the repeated narration – as in a repeated dream narration. On the other hand, the trauma never becomes a past event but rather interferes again and again with the here and now. In this respect, a treatment goal that promotes mentalization in post-traumatic stress disorder with dissociation lies in promoting an association, for example, by asking: "What sentence, what thought do you remember before you were no longer there?" This involves integrating the split-off elements of the trauma into the ongoing narrative of life so that patients can increasingly differentiate between then and now, i.e., regain a valid time structure.

Trauma-related flashbacks activate the right hemisphere (responsible for intuition, emotions, and the visual and tactile systems) and simultaneously deactivate the left hemisphere (responsible for language and sequential and analytical thought), which is why both trauma patients and patients with somatization disorders have difficulty finding words to describe their experience. The finding that not only trauma patients find it difficult to verbalize feelings may rest on the fact that the neurobiological center responsible for self-experience is located relatively far away from the language center. Most trauma patients are better at describing others than themselves. These two facts explain why the altered self-perception of traumatized people causes them to have specific problems talking about their traumatization. Because they have such a hard time putting their feelings into words, they also have a hard time knowing what their physical sensations truly mean. They often fail to deal appropriately with their bodily needs, such as getting enough sleep or nourishment (van der Kolk, 1994, 2014, 2016).

Despite the different psychological and somatic phenomena, up until about the age of four early traumas remain stored in the body's memory, albeit without later recourse to a conscious memory of the actual traumatization. Treatment success regarding the symptom thus may consist only of attenuation or displacement – not of a true resolution of the bodily discomfort, even if progress is made regarding interpersonal and social behavior.

Toward the end of a long-term treatment, a 60-year-old merchant says it bothers him that he can go from a confident attitude to a kind of torpor within seconds, especially on his days off (Wednesday and Sunday mornings). His only biographical memory was that he used to save himself from his classmates in school as a recess clown by freezing. Only in the further course of the interview does he recall that he "felt similarly affected" in group psychotherapy when the topic of his father's abuse of his four sisters came up (of which he only became aware in later adulthood). He himself had often wondered why his father had never touched him. The difference between his experience at the beginning of treatment is that his emotional world used to crash in on him, which once led him to attempt suicide, whereas today he experiences that short-term feeling of paralysis.

Even if patients today do not show the classical symptoms known from Freud's times – dissociative disorders tend to be embedded in their respective historical context and express themselves variously – the historical concepts are still extremely helpful for understanding these disorders. To this day, political or ideological reasons, such as the rejection of a psychodynamic interpretation, are the reason why somatoform and dissociative disorders tend to be underdiagnosed or even misdiagnosed in psychiatry (Bremner, 2009).

We owe much to Hoffmann and Eckhardt-Henn (2017) and the working group around van der Kolk (van der Kolk, 1996) for their successful presentation of the various dynamic models and how they overlap regarding conversion, dissociation, and somatization. They carefully compared and pathogenetically reclassified the different diagnoses based on symptom clusters and somatization disorders, chronic stress disorders, and dissociative disorders. For these authors, the disorders mentioned represent "a spectrum of adaptations to trauma," the common denominator being dysregulation of affect. They propose viewing the various disorder patterns as divergent final forms of a biographical traumatization that applies to all, with the distinctive feature (Figure 3.3) that dramatic stressful experiences are stored in the body as "embodied horrors": "The body keeps the score" (van der Kolk, 2014). According to this understanding, many late effects can only be explained by the fact that, e.g., torture aims at the destruction of an early body-image nucleus. This comes very close to Leikert's (2019a, pp. 27, 181) "encapsulated (kinetic) engrams," which could be recontextualized through intensive work on bodily sensations in the form of verbal images.

From the perspective of the mentalization model, Patrick Luyten and Peter Fonagy (2019) advocate an integrative diagnostic approach. In my opinion, their pioneering proposal lies in not limiting the concept of trauma to post-traumatic stress disorder but using it, as it were, transdiagnostically to view numerous other disorders also based on traumatization. In our opinion, a more frequent psychotherapeutic mistake lies in attributing a "trauma" to patients based on diffuse physical memories without reference to a self-remembered situation.

The stage of life in which trauma (e.g., neglect, experience of violence, sexual abuse) occurs is associated with different consequences and symptoms. Despite great plausibility, it remains relatively unclear how and why they exert such a devastating influence on child development. Thus, affect-regulation disorder can manifest itself as "too much" or "too little" emotion. Indeed, if an individual's affect tolerance is exceeded, they may have to ward off affect through the mechanism of depersonalization or desomatization, i.e., by isolating the affect, they develop a self-chosen "numbing." This corresponds to an early defense mechanism rather than a structural disorder.

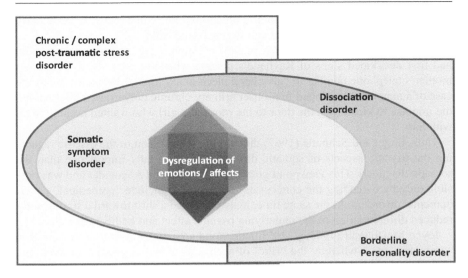

Figure 3.3 Disturbance of affect regulation as a common mechanism of different disturbance patterns with body complaints.

The history of the concept and meaning of somatoform disorders is fraught with conflict and closely associated with the attempt to develop a theory of affect (Landauer, 1991), albeit without much convincing success. Time and again, the debate has centered on whether bodily symptoms have an expressive content. Franz Alexander (1948; Alexander & French, 1948) limited this possibility to the voluntary innervated neuromuscular and sensory-perceptual system, for example, so-called hysterical paralysis or psychogenic blindness. He strictly distinguished this symptomatology from the "vegetative neuroses" (a term developed from the actual neuroses), that is, the "classical" psychosomatic disorders of his time, such as bronchial asthma and essential hypertension. Such disorders are preceded by an activation of the autonomic nervous system as a concomitant of an emotion, such as a sympathetic activation during fight-or-flight or parasympathetic activation during withdrawal. However, if no action is taken to terminate this state, organ damage may result from permanent innervation. Yet, there is no symbolic expression in the sense of a conversion. In this respect, by using these arguments Alexander was one of the first to support an affect theory of somatoform disorders.

Engel and Schmale (1967) did not limit conversion to the sensorimotor system, but rather assumed that *every* organ system could be used as an expression of unconscious-psychic contents. They felt that the presence of an arbitrary or autonomous innervation was not important, but rather whether the organ system or the respective body part was suitable for assuming a mental representation. In particular, they said, the body uses exactly those organ systems or organ functions that have proved significant throughout life under the aspect of object relations, for example, tactile, intestinal, and motoric functions – those that played a particularly important role during the care and upbringing of the child.

Thus, Engel and Schmale (1967, p. 345) mentioned the case of a woman who had first developed signs of Raynaud's disease when she was about to dial her mother's telephone number to "give her a piece of my mind." They also report the case of a man who developed first-onset primary chronic polyarthritis after having the impulse to kick down the door to the room of a girl who wanted nothing to do with him.

Thus, Engel and Schmale (1967) thought the localization of the disease regarding the psychic aspects of somatic diseases was of greater importance than the somatic diagnosis. This viewpoint goes beyond Freud and Alexander and was possible only by extending the concept of conversion to include "preoedipal" developmental disorders. At the same time, it also reflected a shift toward a significantly reduced differentiation of the underlying psychic affect and bodily expression.

Joyce McDougall (1995, p. 153) understood somatization as a regression to a "protolanguage," whereby the "risk" of such a disorder "is greater for everyone whenever there is an unusual increase in internal conflict or external pressures." McDougall advocated the regression model proposed by psychoanalysis: "There is scarcely any patient in psychoanalytic treatment, or any analyst either, who does not display, at one time or another, somatic disturbance due to psychic distress. We are all likely to somatize when internal or external circumstances overflow the containment provided by our usual defenses against mental pain and overwhelming excitement, or depontentiate our habitual ways of discharging stressful emotional experiences" (McDougall, 1995, p. 154). She noticed escapes from her psychotherapies in her countertransference: "The impression that we were going round in circles, that the analysis was treading water or was interspersed with boredom or exhaustion and so on – not to mention that this symptom action threatened to bring about the situation of an endless analysis feared by every analyst" (McDougall, 1997, p. 220). These action symptoms "depend less on language and can be thought of as a regression to an earlier phase of mental organization – the ways of thinking that characterize infancy. Throughout the lifespan, we all have access to this form of primitive mental functioning. Symptoms – whether they be neurotic, psychotic, character organizations, action patterns addictions, or psychosomatic manifestations – are *without exception*, the result of infantile efforts to find solutions to mental pain and psychic conflict" (McDougall, 1995, p. 154).

In the subsequent evolving field of psychoanalytic psychosomatics, which tended to move away from regarding the body toward a metapsychology, sought to understand patients who failed to feel animated and alive by using concepts such as "false self" (Winnicott, 1965), "dead mother" (Green, 1983, 1993), and "unrepresented states" (Levine et al., 2013). Along with Leikert (2019a, p. 21), we find the now canonized term "unrepresented states" rather unhelpful in cases where the autonomic body memory manifests itself in the form of undifferentiated bodily discomforts, paresthesias, or pain. The question is: What form of intervention (it would probably be better to say "what form of interaction?") best does justice to

Table 3.1 Semiotic qualities of psychosomatic symptoms (Küchenhoff, 2019, p. 775)

Model	Semiotic function	Communicative function	Clinical example
Conversion	Iconic function of bodily symptom	Unconscious cathexis of the other and ambivalent work on the object relationship	Conversion disorder, histrionic dynamic
Affect equivalent	Indexical function of bodily symptom	Indication of psychosocial stress	Somatoform disorder
Representational deficit	Semiotic negativity	Protection from intrusions and separations in relationships	Alexithymia
Body as object	Cathexis of the body as an object	Relieving external objects of split-off affects	Hypochondria; self-harm

this early memory formation? Leikert (2019a, p. 22) proposes to "make the body-self of the analysand and of the analyst to the object of attention and reflection." The "semiotic quality" of psychosomatic symptoms and the resulting interactions, of course, depend on our choice of underlying theory, be it ego, self, or object psychology, relational psychoanalysis, or the mentalization model with their respective developmental psychological understanding of drive/affect, attachment, self, and object (Küchenhoff, 2019) (cf. Table 3.1).

The weakness of this classification is that conversion disorder can also lack representations and that affect equivalents can hide in the body as an object.

3.2 The Paris School of Psychosomatics – The Pioneer of the Mentalization Model

> Pierre Marty argues that mental representations are fundamental to human psychological life, serving as the basis for fantasies, dreams, associations of ideas, thoughts, and inner reflections. These representations are constantly employed in direct or indirect relationships with others. The chapter highlights the importance of representations in medical contexts, as a patient's illness history gains meaning and significance when connected to emotional experiences and not limited to mere pathological facts and dates.

> Furthermore, the chapter discusses the historical roots of the concept of mentalizing in Parisian psychosomatics and its connection to somatization. It notes the differences between the Paris and London schools of thought, particularly regarding the understanding of the body and the focus on intrapsychic versus intersubjective perspectives. However, both schools reject the dichotomy between the mind and body and emphasize their continuous interaction.

Between 1960 and 1975, the working group around Pierre Marty developed – (still) on the basis of the Freud's drive concept – first theoretical considerations on mentalization. The booklet "Mentalisation et Psychosomatique" (Marty, 1991) has remained more or less unknown, not having been translated into English or German and rather abstract in content. The central theses declare that the formation of psychosomatic symptoms may be attributed to a lack of "mentalization" and that this deficiency is based primarily on the absence of the development of "representations" – that are not, however, attributed to a developmental-psychological deficit of insecure or missing attachment. Marty's research group came up with the term "mentalization" after carrying out initial interviews and psychotherapies with psychosomatic and even cancer patients and noticing that their weaknesses regarding their individual psychic abilities differed noticeably from those of neurotics under psychoanalysis. Marty forwarded that "mentalization" may not have (yet) been an issue for Freud because he was specifically interested in psychoneuroses as a pathological organization whose representations still proved to be rich in terms of quantity and quality.

They furthered that the dimensions of the mental apparatus, which constituted the "quantity and quality of individual psychic representations," had not been a major research topic. Yet mental representations, Marty claimed, form the basis for the mental/psychological life of every human being: During the day, they provide what we call fantasies; at night, they provide the elements of dreams. Only such representations allow associations of ideas, thoughts, and inner reflection. We also employ them constantly in our direct or indirect relationships with others (Marty, 1991). As an example of "mentalization" – in his work at that time the verb "to mentalize" as a process had not yet occurred – Marty cites the cascade of his own memory triggered by the perception of a handkerchief:

> So, I am . . . holding my handkerchief in my hand. I remember that it came from a cousin who has since died. I think of the death of this cousin, who was taken care of by colleagues. I am grateful to them for their help, back when he was ill. I also think of my family, whom I had just visited in the province, and I feel some guilt for not having visited this cousin's widow. I didn't have time to do that. I will make up for it next summer. . . . Mentalization is a preconscious

ego function that transforms basal bodily sensations and motor patterns into primary . . . representations.

(Marty, 1991, p. 12)

This example starts from an ongoing perception that turns into a representation. This representation in turn connects with associations of ideas and affectively charged inner reflections about the past and future of one's relationships with others. Physicians can appreciate the role of representations when a patient recounts their illness history: Such a story remains dry and with little or no meaning or representation if only pathological facts and dates are voiced. On the other hand, such a tale becomes fruitful if, with the help of the physician, the pathological facts are connected to emotional experiences of the respective episode.

According to Marty, in the case of somatic clinical cases, there are striking differences in both the quantity and quality of the representations, depending on the individual and their momentary situation: Sometimes the representations seemed to be missing completely; sometimes they were diminished in quantity because numerous perceptions present over a longer time did not lead to the formation of representations. Persons who are limited in their ability to think – again, Marty avoids using the word "mentalizing" – see no other way out (if at all possible) than to express this through their behavior, if they are to cope with the various exogenous and endogenous emotions. Thus, Marty proposed speaking of "behavioral neuroses" and, in cases of fewer quantitative and qualitative representations, of "neuroses with deficient mentalization."

Marty and his colleagues, in good Freudian tradition, assumed that individuals are often exposed to a certain quantity of emotions stemming from drives. The events and situations they are exposed to affect their emotional world and cause emotions that they either have to discharge or realize. Such means of discharging or realizing consist either of mentally processing the emotions or of displaying a motor and sensory behavior that is variously bound up in the mental processing. Those emotions that are not discharged or realized accumulate, and sooner or later they will pathologically affect the physical "apparatus." Marty was mainly interested in discovering the means of realization offered by the dynamics of the psyche within the different ongoing individual attempts to process these emotions.

In this context, his research group thus first devised the concept of "mentalization," which referred to representations, to mental images, and to their dynamics. Furthermore, Marty and his group assumed that there is a progressive organization of representations during personal development, probably throughout life, although it may become slower over time (Lecours & Bouchard, 1997). However, the presence of "fundamental insufficiencies" and a "lack of availability of representations . . . constituted an obstacle to mental work" (Marty, 1991).

So, what remains? The historical roots of the concept of mentalizing lie in Parisian psychosomatics, which focused on the connection between mentalization and somatization (Jaeger, 2019; Storck, 2016). Unfortunately, for a long time, this insight was neither sufficiently considered nor duly recognized. The concept of the Paris School formed an important theoretical starting point for the development of the mentalization model, which was subsequently only marginally taken up by the British working group around Fonagy, Target, and Bateman. This explains some interesting differences, especially concerning the understanding of the body: The Paris school of psychosomatics initially understood "mentalization" as the description of a relatively broad mental process of representation connected to drive theory; via Bowlby's concept of attachment, the London group utilized the term "mentalization" to make the connection to an empirically based developmental psychology with concepts of primary and secondary representations, which lead to the development of a self via marked and contingent mirroring of early affects by the primary attachment figures.

Gubb (2013, p. 103) distinguished the Paris school of psychosomatics, calling themselves "psychosomaticiens," and the attachment/mentalization theorists in terms of the former having an intrapsychic focus in contrast to the latter having an intersubjective focus. The former can be characterized in terms of "the speechless mind" and the latter of "the speaking body," where the body attempts to do the work that should be located in the mind. But this has not been elaborated very thoroughly, with the exception of Fonagy and Moran (1990), who turned to self-destructive patients with brittle diabetes from a psychoanalytic treatment perspective, shortly before the development of the mentalization model. Brittle diabetes is a form of insulin-dependent juvenile diabetes in which patients unconsciously or preconsciously fail to control blood glucose so that they put themselves into a hypo- or hyperglycaemic coma in order to regulate proximity or distance to a primary object. What both schools have in common is their rejection of any Cartesian dualism between the psyche and the soma and their understanding that these two entities are in a continuous interaction.

3.3 Alexithymia and/or Autism Spectrum Disorder (ASD)?

> This chapter explores the concept of alexithymia, which is characterized by an inability to recognize and express emotions. The chapter highlights the work of the Paris Psychosomatic School, which suggests that a lack of mentalization, or the ability to understand and interpret one's and others' feelings, is a key factor in the development of alexithymia. It further explores how alexithymic individuals struggle to describe their own physical and emotional states, leading to difficulties in communication and emotional connection with others. The chapter also delves into the neurobiological and developmental aspects of alexithymia, including its association with traumatic experiences and its impact on body perception and touch.

According to the Paris Psychosomatic School, impeded development of mentalization leads to "alexithymia." The term comes from the Greek and means the inability (*a-*) to read (*lexein*) feelings (*thymos*). In the 19th century, its precursor was called "soul blindness" (Lissauer, 1890), which was introduced by Freud as "agnosia" and more recently titled by Lane's research group as "affective agnosia" (Lane et al., 2015). Alexithymia is characterized by "an impoverished fantasy life, a limited imagination, a diminished capacity for empathy, a tendency toward impulsive behavior, a tendency to somatize [!] emotions, and a preference for offering undifferentiated descriptions of emotional experience" (Fain & David, 1963; Fain et al., 1964). "A-lexi-thymia" thus represents the exact opposite model to the ability to "mentalize." Interestingly, the Paris Working Group did not use the processual concept of mentalization in the sense of "mentalizing."

Marty and de M'Uzan (1963; Marty et al., 1963) had observed what they described as operative thinking (*pensée opératoire*) in patients with "classical" psychosomatic disorders as well as in those with unexplained physical symptoms. People with a high degree of alexithymia would know that they were not well, but they would not know how to describe it. They expressed a purposeful, outward-oriented way of thinking, which made them seem to have nothing on the "inside" – an early indication of one of the dimensions of mentalization (cf. Chapter 4.4). These patients were described as "present but empty" (Marty & de M'Uzan, 1963, p. 1348), which is probably why they used the metaphor of the "self as an empty container," where therapists otherwise expect to find a wealth of subjective "material": memories, dreams, hopes, fears, conflicts, and much more.

Psychosomatic patients would have nothing to relate except endless descriptions of their physical symptoms, sometimes without reference to any underlying, medically indicated disease. They were wasting precious therapeutic time with their "detailed descriptions of trivial circumstances" (Apfel & Sifneos, 1979, p. 181). Since, in the eyes of their therapists, they remained stuck on the surface, oriented toward external objects, instead of delving deep, therapists would perceive them as "apathetic, lifeless, colorless, and boring," leading to a feeling of frustration in their conversations (Nemiah & Sifneos, 1970, p. 159). To make matters worse, these patients were insensitive to the boredom and frustration they were evoking and tended to be indifferent to their therapists' interest in their inner lives. The therapists, in turn, felt their own feelings were being ignored: Judging by the patient's behavior, therapists appeared to be nothing more than someone (or something) in whom they can confide their symptoms, but from whom they expect nothing beyond treatment. There is no mutual emotional connection.

Nemiah and Sifneos (1970), who likewise did not expect from these patients a "rich inner life of feeling and fantasy," emphasized that not every silence in the clinical setting need be interpreted in terms of defense, which is why they focused on the "problem of communication." Lind and coworkers (2014) made similar observations in a qualitative study with a semi-structured interview of patients with somatic symptom disorder who had been exposed to major psychosocial stress during childhood and adolescence: Their emotional responses and communications were consistent with an emotional avoidance culture, when they denied their own needs, vulnerabilities, and feelings of sadness and anger, which had also gone unrecognized by their significant adults. They kept an awareness of their stress response divorced from distressing bodily sensations by engaging in avoidant behaviors, such as hyperactivity. A few years earlier, the psychiatrist, trauma specialist, and concentration-camp survivor Henry Krystal opined that "alexithymia is the most common cause of poor outcome or complete failure of psychoanalysis and psychotherapy" (Krystal, 1988, p. XI).

The patients lacked exactly what is usually the subject of psychotherapy. Constricted breathing, a lump in the throat, pressure in the sternum or the chest – these sensations go unrecognized as anxiety symptoms and instead are concretely described as a sore throat or abdominal pain or shortness of breath. In this respect, in the sense of "dementalization," *pensée opératoire* corresponds to a very low level of symbolic activity. Consequently, the idea emerged that these patients were "by no means failing to express their inner selves because powerful inner psychic forces were preventing them from doing so, but because they had nothing to express" (Greco, 2000, p. 269). Today, it is well established that alexithymia exists independent of somatic illness, depression, and anxiety as well as confounding sociodemographic variables (Mattila et al., 2008). Nevertheless, the TAS-20 Factor subscale Difficulty Identifying Feelings of their study proved to be the strongest common denominator of alexithymia and somatization. In patients with psychogenic, nonepileptic seizures, alexithymia correlated directly with seizure frequency and with difficulties in emotion regulation. Such patients showed a poorer understanding of their emotions, expressed negative beliefs about their emotions, and tended to exert control over emotional expression more than healthy individuals (Urbanek et al., 2014). If we consider alexithymia and ASD to be an empathy or affect/emotion regulation disorder (Dell'Osso et al., 2023), it cannot surprise that this mental disorder prevents the proper assessment of reality. Dangers are presumed to exist in situations in which there are none, and when dangers are truly imminent, they go unrecognized. High alexithymia scores, as measured by the Toronto Alexithymia Scale (TAS) or autism spectrum disorders, were found in patients with eating disorders (Cochrane et al., 1993; Nickel et al., 2019), chronic pain disorders (Lumley et al., 1997), dissociations (Grabe et al., 2000), depression, and somatic symptom disorders (Duddu et al., 2003). However, depressives showed even greater difficulty expressing feelings than those with somatization disorders.

Based on studies with institutionalized Romanian children (Chugani et al., 2001), it is now believed that deprivation and maltreatment leave functional "scars" in brain areas involved in the high-level processing of affective impulses. The associated alexithymia is said to be associated with impaired mentalization (Moriguchi et al., 2006). Today, based on clinical and experimental findings, alexithymia is regarded as a dimensional personality trait with a normal distribution in society which arises from suboptimal developmental conditions and is characterized by limitations at the following levels:

- the ability to differentially perceive affective states in oneself and others;
- the ability to represent these states consciously as different feelings;
- the ability to express them at the body level;
- the ability to communicate them linguistically or imaginatively and ultimately to utilize them for adaptive behavior modification (Schäfer & Franz, 2009).

Unresolved to date remains the controversy of whether alexithymia is a genetically determined "psychosomatic" personality structure without progression (in the sense of a maturational disorder), as Ruesch (1948) postulated, or rather an expression of neurotic inhibition and repression – or even a specific neurobiological subset of ASD (Kinnaird et al., 2019).

ASD and alexithymic patients behave opposite to that of psychosis patients regarding their experience of the body-self, which was demonstrated by the so-called rubber hand experiment (Botvinick & Cohen, 1998; Crespi & Dinsdale, 2019). In this sensory illusion, subjects place their right hand on a table. The experimenter covers up the hand and places an artificial, real-looking hand in the subject's field of vision. The examiner then strokes both the hidden real hand and the visible fake hand with a brush using the same manner and rhythm, resulting in a multisensory conflict. After a short time, probands have the feeling that the artificial hand is part of their body.

Neurobiologically, this illusion activates the insula and those brain regions involved in the multisensory integration of visual and tactile stimuli, such as the premotor and parietal cortex. The insula is significant for "self-embodiment" and "self-awareness," which is why it is also considered the center of intero-, extero-, and proprioception (Terasawa et al., 2021).

Whereas alexithymic and ASD patients tend to report lower sensory deprivation, in psychosis patients it is elevated (Crespi & Dinsdale, 2019). Higher levels of alexithymia, in turn, were associated with a decreased (!) illusion of belongingness (Grynberg & Pollatos, 2015). The multisensory integration of the simultaneous processing of tactile, visual, and proprioceptive signals is important for body perception, as it leads to experiencing the body as one's own and to feeling that one's body parts truly belong to oneself.

Since our understanding of mutual touch is neurobiologically based, these embodiment processes are different in the presence of psychosocial impairments, such as deficits in nonverbal communication. While healthy individuals easily grasp the affective meaning of touch in social interactions, this is not true for ASD individuals. How we perceive, understand, and evaluate interpersonal touch (such as a hug or a pat on the buttocks) as nonverbal communication to express emotions and intentions is rooted in multiple neural systems, such as the ToM network and the somatosensory system responsible for embodied resonance. Regarding positive, neutral, and negative touch interactions, male ASD adults showed a greater intact cognitive understanding (i.e., knowledge) than so-called neurotypical healthy individuals, though they exhibited a lack of spontaneous embodied resonance (i.e., feelings) (Lee Masson et al., 2019). This circumstance was attributed to atypical interoception in alexithymia (Shah et al., 2016), expressed as an impaired ability to feel one's own bodily states and emotions, such as pain, temperature, itching, tickling, touch, and muscle tension.

In a cognitive developmental model, somatization is understood as a multilevel developmental deficit associated with a lower level of emotional awareness, whereby undifferentiated emotional arousal is expressed in physical sensations. With their Level of Emotional Awareness-Scale (LEAS), Lane and Schwartz (1987) proposed five levels, the lowest of which (Level 1) describes exclusively the ability of individuals to be aware of their emotional involvement solely through stimulus-reflex patterns. At this level, it is impossible to separate feeling from thinking; perceptual processing functions via unconsciously controlled responses to sensory stimuli. At this developmental level, an increase in stress is experienced exclusively as a physical sensation, with no differences in either the quality or the type of stress perceived.

Only at the sensorimotor-reactive level of development (Level 2) do reactions occur as responses to external or internal stimuli. A reaction points to there already being more scope for action at this level, allowing emotions to accordingly be perceived as bodily sensations and/or action tendencies. The first two levels are compatible with the pre-mentalizing body-mode. Subic-Wrana et al. (2001), who evaluated this instrument for the German-speaking countries, chose two examples to enable a better understanding: A child develops nausea when they experience the mother's leaving the house as threatening; and the child repeatedly goes through the same door the mother has passed through to express their grief.

Level 3 of emotional-cognitive development includes the possibility of replacing "something" with "something else." This means putting consciously perceived emotional states into words for the first time, even without being able to grasp emotional ambivalence. Experienced emotional states flood the consciousness completely and can change only in a set temporal sequence. What cannot yet be grasped here is the simultaneous ambivalence of feelings about a person or situation.

Level 4 of emotional-cognitive development allows the perception of the simultaneous ambivalence of feelings regarding persons and situations, which, in psychodynamic developmental psychology, corresponds to *object constancy*. At this level, someone can, for example, simultaneously love a person and be angry with them too because of a certain behavior.

Level 5 represents the possibility to perceive emotional states of others as different from one's own, including the ability to empathically comprehend feelings that one has not yet experienced. Thus, one's own position becomes relativized, and one's implicit egocentric point of view becomes negotiable. In psychoanalytic developmental psychology, this level corresponds to *self-object differentiation* and in the mentalization model to the ability to change perspectives.

3.4 The Diagnostic Dilemma

> This chapter discusses the development, diagnostic approaches, and challenges associated with somatoform disorders or functional body complaints (FBC). It highlights that the development of these disorders is influenced by various factors, including genetic, epigenetic, developmental, psychodynamic, neurobiological, social, cultural, and transgenerational factors. The passage emphasizes the need to distinguish between predisposing factors, triggers, and maintaining factors in understanding these disorders.
>
> Traditionally, different perspectives have been taken regarding the etiology of somatoform disorders, including psychogenetic, bio-psycho-social, and somatopsychic viewpoints. The *Diagnostic and Statistical Manual of Mental Disorders* (*DSM-5*) introduced the diagnosis of somatic stress disorder (SSD), which replaced the previous somatization disorder. However, the validity of this diagnosis has been questioned due to its broad nature and lack of exclusion criteria. The passage discusses the criticism of *DSM-5*, highlighting the overlap of symptoms between different diagnoses and the neglect of trauma in the diagnostic categories.
>
> The passage also mentions the high comorbidity of somatoform disorders with other mental disorders and the challenges in differentiating between physical and psychological causes. It emphasizes the need for a comprehensive and individualized diagnostic approach, considering both biological and psychological factors. Furthermore, the passage addresses the problem of pseudodiagnoses and somatophilic alibi diagnoses, which may lead to questionable treatment strategies. It mentions various historical and contemporary diagnostic labels associated with somatoform disorders, highlighting the influence of trends and economic interests in the creation of these categories.

The development of functional body complaints (somatizations) and somatoform symptoms is based on genetic, epigenetic, developmental, psychodynamic, neurobiological, social, cultural, and transgenerational factors. It is important to distinguish between predisposing factors, triggers, and maintaining factors (e.g., morbid gain) (Figure 3.4). Although these disorders are likely to be primarily stress-regulatory disorders, they interact in complex ways and call for different diagnostic approaches. Any reference to only one causal factor would necessarily reduce the complexity.

Thus, the theoretical origin and professional orientation point to different traditions regarding somatoform disorders. One psychogenetic line goes back to the Freudian regression model; another line of functional disorders – supported mostly by medical psychotherapists – assumes a multicausal etiopathogenesis in the sense of the bio-psycho-social model; a third line represents a somatopsychic etiology, i.e., the effect of neurobiological diseases on the patient's psychological state. These traditional "either-or" approaches – either psychogenic or somatogenic – have meanwhile been replaced by attitudes tending more toward "both-and." Thus, our understanding now sees a more fluid transition from nonorganic (= psychogenic) to psychosomatic and organically based disorders. This also makes sense because there are always patients who visit their family doctor for a long time with somatization phenomena and then suddenly suffer an organic illness.

In the context of didactics and treatment theory, we should distinguish between three etiopathogenetic levels (Luyten & Fonagy, 2016; Roenneberg et al., 2019):

- *predisposing factors:* such as stressful life circumstances, unfavorable childhood experiences, (underlying) physical diseases, (epi-)genetic factors, and basic cultural assumptions;
- *triggering factors:* such as acute stresses, illnesses, and accidents;
- *maintaining factors:* such as previous (in)appropriate treatments, avoidance and deconditioning, catastrophizing, constantly checking the body for symptoms of any kind (body-checking behavior), and unfavorable experiences in healthcare.

Neurobiological, genetic, epigenetic, molecular biological, immunological, and biochemical factors are significant at each level, with the influence of early experiences of traumatic relationships on attachment style being the best documented. Insecure attachment early in life activates the stress-modulating systems via the hypothalamic-pituitary-adrenal cortex (HPA) axis (Egle, 2016; Maunder & Hunter, 2001). Abuse, maltreatment, and neglect during childhood not only promote somatoform disorders, but leave traces that extend into adulthood, producing a high likelihood of becoming physically ill (Koenig et al., 2018).

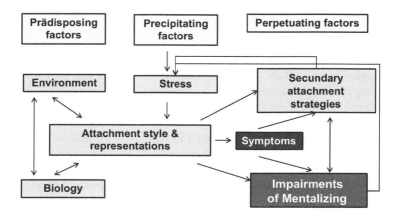

Figure 3.4 A mentalization-based approach to functional somatic disorders.
Source: Luyten et al. (2012).

Unfortunately, contrary to its original intent, the fifth edition of the *Diagnostic and Statistical Manual of Mental Disorders* (*DSM-5*) did not resolve the terminological, conceptual, and practical problems present in the previous classification: Somatization disorder was now replaced by somatic stress disorder (SSD) (APA, 2013). As an innovation, the exclusion of somatic disorders is now no longer required. However, the validity of such a diagnosis is questionable because of its overinclusive nature of far too many different medical conditions. Further points of criticism are the suboptimal selection of psychological disorder characteristics, the abandonment of a uniform concept of hypochondriasis, and deficiencies in the diagnostic criteria through the absence of exclusion criteria.

Somatic stress disorders (SSD) or functional body complaints (FBC) are defined as a broad spectrum of complaints and syndromes that range from temporary ranging from transient disturbances of well-being to so-called Bodily Distress Disorders (BDD) (in ICD-11) or Medically Unexplained (Physical) Symptoms (MU(P)S) – an unfortunate term, seeing as we now have sufficient knowledge to explain the symptoms. The physical symptoms persist over a longer period and go beyond disturbances of well-being. In addition, no organic causes can be proven to *solely* explain these complaints and thus provide patients with reassurance. Because of the frequent association of the complaints with stress, an individual stress model has proven to be particularly suitable. The spectrum is almost unlimited, ranging from mild to severe disorders to anxious-hypochondriac self-observation of one's own body.

In 23% of all patients in primary care (12-month prevalence), no sufficient somatic explanations for complaints are found despite careful diagnostics. Yet, this should not lead to the erroneous conclusion that patients have "nothing," are even imagining their complaints, or that there is only some psychological background to them. The risk physicians run of overlooking a somatic disease, often cited to justify extensive instrumental examinations, is low (0.5–8.8%) (Eikelboom et al., 2016). However, like mistreatments, misdiagnoses should be a particular stimulus for taking an interest in the conditions of origin.

Since the *DSM-5* no longer considers the *absence* of a physical cause as a diagnostic criterion, attention should now be paid to the *presence* of positive symptoms and features (e.g., distressing somatic symptoms as well as abnormal thoughts, feelings, and behaviors in response to these physical symptoms). This, however, means many other diagnoses, such as illness anxiety disorder (formerly "hypochondriasis") and conversion disorder but also psychological factors influencing a physical illness, a feigned disorder, and other unspecified somatic stress disorders, are now subsumed under a single group: SSD.

Illness anxiety disorder is a psychological disorder whereby individuals show great fear of suffering from, and possibly dying from, a serious illness without any plausible medical evidence for such a disease. Frequently feared diseases are, for example, HIV/AIDS, cancer, cardiovascular diseases, or neurological diseases (such as Lyme disease). The psychological strain of such affected persons is great, such that they increasingly avoid activities they consider dangerous and turn their attention to their body, which corresponds to the pre-mentalizing body-mode (Chapter 5.1). They visit a doctor with above-average frequency but without actually being helped by their reassurance. The extent of stress experienced can vary widely, ranging from slight limitations to complete inability to work. Altered body perception is assumed to be a risk factor, that is, the tendency to perceive physical sensations as impairing or pathological instead of as normal physical reactions.

In the meantime, various parties have expressed massive criticism of the *DSM-5* with its new categories (Frances & Chapman, 2013; Hiller & Rief, 2014). On the one hand, the diagnostic labels created the illusion of providing an explanation, whereas, on the other hand, they are scientifically meaningless; furthermore, they promote stigmatization and prejudice (Allsopp et al., 2019). Another problem was that the diagnostic categories used different decision rules, and that there was a large overlap of symptoms between the various diagnoses. Further, almost all diagnoses hide the role of trauma and side effects. Thus, they had little to say about the individual patient and their treatment needs.

Because diagnoses are subject to contemporary trends and zeitgeist as well as economic interests, they can also be seen as "claims" for emerging specialties. This is well evidenced by the emergence of neurasthenia as a nervous disorder in the industrial age of the 19th century and burnout at the end of the 20th century, a term that does not represent a true psychiatric diagnosis. Thus, the treatment of fibromyalgia, listed in ICD-10 under "Other and Unspecified Soft Tissue Disorders, Not Classifiable Elsewhere" (M79.70) and defined since the 1990s as a rheumatologic disorder, lies mainly with the rheumatologist (Egle et al., 2011), although it is primarily a somatoform anxiety disorder. SSD often turn up in institutions, for example, in specialized pain or environmental outpatient clinics; in orthopedic practices they account for more than 50% of all appointments (Nimnuan et al., 2001).

The current diagnostic spectrum includes the newly defined physical stress disorders (somatic symptom disorder [SSD], bodily distress disorder), the so-called functional syndromes (e.g., fibromyalgia syndrome [FMS], irritable bowel syndrome [IBS], chronic fatigue syndrome [CFS], temporomandibular syndrome), and various types of unclear, persistent pain (e.g., chronic, nonspecific back, facial, or myofascial pain). This group does not include physical complaints from clearly defined organic diseases such as joint pain in rheumatism or fatigue in cancer and multiple sclerosis. Although the "physical" pathomechanism in these phenomena is also not clearly clarified, there is a high comorbidity of "organic" and "functional" diseases, and psychosocial factors demonstrably influence the course of the disease, and psychological as well as "body-mind" therapeutic approaches are also demonstrably effective. Therefore, the usual classification of complaints into the categories of "explained/unexplained" or "physical/psychological" should be qualified.

Another difficulty in the diagnosis and treatment of SSD is the frequent comorbidity with other mental disorders, such as affective disorders (depression and anxiety disorders), stress disorders, and personality disorders, which should be considered subgroups of the somatoform disorders. A further problem is that patients with other underlying mental disorders fail to properly attribute their affective-physical symptoms to a depressive episode or anxiety disorder (Staun, 2017). Rather, they report to their family doctor their physical complaints or a general feeling of being unwell. Symptoms such as disturbances of sleep or drive, lack of interest, or nervousness are more likely to suggest a depressive episode.

Such patients express feelings of listlessness more often by saying: "Everything is too much for me, the job, the family. I used to be able to cope more easily." Or they express a sleep disorder as an afterthought: "Sometimes I lie awake all night, and in the morning I'm just exhausted." Signs of lack of interest are expressed with statements such as: "I used to enjoy going to the gym, but now I can't even bring myself to do it."

It is alarming that less than 40% of SSD patients receive adequate psychotherapeutic treatment; in Germany, a higher proportion of untreated patients stem from former East Germany (Pieh et al., 2011). Higher treatment rates are found in regions with university hospitals and psychotherapeutic training institutes.

SSD go under many names, some of them rather adventurous, which almost always refer to a pseudosomatic core (Table 3.2). The narcissistic need to achieve a certain fame or recognition in the professional community and/or among patients as the first to describe a particular nomenclature may also play a role. Thus, "neurocirculatory asthenia" was invented not by a neurologist but by a research group led by the immunologist Shoenfeld (1978). The neurologists Brandt and Dieterich (1986) came up with the strange term of "phobic attack vertigo" for a locomotoric vertigo in anxiety disorders already described by Freud (1895b [1962]) (NB: such a vertigo cannot be phobic as an anxiety equivalent!). The internist Wichmann (1934) introduced the term "vegetative dystonia" to "finally put an end to the psyche." This diagnosis still haunts the occasional doctor's office to this day when the

Table 3.2 Somatophilic alibi diagnoses as iatrogenic diagnostic mentalization failure

---
Irritable heart/soldier's heart (da Costa, 1871)
Neurasthenia (Beard, 1880 [1890])
Fibrositis (Gowers, 1904)
Pseudorheumatism (Bergmann, 1927)
Vegetative dystonia (Wichmann, 1934)
Myofascial pain syndrome (Travell & Rinzler, 1952)
Benign myalgic encephalomyelitis (Acheson, 1959)
Neurocirculatory asthenia (Shoenfeld et al., 1978)
Myalgia-adynamia syndrome (Congy et al., 1980)
Primary fibromyalgia (Yunus, 1983)
Stress neuromyelopathic pain syndrome (Margoles, 1983)
Phobic attack vertigo (Brandt & Dieterich, 1986)
Chronic fatigue syndrome (Holmes et al., 1988)
Multiple chemical sensitivity syndrome (Altenkirch, 1995)
Postural tachycardia syndrome (Diehl, 2003)
Post-Covid syndrome? (Gallegos et al., 2022)

goal is not to be helpful and commit oneself psychosomatically. The use of somatophilic alibi diagnoses point to a lack of psychodynamic understanding. By rejecting a biographical understanding that "somatization is one of the most diverse and clinically relevant coping and defense phenomena" (Lamparter & Schmidt, 2018, p. 26), such physicians come to resemble their patients: They act in a prementalizing mode. Unfortunately, there is little research on which factors promote a mentalization disorder among physicians in diagnostics. Physicians overestimating their own competence seems to be a common factor (Janneck & Krenz, 2018, p. 48).

So, how can diagnostic errors in this regard be minimized? In addition to applying a psychosomatic-holistic approach in specific individual cases, the diagnostic decision among the terms "psychogenic"/"psychosomatic"/"somatopsychic"/"somatogenic" should not be avoided (Lamparter & Schmidt, 2018, p. 31).

The dilemma of diagnostics is also reflected in the fact that, in addition to rather less frequently occurring SSD spectrum disorders, such as Takotsubo syndrome (= "broken heart"), each medical discipline has its own SSD, so that now more than 100 discrete diagnoses belong to this spectrum (Hausteiner-Wiehle et al., 2013). Since these diagnoses are more often than not based on an anxiety disorder or "somatized" depression that is "only" expressed physically – in the past one spoke of "masked" – they are often so-called pseudodiagnoses that are just as often accompanied by questionable treatment strategies, such as hormone treatments. Last but not least, a number of complaints, such as the fashionable "chronic fatigue syndrome," are derived from the physical manifestations of a generalized anxiety and panic disorder ("Fear makes you tired!").

Surprisingly, the fixation on purely biological causes of exhaustion and other bodily complaint symptoms has not been accompanied by any evidence-based therapy based on biological factors, such as medication – here there is only the (basically always justified) hope for further research. The many proofs, on the other hand, that psychotherapy (and mentalization-based therapy) directly helps with severe exhaustion and other body complaint syndromes – and not only with the accompanying anxiety and depressiveness – are fiercely warded off. This is based on the misguided idea that the proven effects of psychotherapy prove psychological causes. It is also based on the fact that psychotherapy is thought to be a spiritual science without natural science. And a somatophilic diagnosis that is stripped of the psychic promises more identitary support.

Concerning subjective symptoms, the most common complaints are pain of various localizations (e.g., headache, back pain, joint pain, and pain in the extremities) as well as dysfunctions of organs or whole systems (e.g., digestive disorders, palpitations, difficulty breathing, dizziness, sexual problems, or difficulty concentrating). Because the previous diagnostic terminology had proven unsatisfactory, a new conceptualization in the diagnosis of somatoform disorders was sought, which is reflected in two S3-guidelines on "Functional Body Complaints" (FBC) (Roenneberg et al., 2020). Diagnostic difficulties arise when, parallel to other somatic and psychological disorders, a not uncommon comorbidity must first be clarified. For example, diffuse whole-body pain previously diagnosed as fibromyalgia syndrome may well occur simultaneously with rheumatoid arthritis, noncardiac chest pain with coronary heart disease, or irritable bowel syndrome with inflammatory bowel disease (Creed et al., 2011, p. 177).

Likewise, as in the case of dissociative disorders, somatic illnesses can favor the development of functional body complaints in the sense of "somatic accommodation," such as when patients with systemic lupus erythematosus, rheumatoid arthritis, or Sjögren's syndrome develop a "tacked-on" fibromyalgia syndrome in the course of their illness; or when epilepsy patients suddenly suffer psychogenic seizures. Stresses of all kinds, such as lack of sleep, which in principle leads to increased sensitivity to pain, as well as serious external life events, such as emigration experiences, lead to complex symptomatology. It therefore does not surprise that somatic symptom disorders are found more frequently among migrants (Ritsner et al., 2000), whereby the respective culture may play a role in whether psychological difficulties are expressed exclusively in the form of bodily symptoms.

How contested the diagnosis of functional body complaints or somatic stress disorder can be is evidenced by a smaller group of patients who have the recalcitrant opinion of suffering from organically caused myalgic encephalomyelitis (ME) or chronic fatigue syndrome (CFS). These patients founded the German ME/CFS Society (www.mecfs.de/was-ist-me-cfs/) to defend the organic etiology against any attempts at psychosomatic or psychological etiopathogenesis – if necessary, even via legal means – although there is no scientific evidence to back this claim up. Presumably, a more detailed analysis could show that pre-mentalizing modes, such as the teleological mode, are at play here (cf. Chapter 5.2).

At the same time, the question of what causes this narrowing of the view, this unification in biologistic reductionism, remains open. Henningsen (2023, p. 10) assumes that the vehement rejection of a possible psychosomatic perspective on physical suffering expresses a general bio-bias, the one-sided preference for biological explanatory factors in medicine. It is also a defense against the past, against a claim that was frequently made by psychosomatics until about 60 years ago, but which is ultimately untenable: that complex clinical pictures with severe physical complaints can have a purely psychological cause. This mirror-image psycho-bias could never be empirically proven; it shares with the bio-bias the attachment to a dualistic either-or thinking ("mental or organic"), which has not been neutral since the beginning of the modern era (Henningsen, 2021). Unfortunately, this also has to do with the weaknesses of the bio-psycho-social model of medicine.

> If, as is so often the case in practice, the individual factors are simply added together, i.e. bio (e.g. immune disorder) plus psycho (e.g. depressive experience) plus socio (perhaps poverty), instead of relating them conceptually in a truly integrative way to one and the same sick person, the model remains part of the problem and not the solution. Because with the addition, the fiction is implied that psycho and socio can be separated from bio – and this opens the door for biologists to leave out the other two factors.
>
> (Henningsen, 2023, p. 10)

3.5 Body-Mode as a Mass Phenomenon

> This chapter explores the phenomenon of somatoform disorders as a sociocultural mass phenomenon, particularly in crisis situations. It examines historical cases such as war neuroses and post-traumatic stress disorders, highlighting the collective breakdown of mentalizing under extreme external pressure. The chapter also discusses the diagnostic challenges, treatment approaches, and societal implications of these disorders, shedding light on the need for further investigation from a mentalization model perspective. Readers will gain insights into the complex dynamics and cultural influences surrounding mass psychogenic illnesses and their impact on individuals and society.

A special phenomenon is the appearance of somatoform disorders (in the sense of a collective body-mode) as a sociocultural mass phenomenon, especially in crisis situations. Well known are the war neuroses of World War I and II as well as the traumatic neuroses that occur following an accident or natural event, now known as post-traumatic stress disorders (Hirschmüller & Kimmig, 1996; Shephard, 2000, 2001). The aforementioned neurasthenia of the 19th century and the burnout syndrome of the 20th century also belong to the category of body-mode as a mass phenomenon. Such disorders occur when – under extreme external pressure – there is a collective breakdown of mentalizing. The conditions surrounding the origin of such a collective "affect contagion" have not yet been investigated from the point of view of the mentalization model.

The history of modern post-traumatic disorders begins in 1860 in the form of somatoform disorders after railroad accidents in patients who had no external injuries. The so-called "railway spine" syndrome, which occurred with a latency of several months to the accident (latency is an important diagnostic feature!) as well as the later "whiplash injury" from car accidents in the 20th century were attributed to the introduction of liability laws and accident insurance, which allowed actionable claims for compensation to be made for the first time (Trimble, 1981). Like the later functional body complaints, the diagnostics here fluctuated between emphasizing somatic causes, such as a concussion of the spinal cord or the brain, and seeking psychogenic causes, right up to simulation. Somewhat later, after the introduction of the telephone, there followed otoneurological health disorders in the form of ringing in the ears, vertigo, headache, and auditory hallucinations, which were attributed to a high level of anxiety and fright as well as to "telephone phobia" (Podoll, 1991). Since the main cause of these very diverse complaints was seen in a weakness of will, psychotherapies for these patients consequently consisted of educational-punitive "will therapies."

So-called "mass hysterias" or "psychogenic mass illnesses" occur largely among schoolchildren and women. They are often accompanied by a change in voice and psychogenic seizures. In so-called developing nations, e.g., East Africa, they are understood as divine possession or the consequences of witchcraft and thus require spiritual action. They occur when an individual from some group presents a "hysterical" manifestation that, not long thereafter, causes all other group members to exhibit the same symptoms. The underlying pathogenesis of mass dissociative phenomena is unknown; the mirror neuron system, which provides the ability to imitate, may form the neural basis for this phenomenon (Lee & Tsai, 2010).

Cultural studies, from the perspective of large group psychology as well as from the perspective of the mentalization model, suggest we are dealing here with a collective "body-mode" (see Chapter 5.1), which could have the function of protecting affected individuals from responsibility or guilt regarding their behavior through the denial of causality and control. At the same time, through their expressive and communicative functions, "obsessions" could serve to mobilize social support and conflict resolution as well as being a coping strategy (Kirmayer & Ramstead, 2017, p. 413). However, this raises the question of how exactly the system of inhibition is reactivated – in each individual – during such dissociative mass phenomena.

The first study of war-related, mass somatoform disorders appeared shortly after the American Civil War by da Costa (1871). The complaints were initially known as "irritable heart syndrome," "effort syndrome," "da Costa syndrome," and, finally, "soldier's heart syndrome." Da Costa, a cardiologist, had encountered many war veterans with anxiety and respiratory problems, an inability to work, and a host of other symptoms that today would probably be diagnosed as anxiety disorder, post-traumatic stress disorder, functional disorder, or perhaps depression. As a cardiologist, however, he diagnosed these conditions as heart problems. Similarly, later during World War I, so-called shell shock symptoms were diagnosed exclusively as physical illnesses, presenting in the form of "legions of 'war tremors'" (Fischer-Homberger, 1975). About 1.5 million soldiers were said to have been affected. The cause was thought to be vibrations on the brain and the destruction of nerve cells by bomb and shell explosions. Only toward the end of the war did most military doctors realize that shell shock was in fact a war neurosis not necessarily caused by literal shell shock.

Another collective "hysteria" manifested itself in World War I in what came to be known as *camptocormia* from the Greek kormos = the torso and champtein = to bend over, in the form of a forward bent-over posture, sometimes even up to 90°. Patients with camptocormia (Hamlin, 1943; Sandler, 1947; Schultz-Venrath, 2023), or "functional bent back," could remain in this posture for weeks, even months, abandoning it only during sleep. Treatment attempts using painful Faraday electric currents were compared to torture methods (Riedesser & Verderber, 1985), proved to be unsuccessful, and even led to numerous deaths (Simmel, 1944). A common feature of these mass somatoform disorders – "psychogenic infections" – was extremely vehement resistance to any kind of therapy of the actual symptomatology (Souques & Rosanoff-Saloff, 1915). They most blatantly challenged the accuracy of physiological concepts of pain. The resistance to therapy sparked a fierce scientific controversy over the proper treatment (Nonne, 1917, 1922). Even so-called war neuroses hospitals were established in reaction to the mass occurrence. Because psychiatrists failed with their treatment methods, from 1916 on these hospitals came to be run by later famous psychoanalysts, such as Karl Abraham in Allenstein, Sándor Ferenczi in Budapest, or Ernst Simmel in Posen. In this respect, somatic symptom disorders during World War I have the "merit" of having become "midwives" to psychoanalytically oriented inpatient psychosomatic medicine (Schultz-Venrath & Hermanns, 2019). It succeeded in treating the mass occurrence of functional disorders in a psychotherapeutically promising way, providing a modicum of respect for psychiatry and the somatic disciplines. Ernst Simmel and numerous other psychoanalysts developed a successful form of focal psychodynamic brief therapy with body-therapeutic elements, which went hand in hand with the destruction of a "dummy" that presumably resembled one's superior (Simmel, 1918). This offered the affect of rage an outlet through a third medium – quite in the sense of triangulation. Although war neuroses largely disappeared with the end of World War I, such patients were later often pejoratively labeled "malingerers," "pension neurotics," or simply "hysterics." Ultimately, however, these designations served only to mask the inadequacy of the prevailing treatment concepts and the lack of treatment success.

Notes

1 This footnote first appeared in the English translation of 1927, in which it was described as having been authorized by Freud. It does not appear in the German editions.
2 This sentence is only found in the German version of the Collected Works (Freud 1923b, p. 253).
3 Not to find in the Standard Edition. Of interest is his differentiation between conversion and obsessive compulsion disorder (OCD): "in hysteria the liberated sum of excitation is transformed into somatic innervation *(conversion hysteria)*; in obsessional neurosis it remains in the psychical field and attaches itself to other ideas which are not incompatible in themselves, and which are thus *substituted* for the repressed idea. The source of the incompatible ideas which are subjected to defense is solely and exclusively sexual life" (Freud 1897, p. 248).

Chapter 4

Bodily or Mental States? On the Development of a Mentalizing Self

In developmental psychology, the question of how a "self" emerges and what constitutes a mentalizing "self" belong to the key concept of *identity development*. Sense of identity is tied to a secure perception of the body and the ability to mentalize. While earlier work emphasized the unique role of dyadic attachment, in terms of promoting or inhibiting the development of mentalization (Fonagy et al., 2002 [2004]; Fonagy et al., 1991), today group experiences involving peers, family structures, and sociocultural factors are considered to be at least as important (Asen et al., 2019). The different developmental stages have been variously well researched, with parents and family members promoting or hindering mentalization depending on their own developmental stage. While we now understand early childhood relatively well via attachment research, there is still a research deficit regarding preadolescence and adolescence. Adolescents are characterized by their becoming increasingly active, self-determined "authors" of their own lives who try out a lot with their bodies for self-discovery. In contrast, preadolescence is focused more on cognitive development regarding the organization and structure of a self. The transition from a self-concept in preadolescence to an identity in adolescence requires making sense of the many different self-(body) concepts to coherently connect the past with the present and the imagined future. Failure to do so results in body dissatisfaction, feelings of being separated from one's body, somatic complaints, and interoceptive deficits. The latter are found significantly more often in self-injuring youth and in those who had recently attempted suicide (Hielscher et al., 2019).

Epistemic trust (Fonagy et al., 2014), an evolutionary capacity to trust others as a source of social information, plays a similarly significant role as the development of tolerance (Berman & Ofer, 2024). It both promotes and facilitates mentalization as well as enhances resilience to life's adversities via a health-promoting process (Fonagy et al., 2019). Epistemic trust is not just a mental phenomenon; it also promotes trust in one's own body, an essential prerequisite for mentalization. Epistemic mistrust of one's own body, on the other hand, manifests itself in the form of misogyny, racism, antisemitism, violence, and right-wing radicalism because of self-hatred (Theweleit, 2009 [1977/1978]). In this respect, a fragmented or unstable body-self because of epistemic mistrust even favors a mentalization failure on the political level and often combines with intolerance and rigidity. This described Frenkel-Brunswik (1949) as intolerance of ambiguity.

Under favorable conditions, a usually radiant mother holds the infant in her arms shortly after birth, quickly begins to scan the infant's face, and gently strokes the little fingers in wonder. Her repetitive vocalizations are accompanied by a loving, bright smile. Even if this is her first baby, she usually knows intuitively what to do. She is proud, has already forgotten her birth pains, and feels that no one has ever taken care of such a beautiful child before. She behaves physically like other mammalian mothers who lick, groom, sniff, smell, touch, poke, and nurse their offspring. A synchronized "dance" of mother and child begins, its unique rhythm forming a resonant relationship: There is much babbling, imaginary scenarios are playfully created, collaboration occurs for the first time, and the pain of the other is understood. Like music, a certain synchronicity emerges involving range, complexity, and timbre, while the basic rhythms convey safety and security. This mother–child dance, which also contains elements of desynchrony, forms the basis for a child's lifelong connection to the rest of the family, including the father and siblings, close friends at school, through adolescence to the first love and the role as a parent of own children.

The success of this early process determines a person's attachments and the conditions of love those attachments set; the empathy, responsibility, cooperation, and self-control with which that person encounters their later fellow human beings, as coworkers, neighbors, or strangers. The neurobiology of belonging, which encompasses the neural, endocrine, and behavioral systems, including the capacity for love, is largely based on the oxytocin system (the neurohormone of attachment). The social brain and the biological synchrony between mother and child are also later responsible for every kind of group formation of great plasticity. Oxytocin is produced by neurons in the hippocampus and, from a neurobiological perspective, represents not only birth, breastfeeding, and bonding, but also prejudice and more aggressive behavior toward nonmembers of one's own group (Buchheim et al., 2009). Oxytocin is released not only by the central part of the neuron, but also by its extensions, the dendrites; ever more oxytocin is released each time attachment memory is invoked. This may be the neurobiological basis for the fact that we spend a lifetime repeatedly seeking echoes of earlier experiences in later relationships, whether we were carried on our mother's back all day or explored nature with our father.

A wide variety of disciplines, such as phenomenology (Husserl and Merleau-Ponty), developmental psychology, and the neurosciences, now agree that the foundations of a mentalizing self and self-consciousness are bodily in nature. They all work within the paradigm of the embodied mind (Fuchs, 2018a; Gallagher, 2005; Leuzinger-Bohleber & Pfeifer, 2013; Varela et al., 1991 [2016]; Zahavi, 2010).

Long before the first definition of embodied mentalization was formulated, Paul Schilder, a neurologist and psychoanalyst, had extended and differentiated Freud's dictum "The ego is primarily a body ego" by adding essential aspects such as the concept of body image and body schema (Schilder, 1923, 1935 [1978]). Schilder's body image consisted of a complex function of psychic experience: physiologically based, libidinously defined, and embedded in the relations between organism and environment, "in which its constitution and effects can be expressed, and external influences retroactively shape its form and performances" (Leuschner, 2017, p. 124). In this context, Schilder emphasized above all the psychic experience rooted in active motor activity (!): There is

> no psychic experience that is not reflected in the mobility and in the vasomotor functions of the body. . . . Every sensation has its own motility, every sensation bears its own motor response. Continuous activity is therefore the basis of our bodily self.
>
> (Schilder, 1935 [1978], p. 105)

The body does not appear to us as a collection of mere optical, kinesthetic, and tactile sensations; rather, the body image is an active director. Through its specific capacity for so-called body intercourse, a body-image transfer mechanism, the body succeeds in incorporating foreign objects or partial objects as representations and, conversely, in reshaping external conditions in its own image. With this model, Schilder became a pioneer of a new theory of the body as well as of defense mechanisms and object relations. His body-image model was to lead "to a new conception of human action," for which the emotional processes were the "driving force and source of energy" (Schilder, 1935 [1978], p. 50). Thus, not only can the body-image reconcile an unlimited variety of things within itself, it is also both variable and stable at the same time; it develops from the experience of pain and motor control over the extremities, while the basis of the body-self is continuous activity and movement.

Antonio Damasio took up this approach: The self, he argued, does not necessarily have to be an immutable cognitive or neural entity, "but rather that it must possess a remarkable degree of structural invariance so that it can dispense continuity of reference across long periods of time. Continuity of reference is in effect what the self needs to offer" (Damasio, 1999, p. 135). "Bodily representations" are a prime example for this stability; they develop from the "automatic regulatory system" already in place at birth, "to ensure that life-threatening deviations do not occur or can be rapidly corrected" (Damasio, 1999, p. 141). In Damasio's view, the earliest origins of the self, including the higher self, comprising identity and personhood, may be found in all those brain mechanisms that continually and unconsciously ensure that bodily states (i.e., not mental states!) remain within a narrow range of relative stability necessary to survival. The state of activity occurring within all these mechanisms corresponds to the "proto-self," the *unconscious* and/or *preconscious* precursor of the core-self and the autobiographical self. Neurobiologically, the proto-self or core-self is most closely associated with the regulatory mechanisms of the brainstem. It remains unclear, however, how representations develop in this model because it lacks the mirroring of bodily states and affects by a primary other. It can therefore be assumed that we can infer the bodily states of others and attach comparable meaning to them only through the representation of our bodily states and their meaning.

Mark Solms (2013a, 2013b) attempted to integrate the previously contradictory positions, albeit without addressing the development of a mentalizing self: Two aspects of the body, he argues, are represented in the brain in two ways: as an outer body and an inner body. The inner body, which represents the inner milieu, sits in the deeper, inner areas of the brain (hypothalamus, circumventricular organs, parabrachial nucleus, area postrema, and the nucleus of the tractus solitarius); the outer body is neuroanatomically represented in the somatotopic maps on the surface of the cortex, which are projections of sensory receptors transmitted via modality-specific thalamic and cranial neural pathways. This body representation is traditionally equated with the cortical homunculus (the upside-down small body map that forms the primary somatosensory area of the cortex). Strictly speaking, however, there are several such maps, each representing a different component of somatic sensations (such as touch, pain, vibration, temperature).

The main difference is that the brainstem mechanisms derived from the autonomic body are associated with affective consciousness, whereas the cortical mechanisms derived from the sensory-motor body are associated with cognitive consciousness. The upper brainstem is said to be intrinsically conscious, the cortex unconscious; the latter derives its consciousness from the brainstem. The upper brainstem (and the associated limbic structures) perform the functions Freud attributed to the Id, whereas the cortex (and the associated forebrain structures) supported the functions Freud attributed to the Ego. Thus, he argued, the Id is the source of consciousness and the Ego as such is unconscious. The inner body, again Freud said, is not an object of perception – inasmuch as it is not externalized and presented to the classical sense organs. Rather, it remains the subject of perception, the background state of consciousness, so to speak, which is of outstanding importance.

Consequently, the development of a mentalizing self begins in the brainstem rather than cortically – if one accepts that "lower"-level affective phenomenal experiences provide the "energy" for the development of higher forms of cognitive consciousness (Solms & Panksepp, 2012). A hungry or thirsty child cries and kicks, and indeed they completely become "hunger" or "thirst"; a feverish child, on the other hand, conserves their last resources and remains rather quiet. Yet, both behaviors are embodied in terms of somatization. In the further course of life, with the maturation of the neuronal system, which reaches its climax with the late adolescence, differentiation of this experience occurs: The child learns to point out what they need, using mimicry or gestures to something they want to eat or unconditionally have. Later they express this – more or less concretely – using language, a developmental step that in psychosomatics has been called "desomatization" (Schur, 1955).

Without the experiences of a (living) body, there can be no mentalization; without a (living) body, there is no psyche. Nor can mentalization occur without movement and action, expressed in various types of vitality (life is movement and movement is life) (Stern, 2010b), because perception and movement are intertwined (von Weizsäcker, 1940). Equally significant is that the perception of movement (in the sense of a physical or mental movement) takes time, the equivalent of a short journey. At the same time, "without movement we cannot read or imagine mental, invisible activity, whether thoughts, emotions, or 'will'" (Stern, 2010b).

The motionlessness of a mother in the form of an expressionless and rigid expression in the so-called still-face experiment by Ed Tronick very quickly triggers massive restlessness in infants up to 12 months of age, which is initially largely expressed physically (www.youtube.com/watch?v=apzXGEb Zht0). The still-face experiment consists of three interaction segments, each lasting 2–3 minutes. In the first episode (face-to-face), mothers are instructed to play with their child as they normally do. In the next episode (expressionless face), mothers are instructed to sit facing their child with unmoving facial expressions and to stop responding to their child. The effects on the infant are dramatic: The infant tries with all the physical (!) means at its disposal to get the mother to respond in the form of eye contact, vocalizations, mimicry and gestures, and raising the arms. Sometimes this cycle is repeated several times over and again. If all attempts fail, the infant withdraws, averts its gaze, and loses control of its posture. Some, but not most, infants cry. In the third episode (reunion), mothers are asked to resume normal interactions with their infants, which can take on very different forms, depending on the relationship (Tronick & Cohn, 1989).

In both mothers and infants, respiratory sinus arrhythmia (RSA) and skin conductance (SC) are directly related to affect regulation and resilience to emotion. RSA measures the parasympathetic influence on heart rate (HR) and heart-rate variability (HRV), which are directly related to emotion-regulation abilities. HRV measures the variation in the time interval between two consecutive heartbeats in milliseconds. A large variation is considered a sign of a healthy heart and is associated with psychological health, higher quality of life, and lower susceptibility to disease. A decrease or even stagnation of HRV is considered prognostically unfavorable in heart-attack patients in intensive-care units.

Infants recovering from a still-face episode showed the greatest increase in RSA at reunion with the mother. The mothers of infants who had recovered from the still-face episode, in turn, showed a decrease in RSA during reunion, suggesting the mobilization of the soothing behavior of the infants. The mothers of infants who did not recover from the still-face episode showed physiological markers of anxiety in the form of a sustained (!) increase in RSA and high SC scores. These mothers failed to pick up on their infant's cues that the infant did not (!) feel connected to them. On the other hand, the results suggest that, when a mother tries to comfort her infant, she physiologically comforts herself. Thus, at the behavioral level, maternal sensitivity is physiologically coherent (Ham & Tronick, 2006, 2009).

Recent research has focused on the phenomenon of synchrony, which occurs at multiple levels between the primary other and the infant:

- behavioral level (e.g., eye contact, touch);
- physiological level (e.g., heart rate, vocal frequency);

- endocrinological level (e.g., cortisol, oxytocin);
- neural level as "interbrain" synchrony (e.g., through the same neural activation patterns in the right prefrontal and temporal cortex) (Miller et al., 2019).

How and whether synchronous interactions occur between the primary others and the infant in the first weeks after birth appears to be crucial for the development of initial (basal) representational structures and thus for the foundation of mentalization. Differences in the formation of these first representational structures are thought to reside in whether, how, and how often a breastfeeding mother looks at the baby and how available she is to the child.

Jonathan Levy and Ruth Feldman (2019) found that synchrony of behavior can explain the capacity for empathy via neural synchrony. The brains of the mother and the infant synchronize via the superior temporal sulcus (STS) in the gamma spectrum of the EEG, a site that constitutes the neural hub for the social brain. Synchrony of behavior is defined here as a process resonant parents enact by adapting to their child's nonverbal cues as well as verbal communication, whereas empathy is considered a process in which an individual resonates and attunes to the affective and cognitive states of another individual. Experiences of synchrony in the context of the mother–infant relationship in the first decade of life form the foundation for the child's later ability to resonate and empathize with the concerns, feelings, and thoughts of others. Incidentally, such "interbrain synchronies" increase especially when both the child and the primary caregiver are involved in a task that requires collaboration (Miller et al., 2019).

However, interaction that promotes development does not always result in a successful coordination; rather, quite a few interactions between mother and infant are also "chaotic." Discrepancies between affective states, misattribution of responses, and misunderstandings of relational intentions must always be resolved (Tronick, 2007). Interactions that complement synchrony consist of repairing mismatches and reestablishing shared relational meaning. These are a central driver of change and have consequences beyond the development of shared meanings. Through reparation, the infant and their primary attachment figure learn that a negative mismatch experience can indeed be transformed into a positive affective match, and that they can act effectively in the world. Mismatch experiences that cannot be repaired, that are conflictual or maladaptive, are also implicitly encoded as emotional processes. These may be reflected as affective memory traces in body memory. Later, through corrective events or in psychotherapy, transformation may become possible, "so that they can become linguistically and reflexively accessible to consciousness as an experiential feeling" (Mertens, 2019, p. 977).

The experiments of Ed Tronick's research group provided very impressive evidence that a newborn infant cannot yet distinguish between its own body and self and that of the mother's body and being. The physical experience of every newborn infant may provide the "universal fantasy . . ., in which there is only one body and only one mind for two people" (McDougall, 1995, p. 156). One's own body lives in a physical fusion – not as an experience of one's own body, but as bodies in connection with each other (intercorporeity); this occurs with the mother already intrauterine and postpartum for long stretches as the fusion of the infant's mouth with the mother's breast or the bottle during breastfeeding. However, when an infant feels hunger, thirst, cold, or pain, satiating these needs succeeds only if the mother or other caregivers are induced by the infant to become active, ultimately to literally save the child from dying (infants are repeatedly in the teleological mode during the oral phase). Already Schilder (1935 [1978], p. 195) assumed that "from the beginning, a core of the body image ... [lies] in the oral zone" and that "head, arms, hands, trunk, legs, and feet" grow only in a "relationship to this core."

Whereas the presence of the other determines the quality of relational experiences, something that eventually finds its way into the body image, borderline experiences are particularly significant for the development of the self. The uniqueness of the body emerges through sometimes painful, quite heterogeneous borderline experiences, most clearly through the skin. On the other hand, a "representation" most likely appears only in the absence of a primary object in the sense of asynchrony or desynchrony, which must have been present at one point.

We are only now beginning to understand the various stages that eventually lead to the ability to mentalize or the ability to understand the inner experience of others to establish successful communication. Infants and toddlers learn relatively quickly to infer from themselves to others and thereby develop a deeper understanding of social situations. Thus, even 15-month-old children can discern the intentions of others, something 9-month-old children cannot. In this respect, ego-other equivalence is the starting point of social learning, something Meltzoff (2007) called the "like-me" assumption. To what extent the differential perception of one, two, or even more bodies also plays a role here has not yet been investigated.

From birth until about the third month of life, infants seek perfect response-stimulus contingencies (relating stimuli in the sense of if . . . , then . . .), which, as physiological states triggered by sensory perception, psychologically form a first mental space, though they do not yet have a structure. A primary mental representation of the body-self forms when the infant has become more and more able to exercise perfect control. Too little contingency seems more likely to lead to discouragement regarding the expression of affect and to an impoverishment of infant contact behavior. Computer-based neuroscientific research and infant research both support the assumption "if the brain is designed to elaborate hierarchical generative models of the world, then the infant brain will fundamentally seek to differentiate between self versus non-self causes of sensations" (Debbané & Nolte, 2019, p. 29). From the third month of life onward, this is accompanied by the infant's search for noncontingent experiences. Through body movements and communicative signals, babies try to produce sensations – something Friston (2017, p. 44) called "self-evidencing" by "producing sensations (e.g. body movements, communicative signals)" – which allows differences between inside/outside and between self/non-self to increasingly be developed and perceived. This is why infants, as early as the third month of life, seem to "know" that anything not perfectly contingent to their actions does not belong to them. They then begin to look for imperfect contingencies, discovering them in the mimicry and (physical) response of their primary attachment figure to their expressions of affect (Gergely & Unoka, 2008a). On the other hand, if the reactions and feedbacks of the primary attachment figures irritate in this developmental phase because they are fuzzy, this can lead to unmarked mirroring.

Without reference to mirror neurons, which were not known at the time, Meltzoff and Moore (1977) published photographs of 12–21-day-old babies imitating the mimicry and facial expressions of an adult in terms of "synchrony," although these imitations occurred based on an incompletely developed neural system. Even more complicated were the questions: To what extent does the imitation of an emotionally happy face lead the infant to perceive the same emotion as that of the adult? And to what extent does this play a significant role in the development of self-efficacy? To date, we have only partial answers to these questions. Children with autism spectrum disorder (ASD) showed significantly poorer results on all psychometric tests regarding social cognition than normally developed children or children with Down syndrome (Gopnik et al., 1993 [2000], p. 61). This was true for both the imitation deficit and the orientation deficit toward social signals. Since this has been observed even in very young children with autistic traits, it is now assumed that ASDs result from a congenital disorder rather than unfavorable early childhood development. In this respect, "psychogenic autism" (Tustin, 1993) is much less common than previously presumed in the psychoanalytic community.

On the other hand, it was once assumed that babies can establish a connection between themselves and others even at birth. Imitation, it was presumed, was how nature solved the body-mind problem. However, such early social behaviors could be explained only based on (obviously already existing!?) representations (Gopnik et al., 1993 [2000], p. 55). By emphasizing the visual aspect of facial expressions, researchers have overlooked the fact that babies also learn to discriminate the internal patterns of physiological and visceral stimulation via the voice of the primary caregiver accompanying the different sensations and emotions.

All these observations suggested that the human infant's capacity for spontaneous and accurate imitation or synchrony with its primary caregivers determines its understanding of others just as essentially as the development of coherent self-experience. What remains difficult to answer is the question of where synchrony originates. Since neuronal development, such as myelination, is not yet complete at this stage of life, one could presume the mirror neuron system (MNS) is most likely responsible for this ability. Mirror neurons explain the phenomena of affect resonance or contagion, such as when one's mouth waters when someone else gleefully laps up their ice cream.

Since, from our point of view, stable representations have not yet formed in this early phase, we cannot yet speak of a jointly *shared representation system* (Fonagy & Bateman, 2019, p. 10). Rather, in the sense of synchrony and imitation (see the following section), it could be a matter of a *shared presentation system*, from which a shared representational system emerges over time via the absence (!) of a primary object. In comparatively early stages, the mirror neuron system serves social information processing and the *recognition* of spatial and physical signals (Vogeley, 2017). In contrast, the neural mentalization system (MENT) develops in later stages of social information processing in the context of *evaluating* the emotional and psychological states of others. In this respect, the mirror neuron system, reminiscent of Merleau-Ponty's intercorporeality, functions as a social recognition system and the mentalization system as a social assessment system.

It is now well established that the face, being a central "interface" for emotional learning, lends itself to imitation and thus to the development of representations at a very early age. This is also true for faces expressing sadness, pain, or disgust. Quite similar "contagions" underlie the everyday phenomena of yawning or laughing, occasionally also sneezing and crying infants. "However, it appears that such resonances do not work equally well for all people and under all circumstances. Under conditions of anxiety and stress . . . the resonance capacity decreases considerably" because "the signal rate of the mirror neurons is massively reduced" (Bauer, 2005, p. 34). This is especially true for people with ASD, whose reduced number of mirror neurons results in a reduced resonance capacity. It manifests itself, among other things, in people with ASD remaining uninfected by the yawning or laughter of others. It is difficult for them to (intuitively) interpret the facial expressions and gestures of others (Williams et al., 2001) because they lack the neuronal structures for this.

4.1 Intersubjective Developmental Conditions for a Body-Self

In this chapter, the multifaceted nature of self-development is explored through the lens of various scientific disciplines, highlighting the crucial role of reciprocal interactions between individuals. Traditional attachment research, focusing on secure attachment and parental sensitivity, once dominated the field. However, recent findings emphasize the significant influence of parental mentalizing on child development. The chapter delves into the concept of the "Skin-Ego" by Didier Anzieu, emphasizing the fundamental role of bodily experiences, particularly the skin, in self-development. The skin serves as a container, a protective barrier, and a means of communication, playing a vital role in establishing meaningful relationships. The profound impact of touch and sensory experiences on human development is underscored, with over 10% of the cerebral cortex dedicated to processing skin-derived information.

The concept of embodiment is discussed within the context of the "embodied self," recognizing that the mind and brain are intrinsically linked to the entire body. Body therapists adopting the mentalization model highlight the parent–infant embodied dance, where the emotional tone is shared

> and co-constructed. Infants demonstrate sophisticated social communication skills and nonverbal language to express their internal states.
>
> The chapter introduces the Parental Embodied Mentalizing (PEM) measurement instrument, which assesses whole-body movements in parent–infant interactions. The study findings reveal that embodied parent mentalizing predicts infant attachment security, social skills, and the absence of internalizing or externalizing problems. These predictions persist even when controlling for traditional measures of parental care.

In various scientific disciplines, such as phenomenological philosophy, modern psychoanalysis, developmental psychology, and the neurosciences, the consensus reigns that a self can emerge only in the presence of and in relation to another self or to a group. This view was supported by traditional attachment research, which focused on secure attachment and maternal or parental sensitivity as key factors. In the meantime, however, it is well documented that the parental ability to mentalize significantly influences child development. This is understood as the ability of parents to consider and treat a child as a " 'psychological agent' motivated by mental states" (Shai & Fonagy, 2014, p. 186).

Subjectivity, psyche, and self-concept, in terms of "normal" development, can emerge only through reciprocal interactions of a responsive and mentalizing caregiver with the infant. Mentalizing parents (or at least one of them) should be able to appreciate that the infant's psyche is separate from their own, but that they influence each other mentally and through their actions. A highly fragile blueprint of the "self" already exists in the child at birth and postnatally, because of sensory experiences toward the end of intrauterine life and because of the genetics that have already programmed the child's development. Interaction with the environment clearly has a biological basis. Didier Anzieu considered skin experience to play a particularly fundamental role in self-development. His experiences with burn victims in intensive-care units deepened his understanding of the interplay between bodily sensations and psychological structure. His Skin-Ego concept is defined as

> a mental image used by the child's Ego during its early stages of development to represent itself as an Ego containing psychical contents, based on its experience of the surface of the body. This corresponds to the moment when the psychical Ego differentiates itself from the bodily Ego in operative terms but remains mixed up with it in figurative terms.
>
> (Anzieu, 2016, p. 43)

However, for the development of the self, various bodily states, such as bodily "envelope systems," "sound-ego," "thermal envelope," "olfactory envelope," "muscular skin," "pain envelope," etc., are required.

According to Anzieu the skin has three functions:

> The first function of the skin is to be the sac that contains and retains inside itself all the good, full material that has accumulated through breastfeeding, everyday care, and the experience of being bathed in words. Its second function is to be the interface that marks the border with the external world, which it keeps on the outside, the barrier that protects one against being penetrated by the aggression and greed of others, whether people or objects. The third function of the skin, which it shares with the mouth and carries out at least as much as the mouth does, is to be a site and primary mode of communication with other people, to establish meaningful relations; in addition, it is a surface for registering the traces left by those others.
> (Anzieu, 2016, p. 44)

This somatopsychic perspective complements the perspective of interactional or attachment theory, and in particular the experience of the body as a container plays a crucial role. It is an anthropological determinant that humans are always in search of a boundary in the space that surrounds them, which is not defined as given or empty, but rather as a continually developing dynamic space, emerging or vanishing through interactions with objects and matter. The importance of the skin and the sense of touch is now well established: More than 10% of the human cerebral cortex is dedicated alone to processing information gathered by the skin (Rullmann et al., 2019).

Eugenio Gaddini (1981b [1998], p. 80), an Italian pediatrician and analyst, suggested that, in the first weeks of life, to the child "perception" means, among other things, "to modify their body in relation to the stimulus." In this way, the child perceives not (only) the real stimulus but the transformation that has occurred in their body. "This involves contact, being held, and a low-stimulus unity with the object." However, only a preponderance of failures intensifies imitative perceptions and makes them last excessively long; in the absence of the satisfying object and with increasing frustration, the object is hallucinated by the child as part of the physical self in the attempt to eliminate the unpleasant sensations deriving from its absence. "The psychological activity that develops from this and strives to restore this state arises in the absence of the object" (Jappe & Strehlow, 1998, p. 12). In this context, how long the absence from the object lasts and the regulation of built-up tension play a decisive role in whether the experiences of " 'now,' 'not now,' 'now again' . . . spawn the development of a sense of time continuity" or whether they are seen rather as "time pathologies" in the complex of disturbed mentalizing processes or even as "disturbed separation processes" (Gutwinski-Jeggle, 2017, p. 196f.).

Imitation, in turn, with its perceptual, fusing, imitative striving to *be the object* and its incorporative, libidinal striving to *have the object*, enables a fundamental distinction (Gaddini, 1969). If this interaction succeeds, the most favorable outcome is a "mouth-connected-with-the-breast" (or "mouth-connected-with-the-bottle") representation as an extended representation of the mouth. In this context,

Kestenberg (1971) spoke of organ-object imagery as the starting point for the development of the self: How the mouth is occupied leaves traces of these interactional experiences. So it is only too justified to transform Winnicott's famous statement by "There is no such thing as a baby [by itself]" (Winnicott, 1952 [1958], p. 99) into the sentence "There is no such thing as a body [by itself], but only and especially a body in connection with another body" (Küchenhoff, 2019, p. 770).

In the current discussion within the embodiment movement, the concept of the "embodied self" dominates, although the term "embodiment" (how is the body represented in the brain?) often neglects the complexity of the issue. The embodiment concept can be explained by a thought experiment: If one could implant the human brain into a frog or a robot, switching the body would also change the consciousness of the affected being. From the proverbial frog's perspective, the world would look very different. Thus, the characteristics of the respective body change the perception of the respective environment. Furthermore, the term "embodiment" serves both to describe implicit/procedural memory contents regarding unconscious resonance processes of intentional actions and to serve an expression of a new holistic movement: Embodiment means "that the mind (i.e., mind, thinking, the cognitive system, the psyche) together with its organ, the brain, is always related to the whole body" (Storch et al., 2010 [2011], p. 12).

Body therapists who use the mentalization model consider the development of a mentalizing self to be based on a parent-embodied, interactive phenomenon localized in the body, implicitly choreographed together through the "embodied dance between parent and child via their dynamic kinesthesia" (Shai & Fonagy, 2014). In this process, during their reciprocal correspondence, the infant and the attachment figure both share and co-construct the emotional tone. Thus, infants have quite sophisticated social communication skills and a rich and subtle nonverbal "language" with which to express internal states such as joy, excitement, curiosity, and frustration.

Experiences with a parent who mentalizes at a low level produce insecure-avoidant or insecure-ambivalent attachment, in which case the anticipatory activation of represented negative consequences automatically exerts an inhibitory effect on the infant. The imminent motor expression of the activated emotion is blocked to prevent the actual occurrence of expected negative consequences. This inhibitory "freezing" of the affective response system is automatic and procedural in nature; it results in the self being overwhelmed by an uncontrolled and persistent state of heightened physiological and psychological arousal and stress, which manifests not only in elevated cortisol levels but also in the development of a rigid and dysfunctional physiological stress regulatory system (Gergely & Unoka, 2008b).[1]

Because it is difficult to use verbal instruments, such as Parental Reflective Functioning (Luyten et al., 2017), Maternal Mind-Mindedness (Meins, 1999), or the Insightfulness Assessment (Oppenheim & Koren-Karie, 2013), to measure the embodied ability of parents to mentalize, Shai and Belsky (2011) developed a nonverbal measurement instrument, the Parental Embodied Mentalizing (PEM). To assess parent–infant encounters, they explicitly focused not on verbal content, but on whole-body movements that unfolded in dyadic interactions. Embodied parent mentalizing, measured 6 months after birth during a free-play interaction at home, was found to predict infant attachment security 15 months later. Mothers who had a high score on embodied mentalizing more frequently had securely attached infants than avoidant or resistant infants. This correlation persisted even when traditional, robust measures of parental care, such as maternal sensitivity, were controlled for. This test also predicted individual differences in social skills, social competence, and level of internalizing and externalizing problems in the infants at 54 months: The infants of mothers with higher scores on embodied mentalizing showed a marked superiority in social skills and fewer internalizing or externalizing problems than the infants of mothers with lower scores on embodied mentalizing.

This corresponds with considerations of Ciaunica and Fotopoulou (2017, p. 180) that the

> early mentalization of one's own body, as opposed to that of another individual, may somewhat paradoxically be caused by social interactions (cosubjectivities). For instance, feeding, sleeping, calming-down, or entertaining routines typically include endless repetitions of multisensory bundles from at least two bodies (e.g. active and passive touch, proprioceptive and vestibular information, smell, temperature, visual and auditory feedback). . . . In this sense, the very first-person experience of my body as mine is constituted by the presence of, and interaction with, other bodies in proximity.

4.2 Body-Mode or Embodied Mentalizing?

> In this chapter, the existing three pre-mentalizing modes proposed by the British research group will be complemented by the fourth pre-mentalizing mode, the body mode. It is proposed to recognize the "body mode" as the earliest and independent mode, which the other three follow as affect regulation strategies. The author delves into the concept of embodied mentalizing, which involves perceiving, reflecting on, and regulating bodily experiences and sensations in relation to mental states. He highlights the importance of primary social perception and the role of physical touch in shaping early attachment and understanding of the world. Through captivating case studies and philosophical insights, this chapter sheds light on the dynamic and intricate relationship between the body and the mind, inviting readers to explore the profound implications for psychology and therapy.

To date, the British research group around Bateman, Fonagy, and Target has introduced three developmental, empirically derived pre-mentalizing modes they assume are able to capture every human being (under certain conditions): the *teleological mode*, which dominates in the first 6 to 9 months of life; the *equivalence mode*, in which the inner and outer worlds are identical; and the *pretend mode*, in which inner and outer worlds are not connected. Scientifically, the current difficulty lies in capturing pre-mentalizing modes in individual and group psychotherapy sessions with a high rater reliability. This is probably because, on the one hand, these modes are context-dependent and do not occur stably over time; on the other hand, they sometimes intermingle with another mode.

Once the ground for the embodied mind had been prepared by cognitive philosophy/psychology through Varela and collaborators (1991 [2016]), representatives of the mentalization model introduced the term "embodied mentalizing" as a key concept to link the neuroscientific and the clinical levels (Debbané & Nolte, 2019). Embodied mentalizing is seen as an ability to "see the body as the seat of emotions, wishes and feelings" and, on the other hand, as an "ability to reflect on one's own bodily experiences and sensations and their relationships to intentional mental states in the self and others" (Luyten et al., 2012, p. 125). Embodied mentalizing thus uses the processes required to perceive, identify, and regulate the signals emerging from one's own body to make them useful for one's own psyche. A famous example from literature is Marcel Proust's struggle to decode initially incomprehensible bodily sensations: A spoonful of tea and a soggy little piece of madeleine suddenly reminded him of the "drama" of his mother's rejection of an expected goodnight kiss (Proust, 1964 [1978], pp. 63–66).

In epileptology, unexpected, inexplicable behaviors triggered by an individualized external trigger, such as the repetition of past actual experiences or the resurgence of memories, are assigned to the so-called kindling model: The intermittent repetition of a merely subliminal stimulus (chemical, physical, or experiential) serves as the kindling to ignite an epileptic seizure (Goddard & McIntyre, 1972). Such brief seizures are associated with an overactivation of the evolutionarily ancient limbic system, which represents the "emotional brain." It is also possible that kindling represents an example of body-mode-related, secondary-attachment deactivation, which is associated with impaired mentalizing, similar to attachment hyperactivation (Luyten et al., 2012, p. 125).

From a neuroscientific perspective embodied mentalizing is defined as a neural process by which primary sensorimotor and multisensory signals are progressively integrated and schematized to represent multiple, predictive models of our embodied states in specific environments. However, these models should not be understood as static neural body representations (in the sense of body schema vs. body image), but rather as hypothetical, dynamic, and generative processes that are continuously being updated vis-à-vis perceived error signals (Fotopoulou & Tsakiris, 2017, p. 8). This once again supports the thesis that, in addition to homeostasis, allostasis in the sense of a predictive brain is necessary for the body to adapt to difficult situations in a survivable way.

This view corresponds with theories that see perception and action as circularly or spirally linked, first formulated in Viktor von Weizsäcker's famous "Gestalt Circle" ("perceiving and moving") of the so-called Heidelberg School (von Weizsäcker, 1940). One cannot describe cognition in an action-neutral way, rather it arises through continuous sensorimotor couplings of the organism with its environment: "Thus, the world is constituted for us only in the course of our continuous interaction with it, by linking perceptual and motoric experiences" (Fuchs, 2017b, p. 152f.). Embodied mentalizing is primarily nonverbal and implicit, i.e., babies find their "psyche" in the arms of their primary others (Shai & Belsky, 2011). This is reminiscent of the "holding" concept of Winnicott (1960), who considered it the origin of other processes, such as intelligence and the mind as something distinct from the psyche. "From this follows the whole story of secondary processes and symbolic functioning as well as the organization of a personal mental content that forms the basis of dreaming and of living relationships" (Winnicott, 1958, p. 589). Although this formulation contains somewhat large steps, which today are viewed in a more nuanced way because of our current state of knowledge in developmental psychology, he was well aware that primary attachment figures use their bodies to communicate their mentalizing of the child's internal mental states. "Sensitive responsiveness and attentive caregiving are not simply the manifestation of internal symbolic processes, they also involve costly effort and physical investment" (Fonagy & Campbell, 2017, p. 40). Physical touch represents a particularly significant form of both communication and metacommunication. Responsive bodily interaction is the first thing to confirm the infant's knowledge of the world as valid.

For philosophers and authors, of course, none of this is breaking news. Anyone who has ever had the experience that taking a long walk inspires creative ideas will agree with the writer Thomas Bernhard: "When we walk," he mused, "the movement of the mind runs parallel to the movement of the body. We make this observation again and again, that, when we walk and put our body into motion, our thinking also comes into motion" (Bernhard, 1971, p. 78). Some philosophers were also aware that the earliest self-representation is a body-representation, as Edmund Husserl boldly formulated it in 1921:

> Thus, the body comprises the most pristine character of what is truly mine; by belonging to me, it stands in contrast to the stranger with whom I am not entangled, i.e., not practical. . . . Of all things, my body is closest to me, closest in perception, closest in terms of feeling and will.
> (Husserl, 1973, p. 58)

Yet, this formulation assumes a self that, as it were, sifts through its possessions and discovers the body as the primary and most important one (perhaps more of a garden than as a foundation of the self).[2]

As mentioned earlier, the German distinction between *Leib* and *Körper* does not exist in the Anglo-Saxon world, which in itself is an interesting phenomenon in cultural studies. The closest thing in English is still *lived embodiment*, although Merleau-Ponty's concept of intercorporeality seems more appropriate with the background of intersubjectivity. He wanted to capture subjective experience and sensation, in the sense of a corporeality of consciousness and a corporeal intentionality with a common experience and sensation of several at the same time. The introduction of the term "body-mode" is supported by the fact that body and psyche are not experienced separately until about the ninth month of life. For this reason, in my opinion, it is justified to replace the previous three pre-mentalizing modes derived from developmental psychology (teleological, equivalence, and pretend mode) by the body-mode as the earliest and independent mode (Diez Grieser & Müller, 2018). This view is also supported by the developmental psychological theory that newborns initially perceive mental states as physiological-bodily sensations and express them automatically because of innate tendencies (Zevalkink et al., 2012, 2015, p. 173f.).

In addition to the notion of intentionality, the notions of corporeality (lived embodiment), empathy, intersubjectivity, and sociality play fundamental roles in the phenomenological philosophy of the 20th century, represented by Husserl, Scheler, Heidegger, Sartre, and Merleau-Ponty (Moran, 2017, pp. 33f.). Their contributions have likely not been duly integrated into the mentalization model to date because of the clash of two philosophical worlds that are difficult to conciliate: the notion of "representation," which derives from Cartesian image theory and thus ultimately from the Platonic second-world theory of body and mind/soul; and, on the other hand, the dynamic concepts of resonance, pattern, matrix, and functional loops, which are based on the Aristotelian theory of perception as a contact theory and refer to his property theory.

Cognitive neuroscience has produced more or less well-founded empirical findings for both theoretical concepts, but their theoretical context remains unknown. Thus, the Heidelberg psychiatrist and philosopher Thomas Fuchs refers to Merleau-Ponty, who sees

> communication, the understanding of gestures . . . as based on the mutual correspondence of my intentions and the gestures of others, of my gestures and the intentions manifested in the behavior of others. It is as if the intentions of others reside in my body and my intentions in their bodies.
> (Merleau-Ponty, 1966, p. 219)

Primary social perception, he argues, is "not based on an internal modeling of the states of others in an observer, but on a connection of two embodied subjects into a common interbody and thus interaffectivity" (Fuchs, 2018b, p. 215). In view of symbiotically embodied agents, this theory, which does without representations, "needs no mind reading, no theory of mind, no mentalization"; rather, one could then also put incest and abuse here. Thus, it is not surprising that this body phenomenology fails to produce a conclusive treatment concept. Such a concept, however, would be especially important for situations in which mutual interactions fail. In our opinion, an exclusively moral dictum that "from a body-phenomenological point of view . . . successful psychotherapy . . . is based on an attitude characterized by the concrete bodily presence and the personal authenticity of the therapist" (Broschmann & Fuchs, 2020) is by no means sufficient for treating patients with somatoform disorders and a lot of others with physical complaints.

Undoubtedly, the mentalization model represents a further development of relational and intersubjective psychoanalysis, even if there has been little exchange between the two fractions so far. Following Merleau-Ponty, *intercorporéité* or intercorporeality comes before intersubjectivity and enables intersubjectivity. Merleau-Ponty extended this concept to include "interanimality" to encompass intercorporeal relations beyond human relations (Moran, 2017, p. 33). Interanimality occurs in the fondling (petting) of animals, in the milking of cows, in the riding of horses, in *doga* (yoga with a dog as a partner!). In even more extreme, albeit very rare, cases, zoophilia may occur, which can go as far as having sexual intercourse with animals. In animal-assisted psychotherapies in the sense of the mentalization model using a horse, donkey, or dog, patients are enabled to understand what could be going on within the animals (Ganser, 2017; Klüwer, 2011). In animal-assisted therapies, the approach of *not knowing* takes on a special relevance because the animal's behavior must first be interpreted to use it to interpret human behavior.

The important question in developmental psychology – at what age of intercorporeality (as a partial aspect of the body-mode) can we assume intersubjectivity? – has encouraged a number of other authors to advocate the concept of a "primary intersubjectivity," which is presumed to take place already in utero, when the fetus and the mother are in "symbiotic" communication, specifically from about the 25th week of gestation (Burrow, 1913 [2013]; Nagy, 2011; Trevarthen, 1979; Trevarthen & Aitken, 2001). If the mother hums, the fetus sometimes even moves to the rhythm of the music, just as it is already responding to the mother's voice, the father's voice, or other external sounds (Malloch & Trevarthen, 2009). Every mother has had such an "interbody" experience when the fetus begins to kick against the abdominal wall, i.e., where one subject perceives the kinesthetic movements of another. In the meantime, ultrasound studies have proven that embryos touch themselves or, in the case of a twin pregnancy, caress or kick the twin (apparently affectionately).

In this context, however, the mother (or father) is not just a (dyadic) individual but is part of a group. The mother's abilities to ascribe meaning to the respective physical state of her embryo and (later) her baby are greatly influenced by how she feels about herself as a mother, whether she is supported in her relationships, how her mother felt when she was her baby's age, and how her physical interactions are complemented by her communicative competence. A crucial prerequisite for the mother's ability to connect with her child seems to be the availability of social support in the sense of surrogate parents (alloparents) (Hrdy, 2000), as found in many African cultures. Thus, the social culture in which the parents and the family are embedded plays a significant role (Brown, 1985, 2006b), which is why we should speak here of a network or better – in the sense of Foulkes – of a physical, psychological, and social matrix. The body of the baby and the later toddler lays the foundation of life, so to speak, which "encompasses all further psychological functions; therefore, it can suffer serious damage if denied emotional, social, and cognitive functioning" (Lemma, 2014, p. 2). In this respect, the psychogenic loss of speech and language in children and adolescents, for example, can be understood as a withdrawal to the body – in terms of attachment deactivation – in the sense of body-mode rather than embodied mentalizing.

Case Vignette

A 4-year-old boy and his sister, who was about a year younger than him, had been sent by his parents to a distant children's home because of the impending birth of another sister. After returning to his parents' home, the boy did not speak for several weeks.

According to Winnicott (1958), the first-year baby is by definition disintegrated, confronted with visual, auditory, tactile, olfactory, and proprioceptive stimuli for which there is no higher-order memory and thus no higher-order processing. However, this view has since been subjected to increasing criticism: It is not the affects that are crude and undifferentiated at birth and only gradually become differentiated as well as cognitively enriching; rather, the self- and object-representations are what remain undifferentiated.

Quite a few authors have been interested in the integration (or failure thereof) of body and psyche in the early relationships between a baby/toddler and its primary attachment figures (Arnott & Meins, 2007; Bion, 1967; Orbach, 2003; Spitz & Wolf, 1946; Stern, 1985 [1992]). In this regard, the nature of attachment, early interactions, and the psychosocial embeddedness of primary attachment figures tended to remain unexamined and unconsidered. Gaddini (1998, p. 198) introduced the notion of "basic psychological organization" to differentiate it from the notion of "structure," which in developmental psychology appears later in life. By basic psychological organization, Gaddini meant the period stretching from biological birth to the psychological separation process, which he defined as the "mental birth," i.e., "the formation of the first mental image of the self, which was, of course, the separate self" (ibid.).

These theoretical outlines have since been superseded by empirical infant and toddler research, which has revealed new and sometimes astonishing findings. The first generation of developmental psychologists still assumed that the basic (primary) emotions of joy, anger, sadness, disgust, surprise, and fear were innate (Ekman et al., 1972; Tomkins, 1962). In contrast, more recent emotion research postulates that affects and emotions are not innate but in fact must be learned by the infant in a specific sociocultural context through marked mirroring of primary attachment figures. Marked mirroring is understood to mean that (ideally) the primary attachment figure(s) respond(s) to the infant's pre- and nonlinguistic expressions of affect in an imitative, slightly emphatic, exaggerated, or relativizing manner. Similarities in this affect mirroring helps the child to classify their own affect experience, and differences help them to differentiate their own self from that of the counterpart. Here, the core of all emotion is communication derived from need (Holodynski, 2006; Krause, 1983), which lies very close to "intentionality." Affects are primarily "felt" as diffuse bodily sensations, so initially they are undifferentiated and holistic at the same time. For example, the expression of joy through mimicry is regularly accompanied by certain types of vocalizations and posture, and the expression of anger with others (Dornes, 1997). However, it has yet to be investigated whether expressions of affect are displayed differently in larger groups (of bodies), such as among spectators at a sports match, than in situations of dyadic, relationship-centered social mirroring (= affect matching). The latter succeeds in 87% of the encounters, because early coordination is often "transmodal": via voice, facial expression, posture, and rhythm (Stern, 2004).

During puberty, in addition to the hormonal development, the body again plays a particularly intensive role, possibly also because of neuronal "pruning" (Giedd, 2003; Giedd et al., 1999). Following an increase in neuronal connections (synaptogenesis) with subsequent synaptic "pruning" – according to the principle of "use it or lose it" – superfluous synapses re-form, creating more efficient brain circuits. At the same time, axonal myelination improves the efficiency of neuronal transmission (Blakemore, 2008, 2010; Giedd, 2004). During adolescence, the prefrontal cortex, the seat of mentalization and affect regulation, undergoes significant structural transformation. At the psychosocial level, it is not unusual for adolescents who are confused and intimidated by the hormonal and physiological changes going on in their bodies to suddenly experience their bodies as something strange, as a threatening monster, even as something alien-like, as an entirely different object that is not part of their selves. This may be why, among other things, the virtual world of the Internet – up to and including cyberaddiction – proves irresistible for many adolescents: It knows no barriers or boundaries. Through fantasized omnipotence, the adolescent replaces experienced helplessness and strangeness, in the sense of the pretend mode (where the inner world and the outer world are not connected), something Alessandra Lemma (2014) convincingly pointed out.

4.3 When the Psychotherapist's Body "Goes on Strike" or "Speaks"

Intercorporeality refers to the phenomena in which the psychotherapist's body becomes involved in the therapeutic process and serves as a bridge between the patient's internal (mental) and external (physical) realities. It suggests that the psychotherapist's body can resonate with the patient's somatic experiences and unspeakable traumas, leading to bodily sensations or symptoms in the therapist.

These psychosomatic symptoms experienced by the therapist can provide valuable insights into the patient's unthought experiences and perinatal traumatization. They go beyond somatic countertransference, which refers to the therapist's emotional reactions to the patient and are seen as "unrepresented" experiences of the patient. The therapist's bodily sensations are considered as early representational enveloping structures, offering a unique perspective into the patient's inner world.

The concept of intercorporeality (*intercorporéité*) also has a clinical *raison d'être* if we consider the many phenomena in which the psychotherapist's body speaks or goes on strike as playing a central role as an intermediary between the internal (mental) and external reality (Hartung & Steinbrecher, 2018). Psychosomatic symptoms such as a spasm in the esophagus or a pressure in the chest (Volz-Boers, 2016) not only spill over sometimes to the analyst's body, but their body may suddenly resonate to an unspeakable trauma and begin to speak itself through somatization. This phenomenon can be used to gain a deeper understanding of the patient. Bodily sensations of the analyst represent more than just somatic countertransference and can be understood as the "unthought experiences" of the patient, while at the same time providing access to their peri-or postnatal traumatization (Volz-Boers, 2009). Of course, it is questionable whether such largely still diffuse bodily sensations are unrepresented if indeed one posits representations as neurodynamic envelope structures! This kind of countertransference is rather a state in which something will be experienced that cannot be grasped using the classical (to date) three pre-mentalizing modes. From our point of view, we should understand such phenomena as the therapist's "body-mode" (cf. Chapter 5.2), which refers to earliest, still undifferentiated representational enveloping structures. Therapeutic success does not consist primarily in the therapist's linking their own bodily sensations during countertransference with feelings, images, thoughts, and words to come up with a meaningful interpretation, but rather in their formulating a meaningful question by first allowing themselves to describe exactly what the patient is feeling at the moment:

"Let's stay with your feeling for a moment. In which situation did it start and where exactly?"

"Could you describe for me what I should be feeling?"

Case Vignette

During an intercollegiate seminar, a colleague experienced in psychosomatics is reporting on a nine-year treatment of a 55-year-old teacher (with numerous interruptions) who, on the advice of his partner, had sought treatment for various physical complaints (tinnitus, back pain, exhaustion). He decided to undergo an analytic, low-frequency therapy. This patient grew up as an illegitimate child living alone with his mother in a village, faced with the well-known problems of social exclusion (the father lived with his family in the same village). Because of this background, he said he did not have a father. His mother, a factory worker, had loved him beyond measure and sewed all his clothes. Thanks to support at school and his good performance, he eventually graduated from high school and started studying to be a teacher (he always able to make the best out of the worst).

He begins treatment with great ("epistemic") distrust and the need for control over the therapist. He not only wants to have a look at the application for long-term therapy, but protests certain formulations there, such as his childhood being filled with "dreariness." During psychotherapy, he develops a life-threatening blood cell disease that leads to a heart attack. The blood cell disease was diagnosed in more detail only at the insistence of the therapist and eventually required a stem-cell transplant. The therapist visits him in the hospital, and the patient survives.

While reporting this case during the lecture, the colleague begins to cough conspicuously and frequently; even a drink of water doesn't help. In addition, he repeatedly falters, overcome by emotion while reading his manuscript aloud. He mentions rather casually that he himself struggled with a serious illness at a later point in time, when this patient was once again in analytical treatment with him. After resuming therapy, the patient, who until then had been difficult to reach emotionally, proved much more accessible. Although the colleagues in the audience are unanimous in their opinion that the therapist had saved the patient's life, the lecturer never once mentions his affective involvement, neither during the entire lecture nor throughout the lively discussion of the casuistry on the part of the therapist – possibly because of shame. It would also be conceivable that a very similar peri- or prenatal fate had inextricably connected the two.

In another case, an analytic trainee suddenly threw up behind the couch when he learned for the umpteenth time about his patient's perverse and self-harming sexual practices, which she continued to engage in addictively despite his repeated friendly attempts to dissuade her – at least until they were understood. Interestingly, the therapist's physical "interaction" abruptly ended the patient's addictive behavior.

Some therapists suggest that such phenomena during the therapeutic process can be deemed the pre-symbolic "language of intrauterine life." These phenomena reflect traumatic relational constellations that appear intersubjectively between the therapist and the patient as implicit relational knowledge of procedural memory. The reactivation of such experiences of fear of annihilation presents a special challenge to the psychotherapeutic relationship, because the two parties must find a language to describe their mutual bodily sensations. There are no immediate words or images available for this purpose in the preverbal sphere. Rather, what is needed is a sensory-intuitive attitude on the part of the therapist, developed through self-experience and appropriately qualified supervision and intervision by colleagues with experience in body processes.

When therapists perceive bodily sensations, they generally assign them to the concept of "countertransference." This concerns the unconscious part of the interactions between therapist and patient, something therapists only slowly become aware of through mostly negative affects ("I feel spellbound," "I feel paralyzed"). Countertransference phenomena are not the same as self-transference: They include the totality of moods, reactions, and attitudes that can be expressed in different degrees of consciousness. The body experience of the psychotherapist reflects not only the attachment style, but also the unconscious communication of the early mother–child relationship as "body empathy" (Jacobs, 1973), a kind of core zone of general embodied empathy, inasmuch as it becomes conscious. If they do not become aware of it, then therapists, too, move in the body-mode and can even become ill from interacting with their patients through nonmentalized countertransference. When therapists struggle to verbally articulate their subjective states, the difference from the analytic technique lies in not providing an interpretation but translating one's own bodily sensations into a mentalizing, preferably affect-focused question.

The latter is all the more justified because Birksted-Breen (2019) has criticized the inflationary and indiscriminate use of the term "countertransference" in the sense of "thought transference" or "affect transference," that is, when the psychoanalyst experiences an affect the patient supposedly cannot express or perceive, which is then termed projective identification. The levels of the unconscious express themselves in different ways and on different levels of transformation, through sensory experiences, affects, emotions, images and dreams, and, in the end, thoughts. Nevertheless, a deep discussion of somatic countertransference – the sensory experiences of nausea, dizziness, heart palpitations, and general malaise on the part of the therapist – is still largely missing in the analytical literature.

4.4 Dimensions of Mentalizing in Somatoform Stress Disorders

> The passage suggests that difficulties in mentalization can arise when individuals or groups excessively focus on one pole of a dimension, neglecting the aspects of the other pole. Successful mentalizing occurs when all dimensions are balanced and used equally. Each pole represents a neural system in the brain, and they compete under stressful conditions, potentially leading to imbalances in mentalizing. Patients with somatization disorders may focus excessively on external factors and laboratory values, lacking interest in internal states and attachment to others. Eating disorder patients may exhibit a hyperfocus on body-related concerns, such as figure and weight. Adverse childhood experiences and trauma often play a role in these difficulties.

To utilize the sensory experiences of both patients and therapists, it is wise to have knowledge of the dimensions of mentalizing. Neurobiological studies that employ imaging to research social cognitions and findings suggesting dysfunctions in individual facets of mentalization underscore the assumption that mentalizing is a multidimensional construct (Lieberman, 2007; Luyten et al., 2019). The dimensions are composed of the following:

- automatic vs. controlled;
- self vs. other;
- internally vs. externally oriented;
- cognitive vs. affective (see Figure 4.1).

Difficulties in mentalizing often go back to the fact that an individual or a group focuses too strongly on one pole of a dimension, whereby the aspects of the other pole of this dimension are neglected; this results in a limitation of mentalization. Successful mentalizing, on the other hand, occurs when *both* poles of a dimension – and indeed all dimensions – are used equally and presented in a balanced way by the individual.

Each of the poles represents a neural system, with all systems interconnected in the structural-functional dynamics of the brain (Debbané & Nolte, 2019). However, each pole competes under stressful conditions of heightened arousal, for example, in the form of a more inward-focused "mentalizing" as thoughts, feelings, and ruminations – or by asking "How does your body feel right now?" with outward-focused "mentalizing" (focusing on observable, external characteristics or features). Patients may exhibit difficulties or deficits in mentalizing in only one domain or in several domains without necessarily being impaired in the other domains. Another polarity is "automatic (implicit)" vs. "controlled (explicit)" mentalizing. Whereas automatic mentalizing (as an emergency response) requires little attention, awareness, or effort because of the rapid processing (it is subcortically localized) and therefore easily leads to erroneous conclusions, controlled mentalizing involves a slow, cortically localized, conscious process of reflection. "Self-oriented" vs. "other-oriented" is directed toward self-reflected mentalizing and other-reflected mentalizing. While cognitive mentalizing refers to the ability to understand mental processes cognitively, affective mentalizing refers to understanding the dimension of the affective core of experience.

Mentalizing occurs when there is a dynamic balance between all four dimensions, especially between all the possible imbalances between the poles of each dimension (Luyten et al., 2019). Non-mentalizing (or impaired mentalizing) manifests itself in borderline patients through overly sensitive reactions to the emotional behavior of others, to the detriment of the reflexive competence of their own mental state (hyperactivation of the attachment strategy). Patients with somatization disorders with alexithymic traits tend to express themselves in a controlling, cognitive manner rather than affectively; they are more interested in laboratory values and external facts than in internal states – and they tend to avoid attachment with a low interest in others (hypoactivation).

Patients with somatoform disorders, eating disorders, and personality disorders, including borderline patients, exhibit numerous phenomena along with their respective specific body experiences. At the level of the body mode, these patients like to deal concretely with laboratory values, externals such as figure and weight, and with hypochondriacal misperceptions that correspond to the dimension internally. Thus, patients with eating disorders have a kind of "hyperembodiment" (Robinson & Skarderud, 2019; Skarderud & Fonagy, 2012), where everything revolves around food. Adverse childhood experiences in the form of neglect, maltreatment, or sexual abuse occur significantly more often in these patients (Maunder et al., 2017; Porter et al., 2019). They are accompanied by constant self-assurance strategies ("body-checking") because their physical and psychological experiences are

128 Bodily or Mental States?

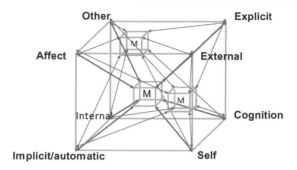

Figure 4.1 Dimensions of mentalizing (whereby M should be imagined as a moving sphere).

insufficiently integrated. Like traumatized patients, patients with somatic symptom disorders have a striking difficulty presenting their stressful experiences as coherent stories with a beginning and an end. A time-grid structure is also very often missing. Nevertheless, the body experience dominates, and any connections to mental processes are far away. Last but not least, "through body manipulations they get caught up in abnormal, subjective, experiential realities, from which they sometimes emerge spontaneously and sometimes only with psychotherapeutic help" (Plassmann, 1993). Before the time of the mentalization model, it was assumed that frequent switching between normal and pathological experiential realities depends on the capacity for symbol formation. Today, we tend to think that it is not the restricted capacity for symbol formation that is causative – which is known to be tied to language – but that the capacity for mentalization determines whether specific attachment activations lead to sudden outbreaks or to gradual, restricted crises of affect regulation.

In addition to the pre-mentalizing modes, the furtherance of mentalizing regarding specific interactions[3] is oriented toward the polar dimensions. These dimensions enable the technique of "contrary move," which means posing questions oriented respectively to the opposite pole to induce mentalizing as so-called contrary-move interactions (Figure 4.1).

Notes

1 Yet cortisol levels are not always elevated by a traumatic event and not in everyone. This phenomenon is attributed to the psychophysiological adaptability of the hypothalamic-pituitary-adrenocortical (HPA) axis.
2 I owe this metaphor to Peter Rottländer.
3 I prefer "interaction" to "intervention" to express the more symmetrical relationship between therapist and patient. Intervention is more reminiscent of technology and military operations and tacitly emphasizes an asymmetry between (knowing) therapists and (not-knowing) patients.

Chapter 5

Somatizing or Mentalizing?

Picture this: A child falls and scrapes a knee on a playground. What is its first reaction? Does the child begin to scream or cry? Does the child look at its knee to regard the extent of the injury, which it internally assesses? Both are possible (Fotopoulou & Tsakiris, 2017). Many parents would confirm that children first turn to their parents and then wait for their response before responding with an "appropriate" behavioral response of their own. Developmental and social psychologists explain such behaviors by referring to a role-model or social-reference system (Bandura, 1967), whereas psychodynamic scholars attribute them to identificatory processes or affect-attunement processes (Stern, 2004) with one or both parents.

From the perspective of the mentalization model, one could hypothesize that this matter concerns a violation of the self and that the child's looking to their primary attachment figures represents an attempt to regain self-coherence. Yet such a behavioral approach raises a fundamental question: Why does the experience of pain, so closely associated with subjectivity and one's body, invite immediate social attention and response? Like Merleau-Ponty, Fotopoulou and Tsakiris (2017, p. 6) assume that even the smallest aspects of selfhood, such as such qualities of feeling "are fundamentally shaped by embodied interactions with other people in early childhood and beyond."

Quite obviously, there are very different modes in the formation of representation: "Besides condensations, overlaps, and references, we also find voids and withdrawals. Something emerges through withdrawal, meaning appears in the meaningless, the unrepresented in the represented" (Kobylinska-Dehe, 2019, p. 525). This aspect of the body-mode plays a central role in mentalization or non-mentalizing. The unrepresented is able to become visible in represented shame; in the form of shame and embarrassment, it inhibits the ability to mentalize and achieve therapeutic progress, something Darwin already suspected:

> Under a keen sense of shame there is a strong desire for concealment. We turn away the whole body, more especially the face, which we endeavour in some manner to hide. An ashamed person can hardly endure to meet the gaze of those present, so that, he almost invariably casts down his eyes or looks askant.... Most persons whilst blushing intensely have their mental powers confused.
>
> (Darwin, 1872 [1934], p. 156)

DOI: 10.4324/9781003345145-5

This is how Darwin described the effect of shame on the ability to mentalize, although that term had not yet been coined. The ability to be ashamed is an important developmental and psychological achievement by higher-order representations. These are characterized by defensive omissions and/or distortions resulting in not having developed representations when experiences with early caregivers are characterized by neglect or abuse. It seems that the intentionality of shame is to hide oneself with the opposite, often hidden desire and hope to finally be seen. Shamelessness and the defence against shame is therefore the opposite of this, the inability to mentalize the feelings of the other and ends therefore often in violence and insult (Schultz-Venrath, 2022, p. 92). Similar to all other affects, "the feeling of shame" has "clearly a social function, moulded according to the social structure" (Elias, 1994, p. 113).

There are numerous reasons why psychotherapies are not successful. One important reason could lie in the failure to recognize and treat shame in clinical work – after all, therapists, too, do not like to be shamed. Unfortunately, despite extensive research, shame remains one of the least-pursued affects in education and training (Küchenhoff, 2018; Schultz-Venrath, 2022).

From a mentalization-based treatment viewpoint, it is of particular importance that the affect of shame, like all affects, is multidimensional, having many faces, running from "the most malignant shame to a necessary and healthy ability to feel the shame in order to be a part of society" (Hadar, 2008, p. 168; Schultz-Venrath, 2022, p. 96) (Figure 1.2). While malignant shame is "nameless" and usually "inexpressible," represented in body dysmorphic disorder or body dysmorphia, the primal shame, blending guilt, disgust, and panic, is a form of shame that goes back to the belief that "something is wrong with me." This is now well conceptualized as "epistemic mistrust" in the mentalization model (Campbell et al., 2021; Fonagy & Allison, 2015; Fonagy & Nolte, 2023).

Case Vignette

In the case of a 24-year-old borderline patient with severe depression, strong feelings of shame and an overbearing, self-critical superego played a central role in her treatment. They made it difficult for her to talk about her difficulties because she found them "so embarrassing." She tried to cope with these overwhelming situations either by binge eating or self-harm.

5.1 Pre-mentalizing Modes

> This chapter justifies the extension of the pre-mentalizing modes of experience. The pre-mentalizing modes are developmental phases that correlate with language development and memory systems. They represent different ways of affect regulation, experiencing and perceiving oneself and the world.

Pre-mentalizing modes progress in developmental phases that correlate with those of language development and the memory systems (Figure 5.1). Under certain psychological stresses, anyone, not just patients, can regress to a pre-mentalizing mode, which manifests itself both mentally and physically, for example, in the form of a steadfast refusal to self-reflect, the avoidance of dealing with the inner states of mind as well as a lack of emotional awareness, whereby the inner state of mind is not, or only slightly, perceived and differentiated. Persistently remaining in the equivalence mode, which equates inner sensitivities and external realities, is currently increasingly reflected in the belief in conspiracies, which is not infrequently also accompanied by a limited ability to regulate and modulate one's affects. A significant correlation between the severity of symptoms and impaired mentalizing ability is well documented for patients with mental disorders, as are differences between patients who self-harmed and those who did not, and between patients with and without suicide attempts (Hausberg et al., 2012).

Diez Grieser and Müller (2018) and Schultz-Venrath (2021) proposed expanding the three previous modes by introducing the body-mode as the earliest mode. The body-mode is defined by the fact that the infant – both prenatally and postnatally – does not experience their body and psyche as something separate until about 9 months of age. Rather, the infant is primarily concerned with their physical and skin sensations (Table 5.3). This mode is particularly helpful for understanding somatic symptom disorders, eating disorders, and other body-related disorders, above all when distinguishing between the "body-having" and "body-being" modes. "Body-being" corresponds to the body-mode in which bodily sensations begin not at birth, but also include intrauterine relationships via procedural memory. Postnatally, in turn, this is accompanied on the neuronal level most likely by the activation

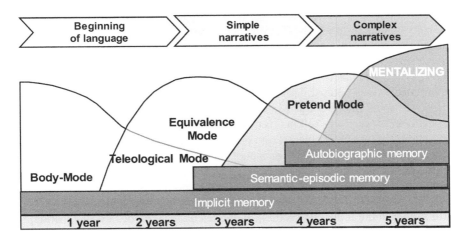

Figure 5.1 Pre-mentalizing modes in relation to the development of language and memory.

of mirror neurons, whereas the "body-having" mode draws on initial body or affect representations: In the "body-having" mode, the child – or even the adult, for example, regarding sexuality, especially onanism – is engaged exclusively with their bodily sensations. Body-dysmorphic disorders also belong to the body-mode: Patients disproportionately regard a supposed physical asymmetry or a small flaw to the extent that they are constantly preoccupied with the respective body part – the skin, hair, teeth, nose, ears, or secondary sexual characteristics. Objective observers would likely not even notice the presumed flaw. However, such patients go to extremes in their anguish, trying desperately to correct the presumed flaw through cosmetic surgery, which can even turn into a "surgery addiction" (Menninger, 1934). While such misperceptions and constant preoccupation with a supposed anomaly may be assigned to the body-mode, the compulsion to undergo an operation better belongs to the teleological mode. A similar differentiation could also be made for tattoos: On the one hand, tattoos project a body boundary; on the other hand, they speak for the mostly unconscious wish to have another body or to be in another body, which is then "acted upon" in this particular way.

Case Vignette

Together with her mother, a 19-year-old female patient accompanied her father in his final days. During her father's dying moments, she had to run back and forth between the deathbed and the bathroom; when her mother called out to her that her father had just died, she bit into her arm and then slid down the wall between the sink and the toilet and collapsed on the floor. She experienced a "meltdown." This initial self-injury was followed by cutting whenever she perceived the seething in her body as too stressful.

The central problem of a psychoanalytic understanding of bodily phenomena is that they are usually immediately attributed to the unconscious system – but before the body-self comes the body. If psychic contents cannot inscribe themselves in the unconscious and conscious system, they are not in the system of the unconscious or even preconscious (Leikert, 2023; Lombardi, 2023). Against this background, it becomes understandable that this breakdown can be understood psychodynamically as an unconscious oedipal desire to want to die herself to be close to her father, today we would interpret this example as speaking more to the body-mode – the desire to feel oneself as a self in this emotionally extremely stressful situation stemming from the loss of an object. From our clinical experience, this difference is significant in that patients at this stage cannot comprehend the psychodynamic context.

Previously, such phenomena were assigned to the teleological mode. In contrast to the teleological mode, the *body-mode is concerned primarily with the self and not with the other*. It thus also differs from Ogden's autistic-contiguous mode (see also further in the following section). In the teleological mode, a well-functioning environment is essential for the infant's survival. Since infants cannot themselves express what they need, the attachment figure must determine whether the infant

Table 5.1 Definitions of the pre-mentalizing modes (Schultz-Venrath, 2021).

Mode	Definition
Body	Pre- and postnatal, the baby cannot experience body and psyche separately until around the ninth month. It is primarily concerned with its body and skin sensations.
Teleological	Mental states such as needs and emotions are expressed in action. Only actions and their available consequences count – not words.
Equivalence	Outer world = inner world. Mental states are experienced as real, as happens in dreams, flashbacks, and paranoid delusions.
Pretend	Mental states are disconnected from reality, retain a sense of unreality because they are not connected and anchored to reality.

feels hunger, thirst, or pain. This experience occurs solely on a physiological level: The environment must be able to alleviate internal states of tension.

Because of the different therapeutic interactions, these two modes should be clearly differentiated. Many patients, such as those with a body-related disorder or eating disorder, accept as reality only what is physically or actually observable, because they are more or less unable to correctly interpret or evaluate their physical sensations. Robinson and Skarderud (2019, p. 370) therefore, in the tradition of Hilde Bruch (1973), speak of anorexia and bulimia patients as having a self-disorder or a deficient sense of self. Because such patients do not know what they feel and what they need, they are in danger of losing touch with their reality.

5.1.1 The Body-Mode – Clinical Examples

Body-oriented affects and mirroring processes moderate psychosexual development. If the various mirroring processes are absent, then neither an "intermediate corporeality" (Merleau-Ponty) nor a capacity for communication develops in the individual concerned, which may explain why linguistic access to patients with somatoform disorders and personality disorders who are in the body-mode is often so difficult (Schultz-Venrath, 2021).

The lack of differentiation between body and psyche manifests itself in numerous clinical symptoms, such as thumb sucking, self-stroking, rumination, eating disorders, skin picking (dermatillomania), nail biting (onychophagia), or nail picking (perionychophagia), up to the phenomenon of occlusal dysesthesia (burning mouth syndrome).[1] Patients and therapists in the body-mode alike perceive "mental states" only as physiological-bodily sensations and express these automatically. The body-mode is part of the nonverbal, largely unconscious interaction, which is differentiated according to posture, gestures, touch behavior, facial expressions, gaze behavior, voice, and speech melody. An essential part of this mode is self-touch, which can appear phasically (e.g., stroking the cheek), repetitively (e.g., scratching the forearm), or irregularly (e.g., nibbling the fingers) (Lausberg, 2018, p. 67). Thus, motor restlessness can manifest itself through irregular hand movements, in other words, fidgeting (nervous restlessness, nibbling, fiddling, and playing around).

One function of the body-mode, analogous to the quality of first relational experiences, lies in boundary experiences. Only through the touching of the skin can a self be reflexively perceived, a circumstance used in various ways in body-therapeutic concepts. Various touch perceptions allow a self to develop so that different kinds of self-injurious behavior can also be understood as an attempt to feel oneself (to prevent fragmentation or unbearable emptiness). Self-injurious behavior is not necessarily tied to an object, as Anzieu (2016) impressively pointed out with his concept of the "Skin-Ego."

In the analytical literature, the body-mode has various theoretical antecedents. The mostly forgotten Paul Schilder was convinced that body images of human beings communicate with each other either in part or in their entirety (Schilder, 1935 [1978], p. 237). He described the exchange of body images as "body-image intercourse" and its effects as "appersonization." Ogden (1989) described the "autistic-contiguous organization" or "position" as the "most primitive state of being" and as a means of "ascribing meaning to experience" (Ogden, 1988, 1989, p. 127). He understands the word "contiguous" as a necessary antithesis to the connotation of the word "autistic," which triggers images of isolation and disconnectedness. In light of recent findings regarding autism spectrum disorders, this word usage may be somewhat confusing for readers less familiar with psychoanalytical thought, but it connotes exclusively (psychological) withdrawal. According to Ogden, this mode ensures limits to extreme (infantile) fears (!), which serve to shape object relations in the form of afferent surface experiences. For Ogden, people in the mode of an autistic-contiguous organization experience sensations mainly taking place on the surface of the skin. This, in turn, prompts the beginnings of self-experience and mental meaning:

> Sensory-contiguity of skin surface and rhythmicity are basic to the most fundamental set of infantile object relations: the experience of the infant being held, nursed and spoken to by the mother.
>
> (Ogden, 1989, p. 128)

If the early mother–child relationship fails to produce forms of sensory experience that "heal" or "make bearable" the awareness of separateness that is an essential component of early infant experience, then this develops into a source of an intolerable process of nonexperience, much like a condition in which the process of ascribing meaning to experience fails, ceases, or is paralyzed. The attribution of meaning, which must be triggered by the patient (and less often by the therapist), can sometimes produce strange linguistic images. For example, in her third, relatively advanced analysis, a depressed female patient described the feeling of tension in her stomach as a sensation of discomfort:

P: "There is a sort of block in my stomach."
Th: "So, there's something in the stomach . . ."
P: "Hm *(pondering)*, yeah, it's like a stone, something really heavy."
Th: "How does that feel?"
P: "Oh, it's like the stone before the tomb of Christ."

This case example quoted by Leikert (2016, p. 163) impressively demonstrates how, given sufficient epistemic trust, the question "How does that feel?" can be used to induce an alternative perspective in the patient by utilizing the method of free body association to promote mentalization. Leikert, who, without referring to the mentalization concept, made it a principle to completely "renounce interpretations in these zones," describes how this "sudden metaphor in the linguistic desert of bodily sensations . . . had an enormously comical effect" on both of them. They burst out laughing at the exact same moment and were subsequently able to analyze the unexpected association together as a fantasy of eternity and indestructibility, which obviously served the purpose of recovery.

Another well-known clinical example of such a "nonexperience" is the body dysmorphic disorder (formerly dysmorphophobia) mentioned earlier, which is accompanied by a pronounced shame effect. Surprisingly, the effect found in this clinical picture as well as the epistemic mistrust have received little attention. Patients are excessively preoccupied with one or more perceived defects or deficiencies in their external appearance, perceiving themselves to be disgusting, ugly, unattractive, abnormal, or disfigured, even though there is no objective reason at all for others to think this. The excessive preoccupation with appearance is perceived as disturbing, unwanted, and time-consuming (occupying an average of 3–8 h/day) (APA, 2013). The basic body feeling is largely negatively determined, accompanied by difficulty speaking in front of and with others, especially with strangers. Body dysmorphic disorder may be accompanied by a relationship ideation or a relationship delusion. It is associated with the high expression of general anxiety, social anxiety, avoidance of social situations, depressed mood, neuroticism, perfectionism, low extraversion, and low self-confidence. Because of the shame these patients feel about their appearance, they long remain reluctant to tell others about their fears.[2]

The body-mode may occur along a kind of continuum or overlap with the teleological mode and even with the pretend mode, especially in patients with multiple conversion symptoms or even with a so-called Munchausen syndrome (Asher, 1951; Eckhardt, 1989). Today, they are counted among the artificial disorders (Hausteiner-Wiehle & Hungerer, 2020), over the years having received a variety of adventurous names, such as "haemorrhagica histrionica" or "neurologica diabolica." This syndrome refers to patients who repeatedly hospitalize themselves – usually after extensive travel – with dramatic symptoms (also called "hospital wanderers") and report medical histories that later turn out to be a mixture of fiction and truth. Occasionally, these patients may provide false names in the emergency room or are even wanted by the police because of a lack of health insurance and incurred costs. Characteristics are countless symptoms with which the patients persuade the doctor to subject them to invasive procedures, only to leave the hospital again at the slightest doubt about the somatic genesis – whether against medical advice or secretly. The repetition compulsion can lead to more than 100 – in one case known to us to 423 – hospital admissions within a short time.

In the neurological and internal medicine literature, one finds numerous colorful complaints and many misdiagnoses. Hausteiner-Wiehle and Hungerer (2020) summarized the variety of typical manifestations. The second most common – following gastrointestinal complaints – are neurological symptoms, preferentially paroxysmal headache, diffuse staggering vertigo, unconsciousness, and peculiar seizures (Eckhardt, 1989). Among the neurological artifact disorders, imaginative diagnoses of epilepsy predominate.

On the other hand, simulated seizures occur much less frequently than might be assumed diagnostically. Because of their purposeful feigning, these patients likely belong to the teleological mode. In 10% of patients with psychogenic nonepileptic seizures (PNES), however, they accumulate to such an extent that they are repeatedly misdiagnosed as status epilepticus (convulsivus), precipitating intensive medical mismanagement. In fact, we are dealing here with a status pseudoepilepticus (SPE), which can last for hours and sometimes days and is now counted among the artifact disorders. Whereas in status epilepticus (convulsivus), several large seizures may occur in succession without the patient becoming conscious in the meantime, we speak of status pseudoepilepticus when nonepileptic seizures repeatedly occur for more than an hour without the patient being responsive although not unconscious (Kütemeyer & Schultz-Venrath, 1997, p. 721f.). Unfortunately, the diagnostic nomenclature is often imprecise. For example, terms such as "pseudo-seizures" and/or "pseudostatus" are problematic because they involve seizures *and* a status. To date, the application of additional apparative diagnostics (CT, MRI, EEG, video-EEG, telemetry, PET, 24 h-EEG) has not reduced the diagnostic difficulties. Serum prolactin levels remain unchanged after PNEA, but this is also true for a few epileptic seizures. No single clinical feature allows a definitive differential diagnosis. Distinguishing a PNES from an epileptic grand mal seizure is usually easier than distinguishing it from psychomotor (focal-complex) seizures (especially those emanating from frontal lobe seizures) or from syncope, hypoglycemic, and tetanic seizures. The motor manifestations of PNES exhibit all variations of expression, ranging from a (playing) dead reflex ("fainting") to a motor storm. Sexual abuse trauma in early development is particularly common in cases of a (playing) dead reflex seizure (Betts & Boden, 1992a, 1992b).

Because of the self-abuse involved, SPE is considered an unconscious reenactment of early trauma. Diagnosis and differential diagnosis can be challenging, among other things, because such patients (being in the teleological mode) may drip belladonna drops into one eye, thus creating a unilateral (and sometimes bilateral) delayed or even absent pupillary response. A tendency toward self-harm, for example, in the form of knife or spoon swallowing, even outside the seizures, as well as chronic suicidal tendencies and other psychiatric abnormalities (also within the family) are the rule in these patients, most of whom work in auxiliary medical professions. We also find several similarities to patients with more severe borderline or antisocial personality disorder; they exhibit increased physiological arousal at rest with abnormal mental processing (Reuber & Mayor, 2012; Wiseman & Reuber, 2015).

The already dramatic and appellative nature of a psychogenic seizure escalates in SPE to the extent that the initially correct assumption of nonepileptic seizure is questioned. Paradoxically, because of the aspects of seizure duration or self-harm, false diagnoses are favored that, on more sober examination, might lead one to consider the correct one. The duration of the seizure increasingly leads to feelings of powerlessness and helplessness on the part of the physician, who tries to compensate by forcing medical measures. A misdiagnosis often results from a misinterpretation of additional findings. Clearly, this is also a failure of medical mentalizing. Thus, both seizure frequency and duration increase in SPE patients following intensive care treatment, whereas a reduction of seizures usually occurs after a communicative intervention. In this respect, SPE can also be a consequence of an activistic, unreflective attitude – and be iatrogenic. Curiously, SPE patients whose seizures are not epileptic almost always continue the antiepileptic treatment despite receiving a correct diagnosis (Kütemeyer et al., 2005; Schultz-Venrath & Masuhr, 1993).

Patients perfect their use of "mimicry" in the service of self-protection in countless hospitalizations. Physicians are more or less forced to go along in the equivalence mode because of the banishment these patients trigger in countertransference, as long as they do not recognize the breakdown of mentalizing. After the end of an SPE, which every therapist should calmly wait for, mentalization-enhancing psychotherapy is indicated, though this rarely materializes. The extremely short length of stay in neurological clinics, along with the massive time pressure put on all employees, leaves little room for early and low-threshold psychotherapy. However, sometimes discontinuing anticonvulsant medication alone brings about freedom from seizures.

Psychodynamic hypotheses have heretofore assumed that artifactual disorders represent a disorder of body image and body experience, since these patients are often not satisfied with their bodies. In unobserved moments, however, they tend to move easily and lively, as if there were no such disorder. From the point of view of the mentalization model, one could argue that the nature of self-damage indicates the consequences of traumatizing social exclusion and a lack of intersubjectivity: Usually, these patients have completely fallen out with their primary family. Artifact disorders serve as the final attempt to connect their body to a helping object (i.e., a physician), as a substitute for a primary parental presence. However, against the background of a disorganized attachment, this cannot be used productively and constructively because, as an unknown experience, a secure binding becomes a threat. The insatiable anger and aggression felt toward the primary attachment figures, responsible – from the patients' vantage point – for the deprivation and/or maltreatment, cannot be transformed into other, more useful behaviors. Therefore, artifact patients often leave the hospital as soon as even rudimentary proximity and understanding develop.

The intensity of the pressure to repeat and stage such disorders indicates that we are dealing here with the acting-out of unconscious fantasies concerning one's own body and involving other persons. One could speak of a sort of "body-acting" or "body-behavior" to feel oneself in the sense of the body-mode and to establish a continuity of the body-self. This is contrasted with the idea that these patients behave toward the fantasies that remain unconscious (Plassmann, 1993). Interestingly, SPE has yet to be studied in epilepsy patients.

Case Vignette

A patient with "status epilepticus" is referred from an intensive care unit following seizures lasting ten days that also led to physical injuries (including a fractured radius). The patient has a subclavian and bladder catheter as well as a cast on the left arm, is unresponsive but twitching violently and irregularly on all four extremities. Head and gaze are turned extremely to the right; from time to time, her body stretches opisthoton; further, salivation, closed eyes, a cyanotic face from minutes of silenced breathing. The diagnosis of status pseudoepilepticus (SPE) – considered because of the overall symptomatology – becomes certain when the patient thwarts testing her pupillary response by squinting her eyelids. The seizures end after the chief physician remarks: "That's enough! We have understood you. You can stop now." Surprisingly, the patient opens her eyes, smiles, and begins to talk about her horse "Sari" in a childlike voice, repeatedly pulling on and stroking the doctor's arm. Over the next few days, individual seizures lasting 20 minutes still occur, but the status is interrupted in this seemingly simple way.

So, from the point of view of the mentalization model, it remains speculative what exactly could have caused the interruption of the SPE. Possibly, in addition to a safe diagnostic attitude of not doubting the psychogenesis of the seizures, it was more the head physician's voice than the content of the statement. From our point of view, a communicative, mentalization-based diagnosis in the sense of a detailed anamnesis of the patient's self-perceptions (including a timely anamnesis by others) and a close observation of the overall course of events, including the reactions of the environment, would be most promising.

It is a therapeutic art to suffer these preverbally acted-out experiences in such patients during therapeutic interactions. The more completely the patient remains in body-mode, the closer the therapist comes to achieving a kind of early "mother–child dyad" in both individual and group settings, although a group can also function as a "mother." Both settings can be understood as an open, dynamic system capable of generating and changing meanings.

5.1.2 The Teleological Mode and the Body

The developmentally "early" mental state of a human being depends on an immediate, physically perceptible satisfaction of their needs and is therefore focused exclusively on this need (cf. Table 5.2). The environment is perceived only insofar as it relates to this need. The teleological mode, often associated with the tendency to externalize non-mentalized traumatic experiences in the sense of an alien self, can be misused tactically to achieve a concrete goal with others. Characteristic of the teleological mode is the "lack of compromise": No substitute, no alternative to the desired goal, is accepted ("If you don't give me your phone number, I'll kill myself!"). Therefore, we often find this mode in patients with antisocial or borderline personality disorder, whose impulsivity is disproportionately stuck in the pre-mentalizing mode of the implicit-automatic dimension. The teleological mode also dominates during simulation, which is defined as purposeful, intentional pretending or exaggerated presentation, very rarely also the generation of symptoms. However, if a high level of suffering is missing, the subjective experience does not correspond to the expressed complaints. In that case, the symptomatology is no longer observable outside the examination setting, and there may be an overlap with the pretend mode.

Depending on the situation in which self-injury occurs, it can be classified as either body-mode or teleological mode. Interestingly, physicians and psychotherapists are often pressured to act with patients suffering from psychogenic seizures, bulimia nervosa, or binge eating – symptomatology associated with the compulsion to eat the entire contents of a refrigerator. At the same time, quite a few eating disorders occur in secret, without a living object. In this respect, the teleological mode most likely has an additional drive quality.

> In adulthood, this mode may manifest in an individual requiring physical or sexual contact from others in order to escape their feeling of being unlovable or worthless, or it may play out in a tendency toward violence or self-harm when feeling overwhelmed or angry.
> (Bateman et al., 2023, p. 36)

Table 5.2 Characteristics of the teleological mode

Uncompromising stance – the doctor/therapist is pressured to do something (e.g., to carry out an operation that is not indicated) that later turns out to be wrong.
- The other person (the object) must fulfill some function.
- Regulation of inner tensions is possible only by acting-out.

5.1.3 The Equivalence Mode and the Body

Colloquial speech has many body-related idioms and metaphors that establish an (intentional) connection between physical sensations and affects/emotions: "It makes my hair stand on end," "I have butterflies in my stomach," "to clench one's teeth" (caution: nocturnal bruxism!), "makes my skin crawl," "to get cold feet" (flight tendencies), "it chills me to the bone," or "turns my stomach."

Patients with somatoform disorders are not the only ones prone to magical thinking. Magical thinking, also called paranormal belief in the Anglo-Saxon literature, is understood as a fusion of thoughts and actions: Events that, according to the usual conceptions of a culture, have no relationship to each other are nevertheless presumed to somehow have one. A well-known example from developmental psychology is the child who tries to hide from others by covering their eyes with the hands, convinced of not being seen. This corresponds to the definition of the equivalence mode: The inner and the outer world are identical. Patients with somatoform pain disorders make no distinction between physical and psychological pain (Table 5.3).

There are plentiful examples of this mode in the psychodynamic literature. Frieda Fromm-Reichmann (1950, p. 92f.), for example, described a unique approach to recording a patient's envy of his pregnant wife. On various occasions, this patient felt compelled to take a deep breath, inflate himself with it, and keep it with him as long as possible (diagnosed as aerophagia). Parallel to this, the patient had the feeling of needing to dispose of something connected to his body. He described this state as extremely pleasant when his wife was expecting their third child. From the confusingly intriguing yet cheerful tone of this narrative, the therapist sensed that it might be essential to understand its meaning at that moment. Without thinking through what it might mean, the therapist decided to simply imitate the patient's physical experience to gain insight into his body language. So, she took as deep a breath as possible and tried to hold it as long as possible. When she tried to dispose of something associated with her body, she was at a loss – until the thought suddenly occurred to her that the pleasurable sensation of filling a bodily cavity to the hilt (while feeling joyfully confused and fascinated at the same time) was the patient's unconscious attempt to experience himself as a pregnant woman.

Joyce McDougall (1995, p. 61) pointed out that pregenital sexuality owed its richness and significance to the fact that it encompassed all five senses and bodily functions. However, certain senses, erogenous zones, and bodily functions are often unconsciously experienced as potentially dangerous and violent or as forbidden sources of pleasure. In this respect, especially among artists, arousal or pleasure at the display of one's own creative production is not infrequently equated with the exhibition of one's body or public masturbation. This is reminiscent of Hanna

Table 5.3 Characteristics of the equivalence mode

- The internal world and external reality are experienced as identical.
- Frightening inner images take on the character of reality.
- Subjective mental experiences (panic attacks, nightmares, flashbacks) are experienced as real.
- Intolerance of alternative perspectives: "I know how it is; nobody can tell me anything!"
- Self-referential negative cognitions seem real – feelings of inferiority are of lesser value.

Segal (1957), who dealt with symbolic equivalents: Segal describes the case of a musician who reacted extremely aggressively to her attempt to analyze his inhibition to give public concerts. He accused her of trying to get him to "masturbate" for all the world to see. Segal saw in the identification of publicly playing a musical instrument as a masturbatory act that the instrument is not really a symbol, but a "symbolic equivalent," in which inner and outer reality are not exchanged but become one. Such an equation – for which, at the time, the concept of the equivalence mode had not yet been found – reminded her of psychotic tints.

The equivalence mode is also dominant in so-called conspiracy theories and beliefs, which are often the result of an individual's supposed loss of control, corresponding with epistemic mistrust.

5.1.4 The Pretend Mode and the Body

From a developmental psychology perspective, pretend play is a developmental stage in which psychic activity replaces direct action (Reddy, 2008). Such play promotes the development of psychological structures because play makes children feel a head taller than they are. In adult patients, however, the pretend mode is not play: Their separation of the inner and outer worlds in the pretend mode results in detailed but finally superficial descriptions and representations of supposed mental states, without personal meaning and without authenticity (Table 5.4).

In such cases, one also speaks of "pseudomentalizing." Often, this is expressed using psychojargon ("I have a superego problem," "I have an introject") or technical metaphors ("My battery is empty," "My memory bank is full!"). Clinically, this mode manifests itself especially often in histrionic personality disorders, but also in group therapies, when external events become more important than the patients' communication about themselves.

The pretend mode plays a prominent role not only in psychogenic and dissociative disorders and histrionic personality disorders, but also in all forms of anxiety or illness anxiety disorders or hyperventilation states, in which the pronounced self-observation of one's own body and the fear of serious illness are "instrumentalized" ("I had a breakdown"). The function of the pretend mode lies in the attempt by the patient to get special attention; not infrequently, it ends in certain

Table 5.4 Characteristics of the pretend mode

- Body and mind are disconnected.
- Absence of affect and pleasure or affectualization.
- Affects and thoughts often do not coincide (belle indifférence).
- Feelings of emptiness and meaninglessness.
- Endless conversations about thoughts and feelings – without leading to any change.
- Dissociation.
- Pseudomentalizing, intellectualizing.

interpersonal encounters failing to come about. Paul Schilder (1935 [1978]) put it aptly: "Feelings are replaced by perceptions." The separation of the inner world and the outer world is found particularly aptly in the phrase attributed to Kurt Tucholsky: "Oh dear, the virgin said and gave birth to her first child!"

One difficulty of "correctly" attributing dissociative states is that they can be understood not only as a pretend mode, but also as an equivalence mode. Hayuta Gurevich, using still-face experiments and her own case studies as examples, pointed out that inner absence can be understood as an imitative response to the absence of the other person. This kind of psychological death – reminiscent of the old psychiatric nomenclature of the "(playing) dead reflex" or type of psychological death – is "the outcome of the absence of a good enough environment in stages of total dependency. Here external absence is also and at the same time internal absence because it is an absence of and from the self, a dissociation (Gurevich, 2008, p. 562). Somewhat simplified, one could also argue that dissociative states of absence represent the final attempt of the self to survive by identifying with the absent primary attachment figure.

People who feel disconnected from their bodies engage more readily in behaviors that are harmful to their bodies since they also care less about their bodies. Disconnectedness from the body can contribute to their claiming reassurance through the "objectification" of the body. This facilitates self-injury to the body, which is seen only as an object.

Notes

1 Patients with occlusal dysesthesia show up in the dental office and report discomfort (and even pain) because of their perception of unfavorable tooth contact. Often, these discomforts begin after dental treatment, which the affected individuals consider having triggered their severe discomforts affecting their quality of life.
2 The body reference could also be understood as a defense against social anxiety, since the body presents a tangible, "external" reason for anxiety; hours of preoccupation with the body are still easier to bear than facing the reasons for (social) anxiety.

Chapter 6

Mentalization Enhancement Therapy

Mentalization-enhancing therapy is based on mentalization-based therapy (MBT), which was initially developed to treat adults with borderline personality disorder and is now evidence-based. In typical British modesty, Bateman and colleagues (2014) emphasized that, in fact, it is not a new therapy but just puts a different focus on things, namely, on mentalizing. Its origins lie in psychodynamic psychotherapies of BPD patients who demanded modifications to the treatment approach because of its modest success. In a Cochrane meta-analysis, MBT was found to be particularly promising for this patient group with regard to various outcome parameters when compared to cognitive-behavioral therapy (CBT), dialectical-behavioral (DBT), and transference-focused psychotherapy (TFP) (Storebo et al., 2020). Mentalization-based therapy proved particularly convincing because of its positive long-term results, something other psychotherapies have yet to show, and the integration of group psychotherapy. The efficacy of MBT for BPD patients, as evidenced in RCT studies, is largely based on mentalization-based group psychotherapy (MBT-G), held four times per week for 75–90 minutes in combination with individual therapy (once per week) (Bales et al., 2015; Bateman & Fonagy, 2008; Morken et al., 2019) and patients with other diagnoses, such as somatoform disorders, anxiety disorders, and depressions, also in a day-treatment setting (Brand et al., 2016; Gypas, 2021; Hecke, 2016) with assessed adherence to MBT (Pries, 2022; Pries et al., 2022).

Surprisingly, for a wide variety of psychotherapies for psychogenic disorders (such as dissociation and adult conversion disorders), the most recent Cochrane meta-analysis "suggest that there is lack of evidence regarding the effects of any psychosocial intervention of conversion and dissociative disorders in adults. Therefore, it is not possible to draw any conclusions about potential benefits or harms from the included studies" (Ganslev et al., 2020). Regarding outcome and process studies in somatoform disorders, this still applies to MBT and MBT-G, even though today they are applied to a wide range of other mental and psychosomatic disorders. Similarly, studies on improving mentalization in comorbid disorders are unfortunately lacking, as somatoform disorders rarely occur alone.

Nevertheless, we do have indirect clinical evidence that MBT and MBT-G are also (particularly) effective in somatoform disorders. Yet, we should note that

DOI: 10.4324/9781003345145-6

whatever method the therapist considers particularly efficacious likely also influences the therapy outcome, something well known from placebo-nocebo research, where facial expressions and clinician interaction influence patients' perceptions (Chen et al., 2019). Before commencing any therapy lies the task of attracting patients with somatoform disorders to engage in such treatment in the first place. In this regard, psychoeducation in MBT/MBT-G with a maximum of ten patients has proven successful. Here, the topic of mentalization and its disorders is taught once a week for 90 minutes for 12 weeks according to a manual. Further topics are preparation for long-term treatment, promoting motivation, explaining what is meant (or not) by mentalizing and by emotions, attachment, interpersonal interactions, mental health, etc.

MBT and MBT-G can help patients with somatization disorders (and others) to find a mentalizing access to their own body. Therefore, one central focus lies in their registering and describing their bodily sensations (pressure, warmth, tingling, muscle tension, muscle relaxation) via specific interactions. Further, they should attempt to determine which sensations of others (via breathing, gestures, movement), including pleasure and relaxation, are associated with positive affect.

6.1 Mentalization in Patients with Somatoform Disorders/Somatic Symptom Disorders (SSD)

This chapter explores the challenges and methods of working with patients suffering from somatoform stress disorders, emphasizing the importance of understanding the body and its expressive peculiarities. The use of "somatic narration" as a therapeutic method, which involves examining the patient's bodily sensations in a systematic manner is an efficient method. The chapter challenges the assumption that explicit mentalizing is contingent on verbal language, showing how it can occur on an embodied level without words. Patients with somatoform disorders often lack insight into the psychodynamic context of their illness, making it essential for therapists to create a safe and friendly space for them to express their bodily experiences. The author highlights the significance of promoting mentalization and addresses the role of empathy, active questioning, and body-based therapies in facilitating the understanding and expression of emotions and affects. The importance of the therapist's attitude, curiosity, and attitude of not knowing for promoting mentalizing cannot be overestimated. The chapter provides practical guidelines and interventions to enhance mentalizing in the therapeutic process, promoting a deeper understanding of the body–mind connection and facilitating the healing process for patients with somatoform disorders.

While among patients with personality disorders the focus lies more on the mental process, in SSD-patients, it should be directed primarily toward the body and its expressive peculiarities. Most patients with somatoform stress disorders lack insight into the psychodynamic context of their illness. Initially, they answer the question posed in the first contact – "How do you feel?" – in the form of non-mentalizing, sometimes stereotypical answers: "What do you mean?" "Well, I . . . ," "Bad . . . ," or "So strange . . ."

Leikert (2023) proposes the method of "somatic narration," with which the patient's bodily sensations are systematically examined, which, however, requires a more active therapeutic stance. Lombardi (2008) criticizes the talk of the body-self, which already implies a higher development and presupposes an integration of the patient's psychological self with their body, which is not self-evident. Most patients today would never have developed a psyche (Lombardi, 2023, pp. 69–70). In this respect, he prefers to speak less of the bodily unconscious and more of the unconscious and the body as two distinct entities. In a real-life interaction analysis from psychotherapy sessions in four cases, based on video data transformed into transcriptions, Jensen and colleagues (2021) demonstrated the gradual development from predominantly implicit mentalizing to predominantly explicit mentalizing. They also found that the mentalizing activity is initiated by the therapist on an embodied level but in an enlarged and complex manner, indicating a higher level of awareness, imagination, and reflection. Thus, this challenges the standard assumption of explicit mentalizing as contingent on verbal language since it demonstrates how processes of explicit mentalizing can take place on an embodied level without the use of words.

Therefore, patients with a low level of structure and high level of attachment avoidance – a constellation frequently found in patients with somatoform stress disorders – run the risk of failing to assert their need for treatment (Nikendei et al., 2020). This is exacerbated by their feeling "pushed away," even sloughed off, by their general practitioner or specialist to the psychotherapist. They fear being stigmatized as "mentally ill" ("I'm not crazy!"), which of course is also a symptom of characteristic maladaptive illness behavior. Such behavior is supported by the fact that some therapists limit themselves to an intellectual exchange of words, for which these patients have little interest. While patients with a borderline personality disorder are often overwhelmed by their affects, expressed in hyperactive facial expressions and body posture, patients with somatization disorders are more likely to have deactivating attachment strategies with avoidance posture and reduced facial expressions because of their previous attachment experiences, which explains their basic rejection of the need for treatment despite great subjective pain. Deactivating attachment strategies exhibit a dissociation between subjective and biological stress, i.e., increased blood pressure without any subjective perception thereof, sweaty and/or restless hands, sometimes with finger-biting. Yet, these patients appear conspicuously calm. It is essential to perceive these somatic markers and address them in a friendly, questioning manner – to discover how the patient understands them but without interpreting them.

Leithner-Dziubas and colleagues (2010), using the Reflective Function Scale (RFS) in patients with chronic lower abdominal complaints, proved that the ability to mentalize is limited in somatic symptom disorders. Their RFS score was 2.3, significantly lower than that of the normal population (~5). The same group mentioned unloving and controlling maternal attachment (36%), neglect (32%), and experiences of violence (54.5%) in early childhood.

Thus, the central question is: How can we come into contact with such patients without becoming their persecutor? The first prerequisite is to maintain a friendly room – a practice or clinic room perceived as a safe place. (This is true especially for modern online video therapies, even if therapists have hardly any control over this, which they should also point out to their patients.) Only in a safe space can patients "use" their psychotherapist as a kind of container. Think of the space as an extension of the patient's body – and from what we know today, one must add: also of the therapist. Given the difficulties, as a therapist, of continually struggling with these patients to keep the conversation alive, maintaining a well-designed, friendly space also has a salutogenetic effect.

Contrary to patients' expectations, therapists should be active rather than passive, supportive and caring, by taking particular interest in the physical complaints and burdens of coping with their disease. Keep in mind that offering such a relationship may promote self-fragmentation in patients with an insecure-associative attachment style – similar to the situation of persons with BPS disorders. The goal, however, is to minimize epistemic mistrust stemming from insecure attachment experiences in childhood and repetitive failed doctor–patient contacts in later development.

Minimizing the risk of a failed contact succeeds through empathy: One way to empathize with the other is through "imitation," as Freud (1921c, p. 121) pointed out in an inconspicuous footnote. In many respects, this differs from unconscious imitation, for which the mirror neurons discovered by Rizzolatti's research group (Rizzolatti & Sinigaglia, 2016) are responsible. Cole and colleagues (2019) showed that people with autism spectrum condition (ASC) showed no increase in functional connectivity between the dorsal medial prefrontal cortex (dmPFC) and the inferior frontal gyrus (IFG) in separate mentalizing and non-mentalizing blocks, regions typically associated with the mirror system. Together, these data emphasized the importance of functional connectivity between the mentalizing and mirror systems when inferring social intentions and show that reduced connectivity between these systems may explain some of the behavioral difficulties experienced by adults with ASC. This primary transfer of bodily behavior ("when the body speaks") is implicit-procedural and not declarative or autobiographical knowledge. Procedural knowledge is resonantly actualized both physically and gesturally by being in contact with others.

In addition to exhibiting empathy, the therapist should ask questions about the patient's subjective theory of illness:

- "Do you have any idea how your illness came about?"
- "How have you understood your illness so far?"

This enables both the motivation to participate in a solution and the accessibility of the mentalization ability. But as a rule, physical sensations cannot really be captured objectively, only communicatively. Therefore, as a first approach, it helps to exactly, actively, and repeatedly listen to the patient's complaints, enhanced by the forward inclination of the body, which signals interest and curiosity.

> The MBT approach seeks to allow the patient to break his/her fluctuating disembodied/hyperembodied states by a process known as "Minding the Body." This technique involves stimulating the patient to investigate his/her concrete experiences with the body . . ., to reconnect them with the emotional, cognitive, and relational experiences.
> (Bateman & Fonagy, 2016, p. 99)

It seems to be helpful to pick up the patient's words as precisely as possible in order to give them a chance to dock with the therapist regarding the therapeutic alliance.

Observational diagnoses are reserved for more experienced therapists, as they can be prone to error. From the point of view of the mentalization model, posing particularly simple questions about which feelings/affects the patient is experiencing regarding the affected body part or which feelings exist beyond those just mentioned spontaneously, enable the conversation to move from the cognitive to an affective level of mentalizing. Putting such an emphasis on affects – or better: feelings – is referred to as "affect focus" (in the sense of mentalizing). Bateman and Fonagy (2016, p. 255f.) use this term to refer to the "atmosphere" or "shared affect" between patient and clinician, "which is present in a session. It is the 'elephant in the room', that is, something that is apparent in the interpersonal/relational domain but is unexpressed."

Case Vignette (Bateman & Fonagy, 2016, p. 257):

Clinician: When we talk about this you start avoiding eye contact and keep looking away. Can you say why?
Patient: I don't know. My mind goes a bit blank.
Clinician: Can you describe it?
Patient: I feel anxious, and I am nervous about talking about it.
Clinician: Perhaps that is something that we share – at the moment I am a bit anxious that if I keep asking about things it will make you more anxious and make you avoid things more. So perhaps both of us are uncertain whether to avoid or not.

Another central focus of mentalizing-promoting interactions in individual and group psychotherapies lies in promoting mentalizing with specific interactions (Table 6.1), for example, by having the therapist develop questions from the perspective of the dimensionally opposite pole in each case.

Thus, if a patient talks about their complaints in a very cognitively oriented way, questions about feelings become necessary: "What feelings do you think this triggers in your wife/partner?"

In this respect, the questions concern the various dimensions of mentalization through the employment of a *contrary move*. Especially in the absence of the conscious perception of emotional expressions, the therapist should pay attention to the usually coherent and valid narrative, which may seem to sound like mentalization but, on the content level, often reflects pseudomentalizing. Currently, such pseudomentalizing appears to be favored by social media and other new communication technologies, for example, when patients resort to spoken or smartphone texts from acquaintances and friends during the initial interview or therapy session, or when they separate from their partner or end psychotherapy via a WhatsApp message.

We also find pseudomentalizing in the pretend mode (see Chapter 5.5), which should be interrupted in both group and individual therapy by appropriate interactions (cf. Table 6.1a): "Wait, stop! I don't understand this yet – can you please explain this in more detail?"

Table 6.1a Therapeutic attitude and interactions aimed at promoting mentalizing

Characteristic	Description
Exploration, curiosity, and not-knowing stance	The therapist asks appropriate, brief questions to promote exploration of the mental states, motives, and emotions of patients and others; the therapist conveys a sincere interest in finding out more about these matters.
Stop and rewind	The therapist identifies an incoherent interpersonal and affect-laden event; the therapist tries – if necessary, with raised hand (the mentalizing hand!) – to slow down the process to discover, together, step by step, something about the event, by going back to the phase before the affect arose. The goal is to stop destructive-affective processes and to initiate the joint exploration of the respective sequence.
Recognition of successful mentalizing	The therapist identifies and explores good mentalizing and expresses recognition.
Focus on the relationship between therapist and patient (relational mentalization)	The therapist comments on how the patient relates to them during the session and attempts to explore this together with the patient; the therapist encourages reflections on alternative perspectives whenever appropriate; the therapist actively uses their own observations and thoughts regarding the relationship and thereby attempts to stimulate a joint process of exploration.
Identifying and mentalizing events	The therapist identifies relevant events and engages the patient in a shared exploration that is both meaningful and clarifying.
Challenging unwarranted beliefs	The therapist adequately challenges the patient's unwarranted beliefs about themselves or others.
The patient is invited to mentalize external events	The therapist asks the patient – implicitly or explicitly – to clarify relevant external events and to better understand them both emotionally and cognitively.

Table 6.1b Therapeutic attitude and interactions aimed at promoting mentalizing

Dealing with the body-mode	The therapist recognizes the body-mode in itself and in the patient and interacts to improve mentalizing by somatic narration.
Dealing with the teleological mode	The therapist recognizes the teleological mode in themselves and the patient and interacts to improve mentalizing.
Dealing with the equivalence mode	The therapist recognizes the equivalence mode in themselves and the patient and interacts to improve mentalizing.
Dealing with the pretend mode	The therapist recognizes the pretend mode in themselves and the patient and interacts to improve mentalizing.
Self-disclosure	The therapist makes his/her own feelings about the events described available for "docking" purposes.

MBT-oriented therapists take an active and playful position to enable an "affective connection" and a modulation of the patient's affective experience. A mentalizing therapist should aim less at inciting insight or producing "correct" results of reflection than at employing therapeutic "stylistic devices" to promote mentalization. The psychotherapy of patients whose early experiences have impaired their ability to mentalize should focus on supporting the building of this ability. Indeed, one might conceptualize all psychotherapeutic work as an activity aimed at restoring this function (Fonagy & Target, 2003).

The therapist would be wise to strive for an improved attitude toward their own body in addition to reducing the suffering of their patients with somatic symptom disorder. Mentalization-promoting interactions and relationship-building with patients with body symptoms also require a special setting, which is generally easier to implement in the clinic than in an outpatient treatment, for example, by combining individual and group psychotherapies with body-oriented special therapies (concentrative movement therapy (KBT), dance therapy, etc.). The observation that patients with somatic symptom disorders hardly react – or even react aversively – to traditional insight-oriented psychotherapies because of their lack of introspection and low ability to perceive feelings makes the application of other therapeutic approaches not uncommon. Body-related therapies of all kinds – breathing therapy, functional relaxation, concentrative movement and dance therapy (Fiedler et al., 2011), all breeding grounds for mentalizing – have meanwhile been proven in RCT studies to be sustainably effective (Geißler & Heisterkamp, 2007; Monsen & Monsen, 2000; Rosendahl et al., 2021; Schreiber-Willnow & Seidler, 2005). We find many mentalization-promoting interactions in their applications, without these having been conceptually identified as such and directly associated with the mentalization model. They awaken in patients with SSD an awareness of emotions and, perhaps for the first time, enable them to find a form of expression, e.g., in music or art therapy.

This gradual differentiation of initially undefined body perceptions resembles "learning vocabulary": It begins with patients learning to perceive and feel themselves through rhythm, body dialogue, or dance movements. Mentalizing interactions bridge the gap between the body, bodily experience, and psychological experience in encounters with other people or fellow patients. They expand the therapeutic space to include the prelinguistic realm, and, in the most favorable cases, body-based therapies develop a triangulating effect, counteracting early fears of fusion or the fear of being engulfed by the object. Body-based therapies allow patients to experience the body (or parts thereof) as both subject and object.

This is because its functional and action-related possibilities may sometimes be to the fore, while on other occasions its phantasy-related and experiential potential will predominate, since the body serves on the one hand for demarcation from and on the other for contact with and relatedness to others.
(Küchenhoff, 2019, p. 788)

Numerous theoretical concepts have given proper psychodynamic attention to the body, such as the concept of proto-mental constitution (Bion, 1952), shared implicit relational knowledge (Stern et al., 2010), the protolanguage of somatization (McDougall, 1974), and embodiment (Leuzinger-Bohleber & Pfeifer, 2016), including body-based psychoanalytic approaches (Geißler & Heisterkamp, 2007; Leikert, 2016, 2022; Lemma, 2014). Lesser-known concepts, such as focusing theory, also argue that "body feelings" contain a variety of preverbal experiences that fundamentally determine a person's psychological life; the human body is a particularly finely tuned organ for perceiving such preverbal experiences (Gendlin, 1991). Nevertheless, most theoretical concepts fail to review the possible interactions and interventions regarding the promotion or inhibition of mentalizing. As psychotherapists, we have mounds of theories at our disposal, but to date, we have distilled only a tiny reservoir of interactions and interventions. In this respect, it has always proved helpful to return to the sharing of feelings in terms of proto-conversations, to promote cooperative communication (pointing gestures and gesture play), and to highlight the shared intentionality of infants, first observed at the age of around 9 to 12 months of age (Tomasello, 2019).

Deep psychosomatic knowledge reveals that we exchange narratives using posture, gestures, facial expressions, movement, and gaze in a body-related and interacting way. This realization is being increasingly received in psychoanalysis and its applications. "Sensorimotor psychotherapy" is the Anglo-Saxon variant of this development (Ogden & Goldstein, 2019), and in the German-speaking countries, we also find various interfaces that employ body-based therapies.

During mentalization-oriented interactions, the actors acknowledge that the body itself "speaks" as a legacy of traumatization and defensive attachment styles. Mentalization-focused interactions enable changing perceptions of the body and its movement patterns. Because bodily habits reflect and maintain implicit processes, not a few of which were formed in the brain and body before language acquisition, "[a] somatic narrative can reveal patterns that cannot be told in words" (Ogden & Goldstein, 2019, p. 47).

Expressions of disappointment, such as "No one supports me!" or "I feel all alone," are accompanied by physiological parameters, such as a toneless voice, decreased eye contact, or a hunched posture. From the point of view of promoting mentalizing, the eye-gaze experience of physical, emotional, and cognitive patterns should not only be considered but should be addressed directly in the form of questions, such as: "Could it be that you have too much on your shoulders right now?"

However, if therapists persist in viewing a conversation as "talking about" things, they themselves are in danger of slipping into the pretend mode (cf. Section 6.2).

Patients with functional body complaints must first be won over to commit to body-related therapies, which form the basis for interactions that promote mentalization. In this context, the playful use of metaphors and linguistic images enables the patient to "dock" with the therapist, facilitating a change of perspective. Suddenly, the "problem appears in a different light," "new doors open," and – if done with humor – for a brief moment, everything seems "transformed."

> Metaphors [have] a central function in the reprocessing of preconscious and unconscious, affectively controlled cognitions into the conscious realm. . . . Their higher frequency is associated with higher treatment satisfaction . . ., whereby the production of interactive metaphors is associated with a reduction in complaints.
> (Fabregat, 2004; Fabregat & Krause, 2008, p. 86)

In this context, it seems favorable that the therapist uses indicative or imitative gestures (such as similarly rhythmic head-nodding paralleling the patient's actions) during the exchange of words to promote connecting, since language ultimately evolved from gestures and primordial sounds (Tomasello, 2008).

Failure to develop an understanding that promotes mentalizing for the derived interactions means people with somatic stress disorders cannot well perceive, differentiate, or articulate their affects and emotions, if at all. Establishing an intersubjective understanding of the formation or prevention of an "affective self" for a mentalization-promoting treatment technique means that the difficulties situated in early development are usually restaged as "difficult situations" during treatment. An early abandonment trauma, for example, the loss of a father who withdrew from his responsibility even before birth, leads to a unique sort of separation vulnerability with a tendency toward somatization, which is then supported by a (mostly) missing triangulation. The structurally weaker patients are, i.e., the fewer affects represented in them, the more diffuse are their expressions of affect and emotion! Therefore, the first step is to identify the respective affect through skillful questioning, without attributing such an affect ("anger," "envy," "sadness") to the patient. Patients with unstable representations are only too happy to use attributions, although these pseudorepresentations do not guarantee much security. Attribution of affect not only fosters the development of a "false self," it also undermines patients' self-efficacy.

This could be one reason why behavioral therapies achieve better short-term but worse long-term follow-up outcomes than psychodynamic therapies.

Mentalization-promoting interactions therefore focus on asking patients where in the body they perceive which feelings. The therapist can further this process by asking questions that probe what the patients remember about these feelings. Greenberg's (2015) emotion-focused therapy also applies this technique. In the sense of "contrary move," the therapist can direct the question to which part of the body the therapist would have to feel what feeling if they were suffering from it, as well as in which situations it would occur, etc. These mentalization-promoting interactions aim to support patients in bringing up nonverbalized or not-yet-verbalizable affects, step by step, to develop a common narrative (see Figure 6.1).

Such specific therapeutic interactions make alexithymic patients more capable of perceiving affects and of relieving them (Vanheule et al., 2007; Verhaeghe et al., 2007). The preferred approach is to perceive the patient's states of arousal and to work out possible explanations for them, i.e., to mirror the affects without interpreting them. Every psychotherapeutic setting offers both patients and therapists the possibility to express ideas, memories, affects, and feelings by staging them "bodily" and situationally. Depending on whether these interactions take place consciously or unconsciously on the part of the two parties, one can speak of "action dialog," "enactment," or "staged interaction" (Scharff, 2007, p. 84). In contrast to other psychotherapies, this method needs no other medium, such as an empty chair, to express the patient's affects and feelings in a less precarious way. Rather, the therapist poses questions focused on the affect until the patient can differentiate the feeling using their own words. If necessary, the therapist can interrupt a frustrating question and continue with it at the next session. One must distinguish here between primary and secondary affects/emotions and between simple and complex affects, such as envy or shame. Shaming should be avoided at all costs.

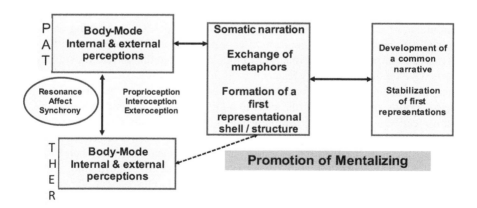

Figure 6.1 Mentalization-based development of representations.
Source: Schultz-Venrath (2021).

Nameless, unbearable body complaints often express themselves in resistance to psychotherapy, in the form of so-called acting-out and typical problem behaviors (e.g., being late, not paying the bill). A mentalization-promoting attitude consists of marking and describing such phenomena without reproach: "How would you feel if I came late to you?" and developing fitting stories, metaphors, and similes.

Macro- and microanalyses of video and audio transcripts can help promote mentalizing, determine during an intervention which interactions inhibited and which promoted mentalizing, and discover whether a true connection or link – and not just a containment – took place between the therapist and the patient. In the case of unawareness and the resulting absence of response (e.g., to blushing during the initial interview), this can lead to the patient failing to show up for the second or third appointment or quitting psychotherapy altogether.

Therapists should possess and foster the ability to let themselves be "touched." Interacting sensitively and touchingly with patients means being resonant toward one's own bodily perceptions, in terms of primary mothering/paternalism. All body-related, mentalization-promoting interactions and interventions have in common that they are transmitted in a language whose words are "touching" by literally (!) "docking" onto the patient's words (Quinodoz, 2002, 2003). Body-anchored language allows meanings to emerge on the physical level of both parties through images; it is all about becoming aware of one's physical-mental state, which is more than becoming aware of one's mental state, as part of a co-existing movement. Patients' early experiences often reflect a sensory dimension associated with the mother's or father's voice. Active listening, speaking, the psychotherapist's voice – all of these can awaken body-related fantasies in patients because they partly remind them of a "good" object from early childhood, in the sense of relational mentalization. It may also enable them to make emotional sense of split-off sensory or bodily experiences, enhancing epistemic confidence. On the other hand, hypervigilance and epistemic distrust dominate when the patient cannot develop memories of a "good" or partial object because of adverse early childhood experiences.

Curiously, patients who have had such experiences often mention their illnesses only when asked. Presumably, they think that they have no psychological significance. Sometimes they fear becoming boring, so they avoid talking about their pain as an affect expression. On the other hand, other patients talk long and loud about their "somatic" suffering because they discovered during childhood that they mattered to someone only when they were sick. In this sense, the therapist needs to reinforce the dominant affect if it pops up in the patient (see the following section).

The body communicates something to the patient, and when the patient can talk about a physiological symptom, it usually reduces epistemic mistrust.

Therapist: "What would I have to do for you to trust me?"

Thus, the dominant affect between patient and therapist must be recognized and acknowledged, which means positively evaluating negative affects as well. The latter offer the chance to bring about a change of perspective regarding epistemic mistrust and misunderstanding (cf. Table 6.2).

Table 6.2 The processual approach to better understanding affect, modified acc. to Luyten (2019)

- Recognition of the affect
- Amplification of the affect
- Differentiation of the affect
- Linking the affect to interpersonal relationships and to the patient's psychodynamics
- Communicating the "emotional cost" of the body-mode to promote change
- Promoting mentalized affectivity
- Promoting the development of a representation

On the other hand, it is to argue that the range of symptoms associated with eating disorders or somatic symptom disorders may share the function of being different attempts at social self-regulation or individual affect regulation. This is important, because the focus of MBT for eating disorders or somatic symptom disorders "is then not so much on body weight and shape, for example, but on dysfunctional relationships and social anxieties, and the mentalizing problems that maintain the disorders" (Bateman et al., 2023, p. 20).

The most important attitude in MBT/MBT-G is focusing on not-knowing, which is also conducive to mentalization in patients with physical complaints. Adopting such an attitude seems particularly difficult following a five- to six-year course of study and a specialist and/or psychotherapeutic training of equally long duration, during which the therapist accumulates a particularly large amount of knowledge. However, if the therapist refrains from subjecting patients to an established theory, but rather understands each patient as an individual human being for whom a theory must first be developed, it becomes easier to show authentic interest in their physical and mental states. Focusing means staying focused and taking small steps along a narrative with an attitude of not-knowing, both in individual and group psychotherapy, using an active questioning technique, and facing the intentionality of bodily symptoms.

Contrary moves have proven to be particularly useful in promoting mentalizing, as have cheeky and surprising questions and humorous statements, often subsumed under the term *"challenging."* Only the successful integration of both the pre-mentalizing modes and the dimensions of mentalizing makes mentalizing possible.

Therapists play a much greater role in therapeutic success than has long been assumed (Wampold, 2015): Empathy showed the second-highest effect size ($d = .63$) among the general and specific therapy factors, and the effect size of the therapist was almost as high ($d = .55$). Compared to their less effective colleagues, effective therapists form stronger alliances across a range of patients, show higher levels of supportive interpersonal skills, and can express professional self-doubt.

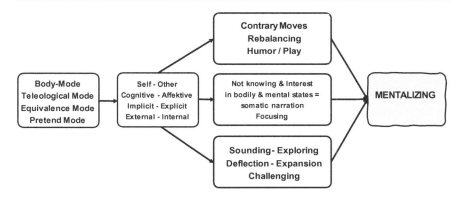

Figure 6.2 Therapeutic stance and techniques to promote mentalizing.

6.2 Interactions That Do Not Promote Mentalization

Interactions that are not conducive to mentalization generally suffer from a lack of flexibility and from rigidity, which, besides certain less favorable personality traits, probably result from a training-related superego fear on the part of therapists of *doing something wrong*. Winnicott (1971) reminded therapists to be creative in their analytic work and to allow play. One of his memorable sentences was: "The creativity of the patient can all too easily be stolen by a therapist who knows too much" (p. 76). In addition to knowing too much, a number of other aspects have proved to be "non-mentalizing":

- Waiting too long or even projecting (ambiguous) silence.
- Overburdening the patient with overly complex explanations, early interpretations, and attributions of feelings ("Your symptoms stem from anxiety!"; "Behind your friendly facade there's some obvious anger"; "What you really mean is . . .").
- Delivering pseudomentalizing explanations (e.g., communicating current research results to persuade the patient to undergo a certain therapy).
- Not daring to interrupt a pre-mentalizing mode.

The urge to remain silent likely stems from an old psychoanalytic tradition. Underlying this transgenerational training introject may be the assumption that silent analysts can do no wrong. However, the opposite seems to be the case: The more severe the patient's disorder is, the more harmful prolonged silence is against the background of missing self and object representations. When therapists say nothing, patients interpret it as disinterest and as distancing, which serves to repeat their past traumatic experience of a missing object, compounded by a breach of trust and loss of binding security. Not infrequently, such patients believe themselves to be the true cause of their therapist's silence and sometimes even feel guilty that their therapists cannot think of anything to say.

In the further course of psychodynamic psychotherapies, it is not enough to assume that the unconscious act exerts a greater influence on somatic processes than the conscious act ever could. The attitude recommended by Freud (1912e, p. 381f.), namely, that therapists address the patient's unconscious by making their own unconscious available to the patient as a receiving organ – like the receiver of the telephone – is too technical and too passive given the numerous findings on intersubjectivity.

For therapists, the central task consists of working with these patients step-by-step to find the words or to invent the metaphors that can (gently) depict their own emotions and recognize the mental states of others. Therein lies the danger, however, that therapists name and attribute emotions that are not yet represented and usually diffuse. Bodily experiences are usually polyphonic and can be variously interpreted. Although the general emotional awareness is intact in many patients with somatoform problems, they still suffer from the specific inability to connect their own emotional and bodily states with the various traumatizing experiences, especially because they cannot interpret bodily sensations as negative emotional states.

6.3 Mentalizing in Group Therapies for SSD Patients

The definition of mentalization as an intrapsychic and simultaneously interpersonal (social) process established a new paradigm for psychotherapies that is especially suitable for understanding group processes and group psychotherapies of all kinds. Mentalizing means that we are in contact with our thoughts, feelings, and motives, that we can put them into perspective and look at them from a distance, that we assume that others also have thoughts, feelings, and motives that underlie their behavior, and that we can guess and infer these thoughts, feelings, and motives without ever really knowing them.

MBT-G is a treatment method applied in clinical and day-clinical settings, if possible, by two therapists with six to nine patients. A treatment duration of 75–90 minutes is recommended, since the ability to mentalize in the group usually begins only after about 45–60 minutes. The high effect sizes of the various RCT studies of MBT are most likely best explained by MBT-G, since group therapies had a higher proportion of intensity (3–4×/week) than individual therapies conducted once a week. Bateman and coworkers (Bateman et al., 2021; Bateman et al., 2019; Karterud, 2015a, 2015b; Karterud et al., 2019) as well as Schultz-Venrath and Felsberger (2016) provided the theoretical bases for these findings.

The significantly higher efficacy of MBT-G compared to other therapies can best be explained by resonance and mirroring phenomena as well as by the possibility of obtaining different perspectives both on oneself and others. In this setting, the primary experience of violent affect can be regulated by the technique of the "mentalizing hand!" (in effect, raising the hand like a stop sign). The messages and observations of copatients reduce the possibility of mistakes on the part of the therapist (pressing too much or too little). Through its cohesion, each (successful) group replicates the development of the reflective function from infant to adult (face-to-face exchange of affective signals as well as the processing of body, teleological, equivalence, and pretend modes). S. H. Foulkes, a pioneer of group analysis who emigrated from Germany, put it succinctly: "In learning to communicate, the group can be compared to a child learning to speak" (Foulkes & Anthony, 1965, p. 263).

For SSD patients, introductory MBT psychoeducation (in a closed outpatient group) with a maximum of ten participants has proven successful before the commencement of day-clinical or clinical treatment (Bales & Bateman, 2012). Over 12 weeks, the topic of mentalization and its disorders is covered once a week for 90–100 minutes using a manual available on the Anna Freud Centre (London) website, primarily for patients with personality disorders. With regard to other patient groups (e.g. ADHD, SSD, Eating disorders), this manual still needs to be adapted. Topics include preparing for long-term treatment, promoting motivation for such treatment, and discerning the meaning of emotions, attachment, interpersonal interactions, and psychosomatic health. It makes sense to reach an understanding with patients about their diagnosis(es), their expectations, and the goals of therapy, which are jointly recorded in writing. This makes clear that psychosomatic changes result from better understanding.

The exercises are structured on flipcharts and can be supported with film clips (e.g., *Good Will Hunting* from 1997), proceeding from more emotionally distant to more personal scenarios. The experiences of the group participants are included only once a certain cohesive atmosphere and trust among the participants have developed. Non-mentalizing expressions should be taken up and referred to repeatedly. The psychoeducational modules, developed and modified for patients with personality disorders, can also be used for somatization disorders and consist of 12 elements that are worked through successively using examples:

1. What is mentalization – what is a mentalizing attitude?
2. What does it mean to have problems with mentalization?
3. Why do we have emotions, and what are the basal types?
4. Mentalizing emotions
5. The importance of attachment relationships
6. Attachment and mentalization
7. What is a personality disorder?
8. Mentalization-based therapy – Part 1 (Dimensions of Mentalizing)
9. Mentalization-based therapy – Part 2 (Pre-mentalizing Modes)
10. Anxiety, attachment, and mentalization
11. Depression, somatization disorders, attachment, and mentalization
12. Recap and summary

In outpatient, day-clinical, and inpatient group therapy, MBT-G therapists do not have the role of telling patients what is going on with them; instead, they are experts in asking (sometimes quite unconventional) questions, with the aim of inducing mentalizing. Their body posture should express an active, curious, and inquisitive attitude. The primary task of MBT-G therapists is to provide a training ground for mentalizing, and to be prepared to restore their own mentalizing ability in case of loss.

MBT-G therapists actively intervene by asking affect-focused questions ("How does this feel to the group?") and maintaining a position of not-knowing, similar to that of the TV detective character Columbo ("I didn't understand that just now – I have another question"). They support the group with curious questions without waiting to see how it would solve a problem ("What do the others think about this?"). They focus their attention on turning implicit (unconscious) dimensions of mentalizing into explicit narratives ("What feelings do you perceive in yourself when you hear this story?").

If we assume that the etiopathogenesis of somatic symptom disorders is multidimensional, then mentalization-enhancing therapeutic interactions should be correspondingly multimodal at different levels. This approach is most successfully implemented in a clinical or day-clinical setting by combining individual and group therapies with body therapies (if possible, in the same group). Mentalization-oriented group therapies provide an excellent opportunity to explore the communicative and relational meaning of psychosomatic disorders and processes. Well trained group therapists know that the body is always part of the group: Participants all look at each other and are looked at by everyone else. The group situation itself represents an embodied situation in the broadest sense (e.g., via the olfactory system). Because of inherent epistemic mistrust, however, it is useful to take particular care to prepare patients with somatoform disorders for group psychotherapy.

Therefore, the following treatment goals for MBT-G should be considered:

Group leaders should start MBT-G actively and with an "open" beginning: "The group has now started." In our opinion, the "flashlight" method used in clinics and day clinics is better suited to binding the fears of the group psychotherapist. A flashlight activates the pretend mode in the group. After a patient's first statement, others usually follow, stereotypically with slight variations, but an open

Table 6.3 MBT-G treatment goals for somatoform stress disorders

- To attract patients to treatment by establishing a trusting therapeutic working relationship through friendly formulations ("There are at least nine therapists in the group").
- To reduce possible fears and misconceptions by conveying information about how a group works ("No one gets the short shrift because everyone's issue is also someone else's issue").
- To improve social and interpersonal functioning.
- To minimize self-harming acts (including suicide attempts).
- To stimulate the adequate utilization of treatment and prevent hospital dependency.

exchange does not develop. Helpful questions include: "What was on your mind after the last session?" "What was meaningful to you in the last session?"

Interaction principles for group leaders should be simple, brief, and affect-focused (e.g., love, desire, hurt, excitement, anger, shame, disgust). It is helpful to refer to current events or actions and current psychological reality as well as to focus on content close to the patients' consciousness. "Psychologizing" about others, i.e., stimulating other perspectives, can be profitable; acknowledge patients' achievements as a group effort once mentalizing has been achieved.

Although the data on group psychotherapies for patients with somatoform disorders are still rather weak, they have a positive impact by improving some alexithymic features, e.g., in patients with rheumatoid arthritis (Poulsen, 1991). One can positively influence the lack of social integration of alexithymic patients with somatoform disorders by providing social support in group therapy and the resulting social relationships, also outside the therapeutic setting (Gündel et al., 2000). If alexithymic symptoms are more pronounced, patients tend to prefer group psychotherapy over individual psychotherapy (Ogrodniczuk et al., 2011).

Positive experiences with group therapy have been described for patients with somatic (!) disorders (Janssen & Wienen, 1995) – even before the mentalization model came around:

> Groups provide an excellent opportunity to explore the communicative and relational meaning of psychosomatic disorders and processes. This statement may seem paradoxical, considering that such disorders and processes often signal the denial or avoidance of direct and complete emotional relationships.
> (Brown, 1985, p. 93f.)

This problem can be minimized by mentalization-based dynamic administration to foster epistemic trust in the group as a whole, in the other participants, in the leader, and last but not least in oneself as leader (Staun & Schultz-Venrath, 2023): The "dynamic administration" according to Foulkes, which has intrapsychic and interpersonal implications, includes the organization of the setting, the space, and the framework, including an explanation of the meaning of this therapeutic procedure as well as the handling of the group rules and any notifications. In particular, it also concerns minimizing the negative expectations and fearful fantasies associated with epistemic mistrust, which are particularly common among SSD patients, through warmth and competence or even by turning them into a positive curiosity. Carefully preparing patients for their group psychotherapy promotes the reduction of epistemic mistrust toward the group. This is best achieved by thoroughly exploring the negative fantasies and mistrust about the (unfamiliar) group and collectively linking them to the underlying early negative dyadic and group relational experiences. Mentalization-based dynamic administration (MDA) should therefore pay the same attention to vertical relationship experiences with early attachment figures as to horizontal relationships with siblings, step-siblings, friends, and the peer group until early adulthood. Regarding lateral relationships, MDA thus has the function, on the one hand of shedding light on negative horizontal transmissions, e.g., through bullying at school or being set back by a sibling, and, on the other hand, of exploring whether and which positive horizontal relationships exist as prognostically important resources for the transmission processes in the group. Especially for patients with more pronounced structural impairments, systematic MDA is necessary to induce epistemic trust in the group and the group leadership. A fixed component here is a psychoeducational preparatory group (MBT-introductory/MBT-i) borrowed from the treatment of borderline disorders (Bateman & Fonagy, 2016; Haslam-Hopwood et al., 2006). From the perspective of the mentalization model, the therapist could ask the patient the following questions:

- What exactly makes you feel so skeptical?
- What could the mistrust of groups you are talking about concern?
- What experiences have you had in your family, in the day care center, at school, in the club, and other group organizations?

Strong outcomes after group psychotherapy for a lot of disorders (Burlingame & Strauss, 2021) suggest that mentalizing succeeds nowhere better than in group sessions. A more recent theoretical development hinges on the development of epistemic trust, defined as trust in the authenticity and personal relevance of knowledge conveyed interpersonally on the functioning of the social environment.

The various effective factors in psychodynamic group therapies enable individuals to become aware of the unity of physical and psychological processes, and to relate more fully to others. Swiller (1988), who recommended the combination of individual and group psychotherapy for alexithymic patients with somatization disorders, suggested repeatedly labeling emotions to provide patients with access to a wider range of emotions. Such a treatment technique maximized their learning opportunities while protecting their self-esteem and minimizing unproductive stress.

Mentalizing is promoted through active, curious listening (Therapist: "Oh! That's interesting what you're saying!" To other group participants: "How does that make you feel?" – "How do you feel when you hear that?"). Making the interactions explicit, e.g., by saying, "You've gotten a lot of feedback now. How do you think the other group participants are doing with this?" promotes group cohesion in terms of connecting, linking, and bridging, which facilitate coming into contact for this group of patients. In contrast to psychodynamic group therapies, MBT-G focuses on explicit mentalization of communication and interaction in the here and now.

Since SSD patients like to question psychotherapeutic offers, group therapists should be able to deal humorously with aggression, e.g., when a patient (unjustifiably) complains about the competence of the group leader (e.g., "Thank you for pointing out that I am the worst group therapist in Germany"). MBT-G therapists should accept the ubiquitous existence of antigroup phenomena (to the other group participants: "Can someone from the group explain to me how that just came about?").

The phenomenon of there always being at least one patient who wants to disturb or even destroy the existence of the group is described as the "antigroup phenomenon" (Nitsun, 1996 [2014]). For this reason, MBT-G therapists should practice turning negative therapeutic processes into positive ones, viewing antigroup phenomena as a natural part of group processes. Tolerance and a friendly repartee toward aggression are beneficial, as the expression of hostility represents an essential therapeutic vehicle and an expression of hope. The more anxious group leaders are, the more likely they are to inhibit aggressive and destructive impulses along with mentalizing. Last but not least, MBT-G therapists should be able to connect and link diverse topics of the group participants.

Mentalization-based group therapies have proved slightly superior to psychodynamic group therapies – albeit without statistical significance – for a mixed patient clientele in short-term group psychotherapies in day-clinics (Brand et al., 2016; Hecke et al., 2016). The nature of group facilitator activity appears to provide a model for the activity among the group participants specifically with somatoform disorders. Higher feedback activity by group therapists induced higher feedback activity among such group participants, which in turn was associated with improvement in important areas of body experience (Tschuschke et al., 2020).

Case Vignette

I greeted an inpatient group (> 12 patients) by asking who would like to inform the newcomers about the rules. This regularly leads to the phenomenon that my third rule fails to be remembered: "Everyone should talk about what they do not like to talk about." After a minute or so, a 35-year-old, relatively good-looking patient, a newcomer to the group, said he was here because he wanted to change his life. He had no professional training, he said, and had been making his money as a callboy for the past 20 years, mostly for rich ladies, but sometimes for older men as well. Under the increased attention of the group, he talked and talked and talked. I remember feeling a little embarrassed at this strange appearance by a newcomer, as I had never experienced anything quite like this before. Suddenly, a 20-year-old participant, whose background included a histrionic borderline mother and a relatively absent father, dramatically sank from his seat slowly to the floor, his eyes closed. Immediately, at least eight or nine other patients jumped from their seats to help him get up. Since the patient was sitting right across from me – I was an epileptologist in my earlier years – I quickly realized that he was having a psychogenic dissociative seizure. I remembered Bateman's "mentalizing hand" and called out loudly, "Stop, please return to your seats, I know Mr. X will manage to return to his seat on his own!" The group seemed to distrust me a bit, but eventually the participants, slowly, followed my instruction. Then I asked the group if they had any idea or could imagine what this seizure could have expressed? Some patients were very angry with me for not allowing anyone to help the "poor little boy" and asked angrily whether I behaved the same way toward my own children, and so on. I stammered something about not having a son who slid off a seat like that and asked again for their ideas. After some time, the group began to work on this question, and to my surprise, they connected the seizure expression to the callboy's story and asked whether this seizure represented his experience of sexuality or sexual abuse. In the meantime, the young patient had begun to take his seat again, and the group members were astonished and asked what had happened to him. After a few minutes, he began to tell them that the callboy patient had reminded him that his father had touched him sexually a long time ago. As the group progressed, he picked up on the thought that this seizure might have something to do with his overwhelming sexual fantasies regarding both parents.

6.4 How Do Psychotherapists Learn to Mentalize?

Mentalizing interactions have always existed, in all psychodynamic and in all behavioral psychotherapies, but especially in the various body psychotherapies. They just have not been designed as such with a focus on mentalization. Nevertheless, one of the most potent means of resistance against MBT is when experienced psychotherapists claim to have *always* worked in this way. Here, we can take our cue from sailing regarding learning and teaching: As the "windforce" increases, therapists are required to have not only nosological-contextual knowledge (analogous to possessing a nautical chart) but also specific skills to keep them from capsizing.

It is now well established that the competence of psychotherapists is more critical for successful treatment than their grasp of theory or the contribution of patients: Even patients who have secure attachment representations with which they can develop a better relationship do not have a better prognosis (Baldwin et al., 2007). Yet even patients with insecure attachment and chaotic interpersonal relationships may benefit from working with therapists who can relate to difficult patients. The impact of individual psychotherapies cannot yet be sufficiently well established in terms of procedure-specific interventions and approaches, because there have been extremely few outcome studies concerning therapist adherence and competence (Perepletchikova et al., 2007; Pries et al., 2019). Thus, the question arises: What can therapists do to improve their mentalizing skills? There certainly seems to be some degree of "natural talent" in the sense of an above-average "social competence"; not surprisingly, those who are interested in the performance in different areas of professional and artistic activity discover that especially the continuous honing of their own skills leads to outstanding work. Such practice best takes place in quiet times without the pressure of performance, and it should also be adopted when training psychotherapeutic skills. During psychotherapeutic work, there is usually little time for thoughtful correction. Thus, good therapists differ from the rest by what they do *before* and *after* meeting with a patient or a group, including building up a tolerance toward their own mentalization failures and accepting their mistakes and deficiencies, all of which should be discussed openly in intervision and supervision groups. Qualified feedback based on video excerpts, audio files, or transcripts of treatment sessions is favorable, but above all role-play helps – and: read, read, read!

The most successful therapists seem to be characterized by their constantly following up on the treatment process, always questioning their own therapy, regularly engaging in intervision and supervision, remaining eager to read and learn, and being responsive, that is, maintaining a genuine interest in their patients (Sperry & Carlson, 2014; Taubner & Evers, 2022). One can address the more common failures in the relationship between the physician/psychotherapist and the patient regarding body complaints by fostering the therapists' confidence in their own psychotherapeutic competence through skilled supervision, which may include role-playing: It has proven very effective to practice therapeutic interactions in small groups using role-play scenes taken from the treatment of patients. It is not a question of right or wrong, but whether mentalizing is being promoted by the kind of therapeutic interaction employed.

It is one of the paradoxes of psychotherapeutic training that, on the one hand, training is so very procedure- and method-oriented, but that, on the other hand, even psychotherapists with the same theoretical orientation differ in numerous ways in their individual work. Just as no two voices sound alike, therapists using the same conceptual approach to treatment can sometimes differ more from each other than therapists with different treatment concepts (Baldwin & Imel, 2013).

With the increasing professionalization of psychotherapy, the question of the teachability and learnability of mentalizing and mentalization-promoting interactions as a competence has come to the forefront. This debate currently also affects all psychodynamically based therapeutic methods. As a complement to the classical triad of the Eitingon model, which for 100 years has comprised the study of *theory*, *self-experience*, and *treatment under supervision*, the concept of experience-based individual or group psychotherapy training is now being complemented in role-play and video analysis in weekend seminars or weekly block events.

In medical training, especially in surgical subjects, it is natural for the learner to observe a "master" before attempting things on their own. Classical psychodynamic training, in contrast, focuses too much on understanding and too little on taking therapeutically based action. At the same time, supervision is always offered posthoc, i.e., there is a lack of direct learning experience with the patient. The question of the teachability of psychodynamic and mentalizing interventions has taken on a new significance with the recent reform of psychological psychotherapy training in Germany (Ehrenthal, 2019). Indeed, it is imperative that future university curricula teach these procedures in a practice-oriented manner, and that they are learned and tested very concretely.

Role-plays with actor-patients – now common in psychosomatic-medicine classes under the reformed medical education regimen – and model learning from video-based initial interviews or therapeutic sessions of clinically experienced MBT therapists have also proven helpful. For the supervision of psychotherapeutic teams, it is also beneficial to employ role-playing, where a therapist plays the patient and the supervisor the therapist. It would be advantageous if the teachers of psychosomatic medicine were trained in didactic competence to better translate their clinical skills into a seminar format, so that the participants are neither overtaxed nor confronted with arbitrary cases. Of particular relevance is the utilization of video-based case histories, which are rarely taught in detail and against the scenic background – although they are of paramount importance to training candidates in clinical or day-clinical settings for treatment planning.

Training in mentalizing skills should have a consistent theoretical frame of reference. Role-playing, theory-teaching, and video-based analysis should be applied early in training, as should supervision. Recent developments in psychoanalysis indicate that self-awareness of the therapist's body is increasingly gaining in importance as a central source of both knowledge and questions, whether implicit or explicit, whether within or outside of sessions.

The goal of mentalizing work regarding the body is to turn the bodily experiences of sensation and feeling into emotions through attentive perception, which is subsequently mentalized into a psychic experience through its connections to images, fantasies, and memories, and through common understanding (Volz-Boers, 2016). This work requires the perceptual capacity of psychotherapists to be sensitized to their own bodily sensations and to those of their patients (Volz-Boers, 2009). This sensitization occurs most effectively in a self-awareness that considers the bodily dimensions. It may also be important that psychotherapists repeatedly expose themselves to such experiences in a kind of continuous education. I was pleased to read that Jörg Scharff (2021) advocates a similar impetus regarding experiential learning for psychoanalysts using role-plays. However, one essential difference to our model is that we do not recommend the couch setting for patients with disturbances on the body mode level: On that level, the patient needs the "whole" therapist to act as a "mirror" in the sense of complete physical presence. Only the therapist's gestures, mimicry, and physical reactions enable the patient to form new and stable representations of self and object. However, this is a topic that classical psychoanalysts like to contradict and therefore needs to be dealt with in a separate paper.

References

Acheson, E. D. (1959). The clinical syndrome variously called benign myalgic encephalomyelitis, Iceland disease and epidemic neuromyasthenia. *Am J Med, 26*(4), 569–595. https://doi.org/0002-9343(59)90280-3.
Adler, A. (1927). *Studie über Minderwertigkeit von Organen*. München: von Bergmann.
Ainsworth, M. D. S., Blehar, M. C., Waters, E., & Wall, S. (1978). *Patterns of Attachment: A Psychological Study of the Strange Situation*. New York: Earlbaum.
Aisenstein, M., & Smadja, C. (2010). Conceptual framework from the Paris psychosomatic school: a clinical psychoanalytic approach to oncology. *Int J Psychoanal, 91*, 621–640.
Alexander, F. (1934). The influence of psychologic factors upon gastro-intestinal disturbances: a symposium. *Psychoanal Q, 3*(4), 501–539. https://doi.org/10.1080/21674086.1934.11925219.
Alexander, F. (1948). Fundamental concepts of psychosomatic research. Psychogenesis, conversion, specifity. *Psychosom Med, 5*, 205–210.
Alexander, F., & French, T. M. (1948) (Eds.). *Studies in Psychosomatic Medicine. An Approach to the Cause and Treatment of Vegetative Disturbances*. New York: Ronald Press Company.
Allen, J. G., Fonagy, P., & Bateman, A. W. (2008). *Mentalizing in Clinical Practice*. Washington, DC: American Psychiatric Publishing.
Allsopp, K., Read, J., Corcoran, R., & Kinderman, P. (2019). Heterogeneity in psychiatric diagnostic classification. *Psychiatry Res, 279*, 15–22. https://doi.org/10.1016/j.psychres.2019.07.005.
Altenkirch, H. (1995). Multiple chemical sensitivity (MCS)-Syndrom. *Gesundh-Wes, 57*, 661–666.
Anzieu, D. (1985 [1995]). *Le Moi-Peau*. Paris: Dunod.
Anzieu, D. (2016). *The Skin-Ego*. London: Routledge.
APA. (2013). *Diagnostic and Statistical Manual of Mental Disorders* (5th ed.). Washington, DC: American Psychiatric Association.
Apfel, R. J., & Sifneos, P. E. (1979). Alexithymia: concept and measurement. *Psychother Psychosom, 32*(1–4), 180–190. www.ncbi.nlm.nih.gov/pubmed/550171.
Arcaro, M. J., Schade, P. F., Vincent, J. L., Ponce, C. R., & Livingstone, M. S. (2017). Seeing faces is necessary for face-domain formation. *Nat Neurosci, 20*(10), 1404–1412. https://doi.org/10.1038/nn.4635.
Argelander, H. (1991). *Der Text und seine Verknüpfungen: Studien zur psychoanalytischen Methode*. Heidelberg, Berlin: Springer.

References

Arnott, B., & Meins, E. (2007). Links between antenatal attachment representations, postnatal mind-mindedness, and infant attachment security: a preliminary study of mothers and fathers. *Bull Menninger Clin, 71*, 132–149. https://doi.org/10.1521/bumc.2007.71.2.132.

Aron, L. (1998 [2015]). Introduction – The body in drive and relational models. In L. Aron & F. S. Anderson (Eds.), *Relational Perspectives on the Body* (Vol. 12, pp. IX–XXVIII). London, New York: Taylor & Francis. Kindle-Version.

Asen, E., Campbell, C., & Fonagy, P. (2019). Social systems. Beyond the microcosm of the individual and family. In A. Bateman & P. Fonagy (Eds.), *Handbook of Mentalizing in Mental Health Practice* (pp. 229–243). Washington, DC: American Psychiatric Association Publishing.

Asher, R. (1951). Munchausen's syndrome. *Lancet, 1*(6650), 339–341. www.ncbi.nlm.nih.gov/pubmed/14805062.

Auster, P. (1982). *The Invention of Solitude*. London: Faber and Faber.

Baldwin, S. A., & Imel, Z. E. (2013). Therapist effects. In M. J. Lambert (Ed.), *Bergin and Garfield's Handbook of Psychotherapy and Behavior Change* (6th ed., pp. 258–297). New York: Wiley & Sons.

Baldwin, S. A., Wampold, B. E., & Imel, Z. E. (2007). Untangling the alliance-outcome correlation: exploring the relative importance of therapist and patient variability in the alliance. *J Consult Clin Psychol, 75*(6), 842–852. https://doi.org/2007-19013-002 [pii];10.1037/0022–006X.75.6.842.

Bales, D. L., & Bateman, A. W. (2012). Partial hospitalization settings. In A. W. Bateman & P. Fonagy (Eds.), *Handbook of Mentalizing in Mental Health Practice* (pp. 197–226). Washington, DC: American Psychiatric Publishing, Inc.

Bales, D. L., Timman, R., Andrea, H., Busschbach, J. J., Verheul, R., & Kamphuis, J. H. (2015). Effectiveness of day hospital mentalization-based treatment for patients with severe borderline personality disorder: a matched control study. *Clin Psychol Psychother, 22*(5), 409–417. https://doi.org/10.1002/cpp.1914.

Bales, D. L., Timman, R., Luyten, P., Busschbach, J. J., Verheul, R., & Hutsebaut, J. (2017). Implementation of evidence-based treatments for borderline personality disorder: the impact of organizational changes on treatment outcome of mentalization-based treatment. *Personal Ment Health, 11*, 118–131. https://doi.org/10.1002/pmh.1381.

Ballespí, S., Vives, J., Alonso, N., Sharp, C., Ramırez, M. S., Fonagy, P., & Barrantes-Vidal, N. (2019). To know or not to know? Mentalization as protection from somatic complaints. *PLoS One, 14*. https://doi.org/https://doi.org/10.1371/journal.pone.0215308.

Ballespí, S., Vives, J., Debbané, M., Sharp, C., & Barrantes-Vidal, N. (2018). Beyond diagnosis: mentalization and mental health from a transdiagnostic point of view in adolescents from non-clinical population. *Psychiatry Res, 270*, 755–763. https://doi.org/https://doi.org/10.1016/j.psychres.2018.10.048.

Bandura, A. (1967). The role of modeling processes in personality development. In W. W. Hartup & N. L. Smothergill (Eds.), *The Young Child: Reviews of Research* (pp. 42–58). Washington, DC: National Association for the Education of Young Children.

Baron-Cohen, S., Leslie, A. M., & Frith, U. (1985). Does the autistic child have a "theory of mind"? *Cognition, 21*(1), 37–46. https://doi.org/0010-0277(85)90022-8 [pii].

Barsky, A. J. (1992). Amplification, somatization, and the somatoform disorders. *Psychosomatics, 33*(1), 28–34. https://doi.org/10.1016/S0033-3182(92)72018-0.

Bateman, A., Bales, D., & Hutsebaut, J. (2014). *A quality manual for MBT*. www.annafreud.org/media/1217/a-quality-manual-for-mbt-edited-april-23rd-2014-2.pdf.

Bateman, A., Campbell, C., & Fonagy, P. (2021). Rupture and repair in mentalization-based group psychotherapy. *Int J Group Psychother*, 1–22. https://doi.org/10.1080/00207284.2020.1847655.

Bateman, A., & Fonagy, P. (2016). *Mentalization-Based Treatment for Personality Disorders – A Practical Guide*. Oxford: Oxford University Press.

Bateman, A., Fonagy, P., Campbell, C., Luyten, P., & Debbané, M. (2023). *Cambridge Guide to Mentalization-Based Treatment (MBT)*. Cambridge: Cambridge University Press.

Bateman, A., Kongerslev, M., & Hansen, S. B. (2019). Group therapy for adults and adolescents. In A. Bateman & P. Fonagy (Eds.), *Handbook of Mentalizing in Mental Health Practice* (pp. 117–133). Washington, DC: American Psychiatric Association Publishing.

Bateman, A. W., & Fonagy, P. (2004). Mentalization-based treatment of BPD. *J Personal Disord*, *18*(1), 36–51. www.ncbi.nlm.nih.gov/pubmed/15061343.

Bateman, A. W., & Fonagy, P. (2008). 8-year follow-up of patients treated for borderline personality disorder: mentalization-based treatment versus treatment as usual. *Am J Psychiatry*, *165*(5), 631–638. www.ncbi.nlm.nih.gov/pubmed/18347003.

Bateman, A. W., & Fonagy, P. (Eds.). (2019). *Handbook of Mentalizing in Mental Health Practice*. Washington, DC: American Psychiatric Association Publishing.

Bauer, J. (2005). *Warum Ich fühle, was Du fühlst. Intuitive Kommunikation und das Geheimnis der Spiegelneurone*. Frankfurt am Main: Hoffmann und Campe.

Beard, G. M. (1880 [1890]). *Die sexuelle Neurasthenie, ihre Hygiene, Aetiologie, Symtomatologie und ihre Behandlung* (2 Aufl.). Leipzig and Wien: Franz Deuticke.

Becker, G., Kempf, D. E., Xander, C. J., Momm, F., Olschewski, M., & Blum, H. E. (2010). Four minutes for a patient, twenty seconds for a relative – an observational study at a university hospital. *BMC Health Serv Res*, *10*, 94. https://doi.org/1472-6963-10-94 [pii];10.1186/1472-6963-10-94.

Beddington, J. (2013). *Foresight Future Identities*. Final Project Report. London: The Government Office for Science.

Bergmann, G. V. (1927). Zum Abbau der "Organneurosen" als Folge interner Diagnostik. *Dtsch med Wschr*, *53*, 2057–2060.

Berman, A., & Ofer, G. (Eds.). (2024). *Tolerance – A Concept in Crisis: Socio-Cultural Psychoanalytic, and Group Analytic Perspectives*. London: Routledge (in press).

Bernhard, T. (1971). *Gehen*. Frankfurt am Main: Suhrkamp.

Betts, T., & Boden, S. (1992a). Diagnosis, management and prognosis of a group of 128 patients with non-epileptic attack disorder. Part I. *Seizure*, *1*(1), 19–26. www.ncbi.nlm.nih.gov/pubmed/1344315.

Betts, T., & Boden, S. (1992b). Diagnosis, management and prognosis of a group of 128 patients with non-epileptic attack disorder. Part II. Previous childhood sexual abuse in the aetiology of these disorders. *Seizure*, *1*(1), 27–32. www.ncbi.nlm.nih.gov/pubmed/1344316.

Bick, E. (1968). The experience of the skin in early object relations. *Int J Psychoanal*, *49*, 484–506.

Bion, W. R. (1952). Group dynamics: a review. *Int J Psychoanal*, *33*, 235–247.

Bion, W. R. (Ed.). (1967). *Clinical Seminars: Brasilia and Sao Paulo and Four Papers*. London: Karnac.

Birksted-Breen, D. (2019). Pathways of the unconscious: when the body is the receiver/instrument. *Int J Psychoanal*, *100*, 1117–1133. https://doi.org/10.1080/00207578.2019.1661253.

References

Blakemore, S. J. (2008). The social brain in adolescence. *Nat Rev Neurosci, 9*(4), 267–277. https://doi.org/10.1038/nrn2353.

Blakemore, S. J. (2010). The developing social brain: implications for education. *Neuron, 65*(6), 744–747. https://doi.org/10.1016/j.neuron.2010.03.004.

Böhme, R. (2019). *Human Touch – Warum körperliche Nähe so wichtig ist.* München: C.H. Beck.

Botvinick, M., & Cohen, J. (1998). Rubber hands 'feel' touch that eyes see. *Nature, 391*(6669), 756. https://doi.org/10.1038/35784.

Bouchard, M.-A., & Lecours, S. (2008). Contemporary approaches to mentalization in the light of Freud's project. In F. N. Busch (Ed.), *Mentalization. Theoretical Considerations, Research Findings and Clinical Implications* (pp. 103–129). New York and London: The Analytic Press, Taylor & Francis Group.

Bowlby, J. (1958). The nature of the child's tie to his mother. *Int J Psychoanal, 39,* 350–373.

Bowlby, J. (1969 [1982]). *Attachment and Loss: Vol. 1 Attachment* (rev. 2nd ed.). New York: Basic Books.

Bowlby, J. (1978). Attachment theory and its therapeutic implications. *Adolesc Psychiatry, 6,* 5–33. www.ncbi.nlm.nih.gov/pubmed/742687.

Brand, T., Hecke, D., Rietz, C., & Schultz-Venrath, U. (2016). Therapieeffekte mentalisierungsbasierter und psychodynamischer Gruppenpsychotherapie in einer randomisierten Tagesklinik-Studie. *Gruppenpsychother Gruppendynamik, 52*(2), 156–175.

Brandt, T., & Dieterich, M. (1986). Phobischer Attacken-Schwankschwindel – ein neues Syndrom? *MMW – Fortschritte der Medizin, 128,* 247–250.

Bremner, J. D. (2009). Neurobiology of dissociation: a view from the trauma field. In P. F. Dell & J. A. O'Neill (Eds.), *Dissociation and the Dissociative Disorders: DSM-V and Beyond.* New York: Routledge.

Brentano, F. (1874 [2008]). *Psychologie vom empirischen Standpunkte. Von der Klassifikation der psychischen Phänomene* (Vol. 1). Frankfurt am Main: Ontos Verlag.

Bretherton, I. (1999). Updating the 'internal working model' construct: some reflections. *Attach Hum Dev, 1*(3), 343–357. https://doi.org/10.1080/14616739900134191.

Breuer, J., & Freud, S. (1956). On the psychical mechanism of hysterical phenomena (1893). *I J Psychoanal, 37,* 8–13.

Broschmann, D., & Fuchs, T. (2020). Zwischenleiblichkeit in der psychodynamischen Psychotherapie – Ansatz zu einem verkörperten Verständnis von Intersubjektivität. *Forum Psychoanal, 36,* 459–475. https://doi.org/https://doi.org/10.1007/s00451-019-00350-z.

Brown, D. (1985). The psychosoma and the group. *Group Anal, 18,* 93–101.

Brown, D. (2006a). Drowsiness in the countertransference. In J. Maratos (Ed.), *Resonance and Reciprocity – Selected Papers by Dennis Brown* (pp. 37–53). London and New York: Routledge, Taylor & Francis.

Brown, D. (2006b). The psychosoma and the group. In J. Maratos (Ed.), *Resonance and Reciprocity* (pp. 15–27). London and New York: Routledge, Taylor & Francis.

Brown, S., & Vaughan, C. (2009). *Play – How It Shapes the Brain, Opens the Imagination and Invigorates the Soul.* New York: Avery.

Bruch, H. (1973). *Eating Disorders: Obesity, Anorexia Nervosa and the Person Within.* London: Routledge & Kegan Paul.

Buchheim, A., Heinrichs, M., George, C., Pokorny, D., Koops, E., Henningsen, P., O'Connor, M. F., & Gündel, H. (2009). Oxytocin enhances the experience of attachment security. *Psychoneuroendocrinology, 34*(9), 1417–1422. https://doi.org/S0306-4530(09)00117-6 [pii];10.1016/j.psyneuen.2009.04.002.

Buchholz, M. B. (2014). Embodiment. Konvergenzen von Kognitionsforschung und analytischer Entwicklungspsychologie. *Forum Psychoanal*, *30*, 109–128.
Budd, S. (2001). 'No sex, please – we're British': sexuality in English and French psychoanalysis. In C. Harding (Ed.), *Sexuality: Psychoanalytic Perspectives* (pp. 52–68). Hove: Brunner-Routledge.
Burlingame, G. M., & Strauss, B. (2021). Efficacy of small group treatments. In M. Barkham, W. Lutz, & L. G. Castonguay (Eds.), *Bergin and Garfield's Handbook of Psychotherapy and Behavior Change: 50th Anniversary Edition* (7th ed., pp. 583–624). Chichester: John Wiley & Sons.
Burrow, T. (1913 [2013]). Psychoanalysis and life. In E. Gatti Pertegato & G. O. Pertegato (Eds.), *From Psychoanalysis to Group Analysis. The Pioneering Work of Trigant Burrow* (pp. 7–16). London: Karnac.
Burton, C., Lucassen, P., Aamland, A., & Olde Hartman, T. (2015). Explaining symptoms after negative tests: towards a rational explanation. *J R Soc Med*, *108*, 84–88.
Campbell, C., Tanzer, M., Saunders, R., Booker, T., Allison, E., Li, E., O'Dowda, C., Luyten, P., & Fonagy, P. (2021). Development and validation of a self-report measure of epistemic trust. *PLoS One*, *16*(4), e0250264. https://doi.org/https://doi.org/10.1371/journal.pone.0250264.
Chen, P. A., Cheong, J. H., Jolly, E., Elhence, H., Wager, T. D., & Chang, L. J. (2019). Socially transmitted placebo effects. *Nat Hum Behav*, *3*(12), 1295–1305. https://doi.org/10.1038/s41562-019-0749-5
Chugani, H. T., Behen, M. E., Muzik, O., Juhasz, C., Nagy, F., & Chugani, D. C. (2001). Local brain functional activity following early deprivation: a study of postinstitutionalized Romanian orphans. *Neuroimage*, *14*(6), 1290–1301. https://doi.org/10.1006/nimg.2001.0917.
Ciaunica, A., & Fotopoulou, A. (2017). The touched self: psychological and philosophical perspectives on proximal intersubjectivity and the self. In C. Durt, T. Fuchs, & C. Tewes (Eds.), *Embodiment, Enaction, and Culture* (pp. 173–192). Cambridge, MA and London: The MIT Press.
Coates, S. W. (2016). Can babies remember trauma? Symbolic forms of representation in traumatized infants. *J Am Psychoanal Assoc*, *64*(4), 751–776. https://doi.org/10.1177/0003065116659443.
Cochrane, C. E., Brewerton, T. D., Wilson, D. B., & Hodges, E. L. (1993). Alexithymia in the eating disorders. *Int J Eat Disord*, *14*(2), 219–222. www.ncbi.nlm.nih.gov/pubmed/8401555.
Cole, E. J., Barraclough, N. E., & Andrews, T. J. (2019). Reduced connectivity between mentalizing and mirror systems in autism spectrum condition. *Neuropsychologia*, *122*, 88–97. https://doi.org/10.1016/j.neuropsychologia.2018.11.008.
Collins, D. T. (1965). Head-banging: its meaning and management in the severely retarded adult. *Bull Menninger Clin*, *29*, 205–211. www.ncbi.nlm.nih.gov/pubmed/14346995.
Congy, F., Hauw, J. J., Wang, A., & Moulias, R. (1980). Influenzal acute myositis in the elderly. *Neurology*, *30*(8), 877–878. www.ncbi.nlm.nih.gov/pubmed/7191071.
Corning, J. L. (1888 [2018]). *A Treatise on Headache and Neuralgia, Including Spinal Irritation and a Disquisition on Normal and Morbid Sleep*. New York: E. B. Treat.
Creed, F., von der Feltz-Cornelis, C., Guthtrie, E., Henningsen, P., Rief, W., Schröder, A., & White, P. (2011). Identification, assessment and treatment of individual patients. In F. Creed, P. Henningsen, & P. Fink (Eds.), *Medically Unexplained Symptoms, Somatisation and Bodily Distress. Developing Better Clinical Services* (pp. 175–216). Cambridge: Cambridge University Press.

Cremerius, J. (1981). Freud bei der Arbeit über die Schulter geschaut. Seine Technik im Spiegel von Schülern und Patienten. In U. Ehenald & F. W. Eickhoff (Hrsg.), *Humanität und Technik in der Psychoanalyse. Jahrbuch der Psychoanalyse, Beiheft 6* (pp. 123–158). Bern: Huber.

Crespi, B., & Dinsdale, N. (2019). Autism and psychosis as diametrical disorders of embodiment. *Evol Med Public Health, 2019*(1), 121–138. https://doi.org/10.1093/emph/eoz021.

Da Costa, J. M. (1871). On irritable heart; a clinical study of a form of functional cardiac disorder and its consequences. *Am J Med Sci, 61*, 18–52.

Damasio, A. R. (1994). *Descartes' Error, Emotion, Reason and the Human Brain*. New York: G. P. Putnam's Son.

Damasio, A. R. (1999). *The Feeling of What Happens. Body and Emotion in the Making of Consciousness*. New York, San Diego and London: Hartcourt Brace & Company.

Darwin, C. R. (1872 [1934]). *The Expression of Emotions in Man and Animals*. London: Watts & Co.

de Lissovoy, V. (1963). Head banging in early childhood: a suggested cause. *J Genet Psychol, 102*(1), 109–114. https://doi.org/10.1080/00221325.1963.10532730.

de Waal, F. B., & Suchak, M. (2010). Prosocial primates: selfish and unselfish motivations. *Philos Trans R Soc Lond B Biol Sci, 365*(1553), 2711–2722. https://doi.org/365/1553/2711 [pii];10.1098/rstb.2010.0119.

Debbane, M., Badoud, D., Sander, D., Eliez, S., Luyten, P., & Vrticka, P. (2017). Brain activity underlying negative self- and other-perception in adolescents: the role of attachment-derived self-representations. *Cogn Affect Behav Neurosci, 17*(3), 554–576. https://doi.org/10.3758/s13415-017-0497-9.

Debbané, M., & Nolte, T. (2019). Contemporary neursoscientific research. In A. Bateman & P. Fonagy (Eds.), *Handbook of Mentalizing in Mental Health Practice* (2nd ed., pp. 21–35). Washington, DC: American Psychiatric Association Publishing.

DeCasper, A. J., & Fiver, V. P. (1980). Of human bonding: newborn prefer their mothers' voices. *Science, 208*, 208.

Dell'Osso, L., Massoni, L., Battaglini, S., De Felice, C., Nardi, B., Amatori, G., Cremone, I. M., & Carpita, B. (2023). Emotional dysregulation as a part of the autism spectrum continuum: a literature review from late childhood to adulthood. *Front Psychiatry, 14*, 1234518. https://doi.org/14:1234518

Dennett, D. (1987). *The Intentional Stance*. Cambridge, MA: The MIT Press.

Dettbarn, I. (2019). Video-Telefonie im Internet – die unheimliche Dritte – und Psychotherapie. *Psychoanalyse im Widerspruch, 61*, 8–26. https://doi.org/10.30820/0941-5378-2019-1-8.

Deutsch, F. (1922). Psychoanalyse und Organkrankheiten. *Int Z Psychoanal, 8*, 290–306.

Deutsch, F. (1926). Der gesunde und der kranke Körper in psychoanalytischer Betrachtung. *Int Z Psychoanal, 12*(3), 493–503.

Deutsch, F., & Murphy, W. F. (1955 [1964]-a). *The Clinical Interview – Volume One: Diagnosis. A Method of Teaching Associative Exploration* (4th ed.). New York: International Universities Press.

Deutsch, F., & Murphy, W. F. (1955 [1964]-b). *The Clinical Interview – Volume Two: Therapy. A method of Teaching Sector Psychotherapy*. New York: International Universities Press.

Diehl, R. R. (2003). Posturales Tachykardiesyndrom. In Deutschland bislang zu selten diagnostiziert. *Dtsch Arztebl, 100*(43), B-2330–B-2335.

Diez Grieser, M. T., & Müller, R. (2018). *Mentalisieren mit Kindern und Jugendlichen*. Stuttgart: Klett-Cotta.
Dornes, M. (1997). *Die frühe Kindheit*. Frankfurt am Main.: Fischer Taschenbuch Verlag.
Duddu, V., Isaac, M. K., & Chaturvedi, S. K. (2003). Alexithymia in somatoform and depressive disorders. *J Psychosom Res*, *54*(5), 435–438. www.ncbi.nlm.nih.gov/pubmed/12726899.
Eckhardt, A. (1989). *Das Münchhausen-Syndrom. Formen der selbstmanipulierten Krankheit*. München: Urban & Schwarzenberg.
Egle, U. T. (2016). Stressinduzierte Schmerzsyndrome. *Physioactive*, *1*, 15–21.
Egle, U. T., Ecker-Egle, M.-L., & Nickel, R. (2011). Fibromyalgie-Syndrom – eine Stressverarbeitungsstörung. *Schweiz Arch Neurol Psychiatr*, *162*(8), 326–337.
Egle, U. T., Heim, C., Strauß, B., & Känel, R. (Eds.). (2020). *Psychosomatik – Evidenzbasiert – Neurobiologisch fundiert*. Stuttgart: Kohlhammer.
Ehrenthal, J. C. (2019). Erfahrungsbasiertes Lernen psychodynamischer Interventionen. *Forum Psychoanal*, *35*(4), 413–428.
Eikelboom, E. M., Tak, L. M., Roest, A. M., & Rosmalen, J. G. M. (2016). A systematic review and meta-analysis of the percentage of revised diagnoses in functional somatic symptoms. *J Psychosom Res*, *88*, 60–66.
Ekman, P. (2003). Emotions inside out. 130 years after Darwin's "the expression of the emotions in man and animal". *Ann N Y Acad Sci*, *1000*, 1–6. www.ncbi.nlm.nih.gov/pubmed/15045707.
Ekman, P., Friesen, W., & Ellsworth, P. (1972). *Emotion in the Human Face*. Oxford: Pergamon Press.
Elias, L. J., Succi, I. K., Schaffler, M. D., Foster, W., Gradwell, M. A., Bohic, M., Fushiki, A., Upadhyay, A., Ejoh, L. L., Schwark, R., Frazer, R., Bistis, B., Burke, J. E., Saltz, V., Boyce, J. E., Jhumka, A., Costa, R. M., Abraira, V. E., & Abdus-Saboor, I. (2023). Touch neurons underlying dopaminergic pleasurable touch and sexual receptivity. *Cell*, *186*, 1–14. https://doi.org/10.1016/j.cell.2022.12.034.
Elias, N. (1939). *Über den Prozeß der Zivilisation. Soziogenetische und psychogenetische Untersuchungen. Erster Band. Wandlungen des Verhaltens in den weltlichen Oberschichten des Abendlandes* (Vol. 1). Basel: Verlag Haus zum Falken.
Elias, N. (1994). *The Civilizing Process*. Oxford: Blackwell.
Engel, G. L., & Schmale, A. (1967). Psychoanalytic theory of somatic disorder. *J Am Psychoanal Assoc*, *15*, 344–365.
Ensink, K., Biberdzic, M., Normandin, L., & Clarkin, J. (2015). A developmental psychopathology and neurobiological model of borderline personality disorder in adolescence. *J Infant Child Adolesc Psychother*, *14*, 46–69.
Fabregat, M. (2004). *Methaphors in Psychotherapy. From Affect to Mental Representations*. Saarbrücken: Philosophische Fakultät der Universität Saarland. http://scidok.sulb.uni-saarland.de/volltexte/2004/417/.
Fabregat, M., & Krause, R. (2008). Metaphern und Affekt: Zusammenwirken im therapeutischen Prozess. *Z Psychosom Med Psychother*, *54*(1), 77–88. www.ncbi.nlm.nih.gov/pubmed/18325245.
Fain, M., & David, C. (1963). Aspects fonctionnels de la vie onirique. *Rev Franç Psychanal*, *27*, 241–243.
Fain, M., David, C., & Marty, P. (1964). Perspective psychosomatique sur la fonction des fantasmes. *Rev Franç Psychanal*, *28*, 609–622.

Federschmidt, H. (2017). Können somatische Erkrankungen einen "symbolischen Ausdrucksgehalt" besitzen? Überlegungen auf der Basis psychoneuroimmunologischer Zusammenhänge. *Ärztliche Psychotherapie, 12*(3), 163–169.

Fenichel, O. (1945). The nature and classification of the so-called psychosomatic phenomena. *Psychoanal Q, 14*, 287–312.

Fiedler, A., Hömberg, R., Oessenich-Lücke, U., Sahm, S., Venrath, D., & Schultz-Venrath, U. (2011). Körperpsychotherapie(n) und Mentalisieren: Wahrnehmen – Vernetzen – Integrieren. In U. Schultz-Venrath (Hrsg.), *Psychotherapien in Tageskliniken. Methoden, Konzepte, Strukturen* (pp. 119–150). Berlin: Medizinisch Wissenschaftliche Verlagsgesellschaft.

Fischer-Homberger, E. (1975). *Die traumatische Neurose. Vom somatischen zum sozialen Leiden.* Bern: Huber.

Fonagy, P. (1991). Thinking about thinking: some clinical and theoretical considerations in the treatment of a borderline patient. *Int J Psychoanal, 72*, 639–656.

Fonagy, P. (2008). A genuinely developmental theory of sexual enjoyment and its implications for psychoanalytic technique. *J Am Psychoanal Assoc, 56*(1), 11–36. https://doi.org/56/1/11 [pii];10.1177/0003065107313025.

Fonagy, P. (2022). Mentalisation based treatment and psychoanalysis. *Gruppenpsychother. Gruppendynamik, 58*, 205–215.

Fonagy, P., & Allison, E. (2015). The role of mentalizing and epistemic trust in the therapeutic relationship. *Psychotherapy, 51*(3), 372–380.

Fonagy, P., & Bateman, A. (2019). Introduction. In A. Bateman & P. Fonagy (Eds.), *Handbook of Mentalizing in Mental Health Practice* (2nd ed., pp. 3–20). Washington, DC: American Psychiatric Association Publishing.

Fonagy, P., & Campbell, C. (2017). What touch can communicate: commentary on "mentalizing homeostasis: the social origins of interoceptive inference" by Fotopoulou and Tsakiris. *Neuropsychoanalysis, 19*, 39–42.

Fonagy, P., Gergely, G., Jurist, E. L., & Target, M. (2002 [2004]). *Affect Regulation, Mentalization and the Development of the Self.* London: Karnac.

Fonagy, P., Luyten, P., Allison, E., & Campbell, C. (2019). Mentalizing, epistemic trust and the phenomenology of psychotherapy. *Psychopathology*, 1–10. https://doi.org/10.1159/000501526.

Fonagy, P., & Moran, G. S. (1990). Severe developmental psychopathology and brittle diabetes: the motivation for self-injurious behaviour. *Bull Anna Freud Centre, 13*, 231–248.

Fonagy, P., & Nolte, T. (Hrsg.). (2023). *Epistemisches Vertrauen – Vom Konzept zur Anwendung in Psychotherapie und psychosozialer Beratung.* Stuttgart: Klett-Cotta.

Fonagy, P., Roussow, T., Sharp, C., Bateman, A. W., Allison, L., & Farrar, C. (2014). Mentalization-based treatment for adolescents with borderline traits. In C. Sharp & J. L. Tackett (Eds.), *Handbook of Borderline Personality Disorder in Children and Adolescents* (pp. 313–332). New York: Springer.

Fonagy, P., Steele, H., & Steele, M. (1991). Maternal representations of attachment during pregnancy predict the organization of infant-mother attachment at one year of age. *Child Dev, 62*(5), 891–905. www.ncbi.nlm.nih.gov/pubmed/1756665.

Fonagy, P., Steele, M., Steele, H., Leigh, T., Kennedy, R., Mattoon, G., & Target, M. (1995). Attachment, the reflective self, and borderline states: the predictive specificity of the adult attachment interview and pathological emotional development. In S. Goldberg, R. Muir, & J. Kerr (Eds.), *Attachment Theory: Social, Developmental, and Clinical Perspectives* (pp. 233–279). Hillsdale, NJ: Analytic Press.

Fonagy, P., & Target, M. (2003). *Psychoanalytic Theories – Perspectives from Developmental Psychopathology*. London: Routledge.

Fonagy, P., & Target, M. (2007). Attachment and reflective function: their role in self-organization. *Dev Psychopathol*, *9*, 679–700.

Fotopoulou, A., & Tsakiris, M. (2017). Mentalizing homeostasis: the social origins of interoceptive inference. *Neuropsychoanalysis*, *19*(1), 3–28. https://doi.org/10.1080/15294145.2017.1294031.

Foulkes, S. H., & Anthony, E. J. (1965). *Group Psychotherapy – The Psychoanalytic Approach*. (2nd ed.). London: Maresfield Reprints.

Fraley, R. C., Roisman, G. I., Booth-LaForce, C., Owen, M. T., & Holland, A. S. (2013). Interpersonal and genetic origins of adult attachment styles: a longitudinal study from infancy to early adulthood. *J Pers Soc Psychol*, *104*(5), 817–838. https://doi.org/10.1037/a0031435.

Frances, A., & Chapman, S. (2013). DSM-5 somatic symptom disorder mislabels medical illness as mental disorder. *Aust N Z J Psychiatry*, *47*, 483–484.

Franke, P., Schleu, A., Hillebrand, V., Welther, M., & Strauß, B. (2016). Beschwerden über Fehlverhalten in der Psychotherapie, Teil 1. Quantitative und qualitative Analyse der Dokumentation des Vereins Ethik in der Psychotherapie 2006–2015. *Psychotherapeut*, *61*(6), 507–515.

Frenkel-Brunswik, E. (1949). Intolerance of ambiguity as an emotional and perceptual personality variable. *J Personality*, *18*, 108–143. https://doi.org/10.1111/j.1467-6494.1949.tb01236.x

Freud, S. (1888b). *Hysterie und Hysteroepilepsie* (*GW* Nachtr., pp. 72–92). Frankfurt am Main: S. Fischer.

Freud, S. (1894). On the grounds for detaching a particular syndrome from neurasthenia under the description 'anxiety neurosis'. In J. Strachey, A. Freud, A. Strachey, & A. Tyson (Eds.), *The Standard Edition of the Complete Psychological Works of Sigmund Freud* (Vol. III, pp. 85–115). London: Hogarth Press.

Freud, S. (1894a). Die Abwehr-Neuropsychosen. Versuch einer psychologischen Theorie der acquirierten Hysterie, vieler Phobien und Zwangsvorstellungen und gewisser halluzinatorischer Psychosen. In *GW I* (pp. 59–74). Frankfurt am Main: Fischer.

Freud, S. (1895b). Über die Berechtigung, von der Neurasthenie einen bestimmten Symptomenkomplex als "Angstneurose" abzutrennen. *Neurol Centralbl*, *14*, 50–66.

Freud, S. (1897). Abstracts of the scientific writings of Dr. Sigm. Freud 1877–1897. In J. Strachey, A. Freud, A. Strachey, & A. Tyson (Eds.), *The Standard Edition of the Complete Psychological Works of Sigmund Freud* (Vol. III, pp. 223–257). London: Hogarth Press.

Freud, S. (1905 [1953]). Fragment of an analysis of a case of hysteria. In J. Strachey, A. Freud, A. Strachey, & A. Tyson (Eds.), *The Standard Edition of the Complete Psychological Works of Sigmund Freud* (Vol. VII, pp. 1–122). London: Hogarth Press.

Freud, S. (1905d). *Drei Abhandlungen zur Sexualtheorie*. In *GW Bd. V* (pp. 27–145). Frankfurt am Main: S. Fischer.

Freud, S. (1910). The psycho-analytic view of psychogenic disturbance of vision. In J. Strachey, A. Freud, A. Strachey, & A. Tyson (Eds.), *The Standard Edition of the Complete Psychological Works of Sigmund Freud* (Vol. XI, pp. 209–218). London: Hogarth Press.

Freud, S. (1912e). *Ratschläge für den Arzt bei der psychoanalytischen Behandlung*. In *GW Bd. VIII* (pp. 376–387). Frankfurt am Main: S. Fischer.

Freud, S. (1915c). Triebe und Triebschicksale. In *GW 10* (pp. 210–232). Frankfurt am Main: S. Fischer.
Freud, S. (1917). Introductory lectures on psycho-analysis. In J. Strachey, A. Freud, A. Strachey, & A. Tyson (Eds.), *The Standard Edition of the Complete Psychological Works of Sigmund Freud* (Vol. XVI, pp. 241–463). London: Hogarth Press.
Freud, S. (1921c). Massenpsychologie und Ich-Analyse. In *GW 13* (pp. 71–161). Frankfurt am Main: S. Fischer.
Freud, S. (1923). The ego and the id. In *The Standard Edition of the Complete Psychological Works of Sigmund Freud* (Vol. XIX, pp. 1–66). London: Hogarth Press.
Freud, S. (1923b). Das Ich und das Es. In *Gesammelte Werke* (GW XIII, pp. 237–289). Frankfurt am Main: Fischer.
Freud, S. (1955). *Studies on Hysteria* (Vol. II). London: Hogarth Press.
Freud, S., & Breuer, J. (1895d). Studien über Hysterie. Gesammelte Werke I. In *Gesammelte Werke* (Vol. 1, pp. 75–312). Frankfurt am Main: S. Fischer.
Friedman, M., & Rosenman, R. H. (1971). Type A behavior pattern: its association with coronary heart disease. *Ann Clin Res*, *3*(6), 300–312. www.ncbi.nlm.nih.gov/pubmed/5156890.
Friedman, R. (2007). In der Gruppenanalyse heilen die Störungen einander – eine Beziehungsperspektive. *Psychosozial*, *107*, 57–76.
Friston, K. J. (2017). Self-evidencing babies: commentary on "mentalizing homeostasis: the social origins of interoceptive inference" by Fotopoulou and Tsakiris. *Neuropsychoanalysis*, *19*, 43–47.
Fromm-Reichmann, F. (1950). *Principles of Intensive Psychotherapy*. Cambridge: Cambridge University Press.
Fuchs, T. (1995). Coenästhesie. Zur Geschichte des Gemeingefühls. *Z Klin Psychol Psychother*, *43*, 103–112.
Fuchs, T. (2017a). *Das Gehirn – ein Beziehungsorgan. Eine ohänomenologisch-ökologische Konzeption* (5. akt. und erw. Aufl.). Stuttgart: Kohlhammer.
Fuchs, T. (2017b). Embodiment – Verkörperung, Gefühl und Leibgedächtnis. *Psychoanalyse im Widerspruch*, *57*(29 (1)), 9–28.
Fuchs, T. (2018a). *Ecology of the Brain: The Phenomenology and Biology of the Embodied Mind*. Oxford: Oxford University Press.
Fuchs, T. (2018b). Zwischenleibliche Resonanz und Interaffektivität. *PPT – Persönlichkeitsstörungen*, *17*, 211–221.
Gaddini, E. (1969). On imitation. *Int J Psychoanal*, *50*, 475–484.
Gaddini, E. (1981a). Note sul problema mente-corpo. *Riv Psicoanal*, *27*(1), 3–29.
Gaddini, E. (1981b [1998]). Bemerkungen zum Psyche-Soma-Problem. In G. Jappe & B. Strehlow (Hrsg.), *Eugenio Gaddini: "Das Ich ist vor allem ein Körperliches". Beiträge zur Psychoanalyse der ersten Strukturen* (pp. 21–51). Tübingen: Edition Diskord.
Gaddini, E. (1998). Die präsymbolische Aktivität der kindlichen Psyche. In G. Jappe & B. Strehlow (Hrsg.), *Eugenio Gaddini: "Das Ich ist vor allem ein Körperliches. Beiträge zur Psychoanalyse der ersten Strukturen* (pp. 198–215). Tübingen: Edition Diskord.
Gaddini, R., & Gaddini, E. (1970). Transitional objects and the process of individuation: a study in three different social groups. *J Am Acad Child Psychiatry*, *9*(2), 347–365.
Gallagher, S. (2005). *How the Body Shapes the Mind*. Oxford: Oxford University Press.
Gallegos, M., Martino, P., Caycho-Rodriguez, T., Calandra, M., Razumovskiy, A., Arias-Gallegos, W. L., Castro-Pecanha, V., & Cervigni, M. (2022). What is post-COVID-19 syndrome? Definition and update (Que es el sindrome pos-COVID-19?

Definicion y actualizacion). *Gac Med Mex*, *158*(6), 442–446. https://doi.org/10.24875/GMM.M22000725.
Gallese, V., & Caruana, F. (2016). Embodied simulation: beyond the expression/experience dualism of emotions. *Trends Cogn Sci*, 1. https://doi.org/10.1016/j.tics.2016.03.010.
Ganser, G. (2017). *Hundegestützte Psychotherapie. Einbindung eines Hundes in die psychotherapeutische Praxis*. Stuttgart: Schattauer.
Ganslev, C. A., Storebø, O. J., Callesen, H. E., Ruddy, R., & Søgaard, U. (2020). Psychosocial interventions for conversion and dissociative disorders in adults. *Cochrane Database Syst Rev* (7). https://doi.org/10.1002/14651858.CD005331.pub3.
Geißler, P., & Heisterkamp, G. (2007). Psychoanalyse der Lebensbewegungen. Zum körperlichen Geschehen in der psychoanalytischen Therapie. In P. Geißler & G. Heisterkamp (Hrsg.), *Ein Lehrbuch*. Wien and New York: Springer.
Geisthövel, A., & Hitzer, B. (Eds.). (2019). *Auf der Suche nach einer anderen Medizin – Psychosomatik im 20. Jahrhundert*. Berlin: Suhrkamp.
Gendlin, E. T. (1991). Thinking beyond patterns: body, language, and situations. In B. den Ouden & M. Moen (Eds.), *The Presence of Feeling in Thought* (pp. 21–151). New York: Peter Lang.
Gergely, G. (2005). The obscure object of desire-'Nearly, but clearly not, like me': contingency preference in normal children versus children with autism. *Bull Menninger Clin*, *65*(3). https://doi.org/https://doi.org/10.1521/bumc.65.3.411.19853.
Gergely, G., & Unoka, Z. (2008a). Attachement and mentalization in humans. The development of the affective self. In E. L. Jurist, A. Slade, & S. Bergner (Eds.), *Mind to Mind. Infant Research, Neuroscience, and Psychoanalysis* (pp. 50–87). New York: Other Press.
Gergely, G., & Unoka, Z. (2008b). The development of the unreflective self. In F. N. Busch (Ed.), *Mentalization. Theoretical Considerations, Research Findings, and Clinical Implications* (pp. 57–102). London: Taylor & Francis.
Gergely, G., & Watson, J. S. (1996). The social biofeedback theory of parental affect-mirroring: the development of emotional self-awareness and self-control in infancy. *Int J Psychoanal*, *77*(6), 1181–1212. www.ncbi.nlm.nih.gov/pubmed/9119582.
Gergely, G., & Watson, J. S. (1999 [2014]). Early socio-emotional dvelopment: contingency perception and the social-biofeedback model. In P. Rochat (Ed.), *Early Social Cognition – Understanding Others in the First Months of Life*. London: Taylor & Francis, Psychology Press.
Giedd, J. N. (2003). The anatomy of mentalization: a view from developmental neuroimaging. *Bull Menninger Clin*, *67*(2), 132–142. www.ncbi.nlm.nih.gov/pubmed/14604098.
Giedd, J. N. (2004). Structural magnetic resonance imaging of the adolescent brain. *Ann N Y Acad Sci*, *1021*, 77–85. https://doi.org/10.1196/annals.1308.009.
Giedd, J. N., Blumenthal, J., Jeffries, N. O., Castellanos, F. X., Liu, H., Zijdenbos, A., Paus, T., Evans, A. C., & Rapoport, J. L. (1999). Brain development during childhood and adolescence: a longitudinal MRI study. *Nat Neurosci*, *2*(10), 861–863. https://doi.org/10.1038/13158.
Gleichgerrcht, E., & Decety, J. (2013). Empathy in clinical practice: how individual dispositions, gender, and experience moderate empathic concern, burnout, and emotional distress in physicians. *PloS One*, *8*(4), e61526. https://doi.org/10.1371/journal.pone.0061526.
Gleichmann, P. R. (1979). Die Verhäuslichung körperlicher Verrichtungen. In P. Gleichmann, J. Goudsblom, & H. Korte (Hrsg.), *Materialien zu Norbert Elias' Zivilisationstheorie* (pp. 254–278). Frankfurt am Main: Suhrkamp.

Goddard, G. V., & McIntyre, D. D. (1972). Some properties of a lasting epileptogenic trace kindled by repeated electrical stimulation of the amygdala in mammals. In L. V. Lattinen & K. E. Livingston (Eds.), *Surgical Approaches in Psychiatry* (pp. 109–117). Baltimore, MD: University Park Press.

Goldstein, E., McDonnell, C., Atchley, R., Dorado, K., Bedford, C., Brown, R. L., & Zgierska, A. E. (2019). The impact of psychological interventions on posttraumatic stress disorder and pain symptoms: a systematic review and meta-analysis. *Clin J Pain*, *35*(8), 703–712. https://doi.org/10.1097/ajp.0000000000000730.

Gopnik, A., Capps, L., & Meltzoff, A. N. (1993 [2000]). Early theories of mind: what the theory theory can tell us about autism. In S. Baron-Cohen, H. Tager-Flusberg, & D. J. Cohen (Eds.), *Understanding Other Minds. Perspectives from Developmental Cognitive Neuroscience* (pp. 50–72). Oxford: Oxford University Press.

Gowers, W. R. (1904). A lecture on lumbago: its lessons and analogues: delivered at the national hospital for the paralysed and epileptic. *Br Med J*, *1*(2246), 117–121. www.ncbi.nlm.nih.gov/pubmed/20761312.

Grabe, H. J., Rainermann, S., Spitzer, C., Gansicke, M., & Freyberger, H. J. (2000). The relationship between dimensions of alexithymia and dissociation. *Psychother Psychosom*, *69*(3), 128–131. https://doi.org/10.1159/000012380.

Greco, M. (2000). Homo Vacuus: Alexithymie und das neoliberale Gebot des Selbstseins. In U. Bröckling, S. Krasmann, & T. Lemke (Hrsg.), *Gouvernementalität der Gegenwart* (pp. 265–285). Frankfurt am Main: Suhrkamp.

Green, A. (1983). *Narcissisme de vie, narcissisme de mort*. Paris: Minuit.

Green, A. (1993). Die tote Mutter. *Psyche – Z Psychoanal*, *47*, 205–240.

Green, A. (2017). *Illusionen und Desillusion der psychoanalytischen Arbeit*. Frankfurt am Main: Brandes & Apsel.

Greenberg, L. (2015). *Emotion-Focused Therapy: Coaching Clients to Work Through Their Feelings* (2nd ed.). Washington, DC: American Psychological Association.

Gretenkord, S., Kostka, J. K., Hartung, H., Watznauer, K., Fleck, D., Minier-Toribio, A., Spehr, M., & Hanganu-Opatz, I. L. (2019). Coordinated electrical activity in the olfactory bulb gates the oscillatory entrainment of entorhinal networks in neonatal mice. *PLoS Biol*, *17*(1), e2006994. https://doi.org/10.1371/journal.pbio.2006994.

Grosse Wiesmann, C., Friederici, A. D., Singer, T., & Steinbeise, N. (2020). Two systems for thinking about others' thoughts in the developing brain. *PNAS*, *117*(12), 6928–6935.

Grossmann, K. E., Grossmann, K. E., & Waters, E. (Eds.). (2006). *Attachment from Infancy to Adulthood. The Major Longitudinal Studies*. New York and London: Guilford.

Grünewald-Zemsch, G. (2019). *Die psychoanalytische Ausbildungssupervision – "Thinking under fire". Geschichte, Methoden und Konflikte*. Gießen: Psychosozial Verlag.

Grynberg, D., & Pollatos, O. (2015). Alexithymia modulates the experience of the rubber hand illusion. *Front Hum Neurosci*, *9*, 357. https://doi.org/10.3389/fnhum.2015.00357.

Gubb, K. (2013). Psychosomatics today: a review of contemporary theory and practice. *Psychanal Rev*, *100*(1), 103–142.

Gündel, H., Ceballos-Baumann, A. O., & von Rad, M. (2000). Aktuelle Perspektiven der Alexithymie. *Nervenarzt*, *71*(3), 151–163.

Gurevich, H. (2008). The language of absence. *Int J Psychoanal*, *89*, 561–578.

Gutwinski-Jeggle, J. (2017). *Unsichtbares sehen – Unsagbares sagen. Unbewusste Prozesse in der psychoanalytischen Begegnung*. Gießen: Psychosozial-Verlag.

Gypas, R. (2021). *Gruppenpsychotherapie bei Angstpatienten in einer Tagesklinik – Einfluss der Mentalisierungsfähigkeit auf den Behandlungsverlauf*. Fakultät für Gesundheit, Witten: Universität Witten/Herdecke.

Hadar, B. (2008). The body of shame in the circle of the group. *Group Anal, 41*(2), 163–179.
Ham, J., & Tronick, E. (2006). Infant resilience to the stress of the still-face: infant and maternal psychophysiology are related. *Ann N Y Acad Sci, 1094*, 297–302. https://doi.org/1094/1/297 [pii];10.1196/annals.1376.038.
Ham, J., & Tronick, E. (2009). Relational psychophysiology: lessons from mother-infant physiology research on dyadically expanded states of consciousness. *Psychother Res, 19*(6), 619–632. https://doi.org/908926018 [pii];10.1080/10503300802609672.
Hamlin, P. G. (1943). Camptocormia: hysterical bent back of soldiers. Report of two cases. *Mil Surg, 92*, 295–300.
Hartmann, M., Finkenzeller, C., Boehlen, F. H., Wagenlechner, P., Peters-Klimm, F., & Herzog, W. (2018). Psychosomatische Sprechstunde in der Hausarztpraxis – ein neues Kooperationsmodell von Psychosomatik und Allgemeinmedizin. *PPmP – Psychosomatik Psychotherapie Medizinische Psychologie* (8). https://doi.org/10.1055/a-0668-1019.
Hartung, T., & Steinbrecher, M. (2018). From somatic pain to psychic pain: the body in the psychoanalytic field. *Int J Psychoanal, 99*(1), 159–180. https://doi.org/10.1111/1745-8315.12651.
Haslam-Hopwood, G. T. G., Allen, J. G., Stein, A., & Bleiberg, E. (2006). Enhancing mentalizing through psycho-education. In J. G. Allen & P. Fonagy (Eds.), *Handbook of Mentalization-Based Treatment* (pp. 249–267). Chichester: John Wiley & Sons.
Hausberg, M. C., Schulz, H., Piegler, T., Happach, C. G., Klopper, M., Brutt, A. L., Sammet, I., & Andreas, S. (2012). Is a self-rated instrument appropriate to assess mentalization in patients with mental disorders? Development and first validation of the mentalization questionnaire (MZQ). *Psychother Res, 22*(6), 699–709. https://doi.org/10.1080/10503307.2012.709325.
Hausteiner-Wiehle, C., Henningsen, P., Häuser, W., Herrmann, M., Ronel, J., Sattel, H., & Schäfert, R. (2013). *Umgang mit Patienten mit nicht-spezifischen, funktionellen und somatoformen Körperbeschwerden: S3-Leitlinien mit Quellentexten, Praxismaterialien und Patientenleitlinie.* Stuttgart: Schattauer.
Hausteiner-Wiehle, C., & Hungerer, S. (2020). Factitious disorders in everyday clinical practice. *Dtsch Arztebl, 117*, 452–459. https://doi.org/10.3228/aerzteb l.2020.0452.
Hausteiner-Wiehle, C., & Sokollu, F. (2011). Magical thinking in somatoform disorders: an exploratory study among patients with suspected allergies. *Psychopathology, 44*(5), 283–288. https://doi.org/000322795 [pii];10.1159/000322795.
Hecke, D., Brand, T., Rietz, C., & Schultz-Venrath, U. (2016). Prozess-Outcome-Studie zum Gruppenklima in psychodynamischer (PDGT) und mentalisierungsbasierter Gruppenpsychotherapie (MBT-G) in einem tagesklinischen Setting – Was verändert wen? *Gruppenpsychother Gruppendynamik, 52*(2), 175–193.
Hecker, E. (1893). Ueber larvirte und abortive Angstzustände bei Neurasthenie. *Centralbl Neurol Psychiat, 16*, 565–572.
Heim, C., Young, L. J., Newport, D. J., Mletzko, T., Miller, A. H., & Nemeroff, C. B. (2009). Lower CSF oxytocin concentrations in women with a history of childhood abuse. *Mol Psychiatry, 14*, 954–958. https://doi.org/mp2008112 [pii];10.1038/mp.2008.112.
Henningsen, P. (2003). Der Kampf um Schmerz: Gesprächsanalyse zur interpersonellen Repräsentanz somatoformer Schmerzen. *Psychother Soz, 5*(3), 194–202.
Henningsen, P. (2021). *Allgemeine Psychosomatische Medizin. Krankheiten des verkörperten Selbst im 21. Jahrhundert.* Berlin: Springer.
Henningsen, P. (2023, February 22). *Cancel Culture in der Medizin. Viel mehr als nur Biologie: Bei der Therapie von Syndromen wie Long Covid könnte die Psychosomatik einen wichtigen Beitrag leisten – wenn man sie denn ließe.* München: Süddeutsche Zeitung.

Henrich, J. (2020). *The Weirdest People in the World: How the West Became Psychologically Peculiar and Particularly Prosperous*. New York: Allen Lane, Penguin Random House.
Henrich, J., Heine, S. J., & Norenzayan, A. (2010). Most people are not WEIRD. *Nature*, *466*(7302), 29. https://doi.org/10.1038/466029a.
Hielscher, E., Whitford, T. J., Scott, J. G., & Zopf, R. (2019). When the body is the target – representations of one's own body and bodily sensations in self-harm: a systematic review. *Neurosci Biobehav Rev*, *101*, 85–112. https://doi.org/10.1016/j.neubiorev.2019.03.007.
Hill, D. (2015). *Affect Regulation Theory – A Clinical Model*. New York and London: Norton & Company.
Hiller, W., & Rief, W. (2014). Die Abschaffung der somatoformen Störungen durch DSM-5 – ein akademischer Schildbürgerstreich? *Psychotherapeut*, *59*, 448–455. https://doi.org/ https://doi.org/10.1007/s00278-014-1081-1.
Hiller, W., Rief, W., & Brähler, E. (2006). Somatization in the population: from mild bodily misperceptions to disabling symptoms. *Soc Psychiatry Psychiatr Epidemiol*, *41*(9), 704–712. https://doi.org/10.1007/s00127-006-0082-y.
Hirschmüller, A., & Kimmig, R. (1996). "Pénétration pacifique"? Zur Rezeption der Psychoanalyse in der deutschen Psychiatrie der zwanziger Jahre. *Fundamenta Psychiatrica*, *10*, 67–72.
Hoff, H., Ringel, E., Cremerius, J., Elhardt, S., Hose, W., Klüwer, R., Seitz, W., Jores, A., Schultz, J. H., Baumeyer, F., Kühnel, G., Schwidder, W., & Binswanger, H. (1958). Stellungnahmen zum Problem der Spezifität der Persönlichkeitstypen und der Konflikte in der psycho-somatischen Medizin. *Psychosom Med*, *4*, 168–186.
Hoffmann, S. O., & Eckhardt-Henn, A. (2017). Konversion, Dissoziation und Somatisierung – Abgrenzbare dynamische Modelle mit Schnittmenge. In A. Eckhardt-Henn & C. Spitzer (Hrsg.), *Dissoziative Bewusstseinsstörungen. Grundlagen – Klinik – Therapie* (pp. 23–44). Stuttgart: Schattauer.
Holmes, G. P., Kaplan, J. E., Gantz, N. M., Komaroff, A. L., Schonberger, L. B., Straus, S. E., Jones, J. F., Dubois, R. E., Cunningham-Rundles, C., & Pahwa, S. (1988). Chronic fatigue syndrome: a working case definition. *Ann Intern Med*, *108*(3), 387–389. www.ncbi.nlm.nih.gov/pubmed/2829679.
Holodynski, M. (2006). *Emotionen – Entwicklung und Regulation*. Heidelberg: Springer Medizin Verlag.
Hrdy, S. B. (2000). *Mother Nature: Maternal Instincts and How They Shape the Human Species*. New York, NY: Ballantine Books.
Husserl, E. (1900 [1922]). *Logische Untersuchungen*. Halle: Niemeyer.
Husserl, E. (1973). *Zur Phänomenologie der Intersubjektivität: Texte aus dem Nachlass; Zweiter Teil, 1921–1928. Husserliana XIV*. Kern: Martinus Nijhoff.
Jackson, J. C., Watts, J., Henry, T. R., List, J. M., Forkel, R., Mucha, P. J., Greenhill, S. J., Gray, R. D., & Lindquist, K. A. (2019). Emotion semantics show both cultural variation and universal structure. *Science*, *366*(6472), 1517–1522. https://doi.org/10.1126/science.aaw8160.
Jacobs, T. J. (1973). Posture, gesture, and movement in the analyst: cues to interpretation and countertransference. *J Am Psychoanal Assoc*, *21*, 77–92.
Jaeger, P. (2019). The ideas of the Paris Psychosomatic School. *Int J Psychoanal*, *100*(4), 754–768. https://doi.org/10.1080/00207578.2019.1590779.
Jank, R., Liegl, G., Böckle, M., Vockner, B., & Pieh, C. (2017). Häufigkeit somatoformer Syndrome in der Allgemeinmedizin. *Z Psychosom Med Psychother*, *63*, 202–212.

Janneck, M., & Krenz, I. (2018). Mustererkennung und diagnostische Fehler. In U. Lamparter & H. U. Schmidt (Hrsg.), *Wirklich psychisch bedingt? Somatische Differenzialdiagnosen in der Psychosomatischen Medizin und Psychotherapie*. Stuttgart: Schattauer.

Janssen, P. L. (2017). *Als Psychoanalytiker in der Psychosomatischen Medizin. Eine persönliche berufspolitische Geschichte der Psychotherapien, Psychiatrie und Psychosomatik*. Gießen: Psychosozial-Verlag.

Janssen, P. L., & Wienen, G. (1995). Group analysis with ulcerative colitis and regional ileitis: the discovery of the scream. *Group Anal*, 28, 87–96.

Jappe, G., & Strehlow, B. (Hrsg.). (1998). *Eugenio Gaddini: "Das Ich ist vor allem ein körperliches" – Beiträge zur Psychoanalyse der ersten Strukturen*. Tübingen: Edition Diskord.

Jensen, T. W., Høgenhaug, S. S., Kjølbye, M., & Bloch, M. S. (2021). Mentalizing bodies: explicit mentalizing without words in psychotherapy. *Front Psychol*, 12, 577702. https://doi.org/10.3389/fpsyg.2021.577702.

Joksimovic, L., Bergstein, V., & Rademacher, J. (2019). *Mentalisierungsbasierte Psychotherapie und Beratung von Geflüchteten. Grundlagen und Interventionen für die Praxis*. Stuttgart: Kohlhammer.

Jurist, E. (2018). *Minding Emotions – Cultivating Mentalization in Psychotherapy*. New York and London: Guilford.

Jurist, E. (2022). Mentalizing from/to/with the body. In J. Mills (Ed.), *Psychoanalysis and the Mind-Body Problem* (pp. 186–203). Milton Park and New York: Routledge.

Karterud, S. (2015a). *Mentalization-Based Group Therapy (MBT-G)*. Oxford: Oxford University Press.

Karterud, S. (2015b). On structure and leadership in MBT-G and group analysis. *Group Anal*, 48(2), 137–149.

Karterud, S., Folmo, E., & Kongerslev, M. T. (2019). Personality and the group matrix. *Group Anal*, 52(4), 503–519. https://doi.org/10.1177/0533316418824210.

Katz, L. F., & Windecker-Nelson, B. (2004). Parental meta-emotion philosophy in families with conduct-problem children: links with peer relations. *J Abnorm Child Psychol*, 32(4), 385–398. https://doi.org/10.1023/b:jacp.0000030292.36168.30.

Katznelson, H. (2014). Reflective functioning: a review. *Clin Psychol Rev*, 34(2), 107–117. https://doi.org/10.1016/j.cpr.2013.12.003.

Kazantzakis, N. (1965). *Report to Greco*. New York: Simon & Schuster.

Kealy, D., Rice, S. M., Ogrodniczuk, J. S., & Cox, D. W. (2018). Investigating the link between pathological narcissism and somatization. *J Nerv Ment Dis*, 206(12), 964–967. https://doi.org/10.1097/nmd.0000000000000903.

Keller, H. (2014 [2018]). Introduction: understanding relationships – what we would need to know to conceptualize attachment as the cultural solution of a universal developmental task. In H. Otto & H. Keller (Eds.), *Different Faces of Attachment. Cultural Variations on a Universal Human Need*. Cambridge: Cambridge University Press.

Keller, H. (2017). Cultural and historical diversity in early relationship formation. *Eur J Dev Psychol*, 14(6), 700–713. https://doi.org/10.1080.

Kestenberg, J. S. (1971). From organ-object imagery to self and object representation. In J. B. McDevitt & C. F. Settlage (Eds.), *Separation – Individuation. Essays in Honor of Margaret S. Mahler* (pp. 75–99). New York, NY: International Universities Press.

Kinnaird, E., Stewart, C., & Tchanturia, K. (2019). Investigating alexithymia in autism: a systematic review and meta-analysis. *Eur Psychiatry*, 55, 80–89. https://doi.org/10.1016/j.eurpsy.2018.09.004.

Kirmayer, L. J., & Ramstead, M. J. D. (2017). Embodiment and enactment in cultural psychiatry. In C. Durt, T. Fuchs, & C. Tewes (Eds.), *Embodiment, Enaction, and Culture* (pp. 397–422). Cambridge, MA and London: The MIT Press.

Klüwer, B. (2011). Psychotherapie mit dem Pferd – Bindungsrelevante Wahrnehmungsübungen auf körpersprachlicher Ebene. In U. Schultz-Venrath (Hrsg.), *Psychotherapien in Tageskliniken. Methoden, Konzepte, Strukturen* (pp. 151–165). Berlin: Medizinisch Wissenschaftliche Verlagsgesellschaft.

Kobylinska-Dehe, E. (2019). Vom Leib zum phantasmatischen Körper – Bewegung, Berührung, Phantasie. *Psyche – Z Psychoanal, 73*, 523–545. https://doi.org/10.21706/ps-73-7-523.

Koenig, A. M., Karabatsiakis, A., Stoll, T., Wilker, S., Hennessy, T., Hill, M. M., & Kolassa, I. T. (2018). Serum profile changes in postpartum women with a history of childhood maltreatment: a combined metabolite and lipid fingerprinting study. *Sci Rep, 8*(1), 3468. https://doi.org/10.1038/s41598-018-21763-6.

Koerfer, A., Köhle, K., & Obliers, R. (1994). Zur Evaluation von Arzt-Patienten-Kommunikation. Perspektiven einer angewandten Diskursethik in der Medizin. In A. Redder & I. Wiese (Eds.), *Medizinische Kommunikation: Diskurspraxis, Diskursethik, Diskursanalyse* (pp. 53–116). Opladen: Westdeutscher Verlag.

Kollbrunner, J. (2001). *Der kranke Freud*. Stuttgart: Klett-Cotta.

Kovacs, A. M., Teglas, E., & Endress, A. D. (2010). The social sense: susceptibility to others' beliefs in human infants and adults. *Science, 330*(6012), 1830–1834. https://doi.org/10.1126/science.1190792.

Krause, R. (1983). Zur Onto- und Phylogenese des Affektsystems und ihrer Beziehungen zu psychischen Störungen. *Psyche – Z Psychoanal, 37*, 1016–1043.

Krause, R. (2012). *Allgemeine psychodynamische Behandlungs- und Krankheitslehre. Grundlagen und Modelle*. Stuttgart: Kohlhammer.

Krause, R. (2016). Auf der Suche nach dem "missing link" zwischen Analytiker und Analysand, ihren Körpern und ihrer gemeinsamen Seele. Oder wie ist der intersubjektive Raum konstruiert und tapeziert? In K. Nohr & S. Leikert (Hrsg.), *Zum Phänomen der Rührung in Psychoanalyse und Musik – Eine Publikation der Deutschen Gesellschaft für Psychoanalyse und Musik*. Gießen: Psychosozial-Verlag.

Kroll, S. (1932). Eine ungewöhnliche Somatisation. Eine geheime Todesklausel. *Psychoanal Praxis, 2*, 53.

Krystal, H. (1978). Trauma and affects. *Psychoanal Study Child, 33*, 81–116. www.ncbi.nlm.nih.gov/pubmed/715118.

Krystal, H. (1988). *Integration and Self Healing. Affect, Trauma and Alexithymia*. New York, NY: Hillsdale.

Küchenhoff, J. (2012). *Körper und Sprache. Theoretische und klinische Beiträge zu einem intersubjektiven Verständnis des Körpererlebens*. Gießen: Psychosozial-Verlag.

Küchenhoff, J. (2018). Scham und Beschämung – auch in psychoanalytischen Institutionen. *Forum der Psychoanalyse, 34*, 329–342. https://doi.org/https://doi.org/10.1007/s00451-017-0293-8.

Küchenhoff, J. (2019). Intercorporeity and body language: the semiotics of mental suffering expressed through the body. *Int J Psychoanal, 100*(4), 769–791. https://doi.org/10.1080/00207578.2019.1590780.

Kütemeyer, M., & Masuhr, K. F. (2013). Körperliche Empfindungen als Leitfaden der Diagnostik in der Psychiatrie, Neurologie und Psychosomatik. *Ärztliche Psychotherapie, 8*, 229–237.

Kütemeyer, M., Masuhr, K. F., & Schultz-Venrath, U. (2005). Kommunikative Anfallsunterbrechung – Zum ärztlichen Umgang mit Patienten im Status pseudoepilepticus. *Z Epileptol, 18,* 71–77.
Kütemeyer, M., & Schultz-Venrath, U. (1989). Frühe psychoanalytische Schmerzauffassungen. *PPmP – Psychosomatik Psychotherapie Medizinische Psychologie, 39,* 185–192.
Kütemeyer, M., & Schultz-Venrath, U. (1996). Neurologie. In R. H. Adler, J. M. Herrmann, K. Köhle, O. W. Schonecke, T. von Uexküll, & W. Wesiack (Hrsg.), *Psychosomatische Medizin* (5. Aufl., pp. 1067–1086). München: Urban & Schwarzenberg.
Kütemeyer, M., & Schultz-Venrath, U. (1997). Pictures of disease in neurology. In T. von Uexküll (Ed.), *Psychosomatic Medicine* (pp. 704–722). München: Urban & Schwarzenberg.
Lamparter, U., & Schmidt, H. U. (Hrsg.). (2018). *Wirklich psychisch bedingt? Somatische Differenzialdiagnosen in der Psychosomatischen Medizin und Psychotherapie.* Stuttgart: Schattauer.
Lancy, D. F. (2008). *The Anthropology of Childhood: Cherubs, Chattel, Changelings.* Cambridge: Cambridge University Press.
Landauer, K. (1991). *Theorie der Affekte und andere Schriften zur Ich-Organisation, herausgegeben von Hans-Joachim Rothe.* Frankfurt am Main: Fischer Taschenbuch Verlag.
Lane, R. D., & Schwartz, G. E. (1987). Levels of emotional awarness: a cognitive-developmental theory and its application psychopathology. *Am J Psychiatry, 144,* 113–143.
Lane, R. D., Weihs, K. L., Herring, A., Hishaw, A., & Smith, R. (2015). Affective agnosia: expansion of the alexithymia construct and a new opportunity to integrate and extend Freud's legacy. *Neurosci Biobehav Rev, 55,* 594–611. https://doi.org/10.1016/j.neubiorev.2015.06.007.
Lausberg, H. (2018). Selbstberührungen und andere nonverbale Zeichen im ärztlichen Gespräch. Non-, para- und verbale Kommunikationsaspekte. In J. Jünger (Hrsg.), *Ärztliche Kommunikation – Praxisbuch zum Masterplan Medizinstudium 2020* (pp. 64–69). Stuttgart: Schattauer.
Lecours, S., & Bouchard, M. A. (1997). Dimensions of mentalization: outlining levels of psychic transformation. *Int J Psychoanal, 78*(Pt 5), 855–875. www.ncbi.nlm.nih.gov/pubmed/9459091.
LeDoux, J. (1996). *The Emotional Brain.* New York: Simon and Schuster.
Lee Masson, H., Pillet, I., Amelynck, S., Van De Plas, S., Hendriks, M., Op de Beeck, H., & Boets, B. (2019). Intact neural representations of affective meaning of touch but lack of embodied resonance in autism: a multi-voxel pattern analysis study. *Mol Autism, 10,* 39. https://doi.org/10.1186/s13229-019-0294-0.
Lee, Y. T., & Tsai, S. J. (2010). The mirror neuron system may play a role in the pathogenesis of mass hysteria. *Med Hypotheses, 74*(2), 244–245. https://doi.org/10.1016/j.mehy.2009.09.031.
Lehtonen, J. (2006). In search of the early mental organization of the infant: contributions from the neurophysiology of nursing. In M. Mancia (Ed.), *Psychoanalysis and Neuroscience* (pp. 419–431). New York: Springer.
Leikert, S. (2016). Das kinästhetische Unbewusste in der psychoanalytischen Arbeit. Die Methode der freien Körperassoziation. In S. Walz-Pawlita, B. Unruh, & B. Janta (Hrsg.), *Körper-Sprachen* (pp. 153–166). Gießen: Psychosozial-Verlag.
Leikert, S. (2019a). *Das sinnliche Selbst: Körpergedächtnis und psychoanalytische Behandlungstechnik.* Frankfurt am Main: Brandes & Apsel.

Leikert, S. (2019b). Wie viel Body überträgt sich via Internet? Leibliche Aspekte der Behandlungstechniken im klassischen Setting und in der Teleanalyse. *Psychoanalyse im Widerspruch, 61*(31), 27–47.

Leikert, S. (Hrsg.). (2022). *Das körperliche Unbewusste in der psychoanalytischen Behandlungstechnik*. Frankfurt am Main: Brandes & Apsel.

Leikert, S. (2023). Die analytische Haltung und das körperliche Unbewusste. Bemerkungen zu einer Behandlung technischen Kontroverse. In B. Nissen, U. Zeitzschel, W. Hegener, & U. Karacaoglan (Hrsg.), *Jahrbuch der Psychoanalyse – Analytische Haltung im Umbruch?* (Vol. 86, pp. 37–65). Gießen: Psychosozial-Verlag.

Leithner-Dziubas, K., Bluml, V., Naderer, A., Tmej, A., & Fischer-Kern, M. (2010). Mentalisierungsfähigkeit und Bindung bei Patientinnen mit chronischen Unterbauchschmerzen – eine Pilotstudie. *Z Psychosom Med Psychother, 56*(2), 179–190. www.ncbi.nlm.nih.gov/pubmed/20623462.

Lemma, A. (2014). *Minding the Body. The Body in Psychoanalysis and Beyond*. London: Institute of Psychoanalysis.

Leuschner, W. (2017). Paul Schilders Körperbild-Modell und der "body intercourse". *Psyche – Z Psychoanal, 71*(2), 123–150. https://doi.org/10.21706/ps-71-2-123.

Leuzinger-Bohleber, M., & Pfeifer, R. (2013). Embodiment: Den Körper in der Seele entdecken – Ein altes Problem und ein revolutionäres Konzept. Thematische Einführung und Überblick über die Beiträge dieses Bandes. In M. Leuzinger-Bohleber, R. N. Emde, & R. Pfeifer (Hrsg.), *Embodiment – Ein innovatives Konzept für Entwicklungsforschung und Psychoanalyse* (pp. 39–74). Göttingen: Vandenhoeck & Ruprecht.

Leuzinger-Bohleber, M., & Pfeifer, R. (2016). Embodiment. In S. Walz-Pawlita, B. Unruh, & B. Janta (Hrsg.), *Körper-Sprachen* (pp. 125–140). Gießen: Psychosozial-Verlag.

Levine, H. B., Reed, G. S., & Scarfone, D. (2013). *Unrepresented States and the Construction of Meaning. Clinical and Theoretical Contributions*. London: Karnac.

Levy, J., & Feldman, R. (2019). Synchronous interactions foster empathy. *J Exp Neurosci, 13*, 1179069519865799. https://doi.org/10.1177/1179069519865799.

Lieberman, M. D. (2007). Social cognitive neuroscience: a review of core processes. *Ann Rev Psychol, 58*, 1811–1831.

Lind, A. B., Delmar, C., & Nielsen, K. (2014). Struggling in an emotional avoidance culture: a qualitative study of stress as a predisposing factor for somatoform disorders. *J Psychosom Res, 76*(2), 94–98. https://doi.org/10.1016/j.jpsychores.2013.11.019.

Lissauer, H. (1890). Ein Fall von Seelenblindheit nebst einem Beitrag zur Theorie derselben. *Arch Psychiatrie, 21*, 222–270.

Loewald, H. W. (1980). *Papers on Psychoanalysis*. New Haven, CT: Yale University Press.

Lombardi, R. (2008). The body in the analytic session: focusing on the body-mind link. *Int J Psychanal, 89*, 89–109.

Lombardi, R. (2023). Übertragung auf den Körper und die Sprachregister der Analysesitzung. In B. Nissen, U. Zeitzschel, W. Hegener, & U. Karacaoglan (Hrsg.), *Jahrbuch der Psychoanalyse - Analytische Haltung im Umbruch?* (Vol. 86, pp. 67–75). Gießen: Psychosozial-Verlag.

Lumley, M. A., Asselin, L. A., & Norman, S. (1997). Alexithymia in chronic pain patients. *Compr Psychiatry, 38*(3), 160–165. www.ncbi.nlm.nih.gov/pubmed/9154372.

Luyten, P. (2019). *Working with Somatoform Patients: An Integrative, Neuroscience Informed Perspective the Future of Neuroscience, Attachment and Mentalizing – from Research to Clinical Practice*. London: UCL.

Luyten, P., Campbell, C., Allison, C., & Fonagy, P. (2020). The mentalizing approach to psychopathology: state of the art and future directions. *Annu Rev Clin Psychol, 16*, 297–325.
Luyten, P., & Fonagy, P. (2015). The neurobiology of mentalizing. *Pers Disord, 6*(4), 366–379.
Luyten, P., & Fonagy, P. (2016). An integrative, attachment-based approach to the management and treatment of patients with persistent somatic complaints. In R. Hunter & R. Maunder (Eds.), *Improving Patient Treatment with Attachment Theory: A Guide for Primary Care Practitioners and Specialists* (pp. 127–144). Springer International Publishing. https://doi.org/DOI 10.1007/978-3-319-23300-0_9.
Luyten, P., & Fonagy, P. (2019). Mentalizing and trauma. In A. Bateman & P. Fonagy (Eds.), *Handbook of Mentalizing in Mental Health Practice* (2nd ed., pp. 79–99). Washington, DC: American Psychiatric Association Publishing.
Luyten, P., Houdenhove, V. B., Lemma, A., Target, M., & Fonagy, P. (2012). A mentalization-based approach to the understanding and treatment of functional somatic disorders. *Psychoanal Psychother, 26*(2), 121–140.
Luyten, P., Malcorps, S., Fonagy, P., & Ensink, K. (2019). Assessment of mentalizing. In A. Bateman & P. Fonagy (Eds.), *Handbook of Mentalizing in Mental Health Pracice* (pp. 37–62). Washington, DC: American Psychiatric Association Publishing.
Luyten, P., Mayes, L. C., Nijssens, L., & Fonagy, P. (2017). The parental reflective functioning questionnaire: development and preliminary validation. *PLoS One, 12*(5). https://doi.org/https://doi.org/10.1371/journal.pone.0176218.
Mackes, N. K., Golm, D., Sarkar, S., Kumsta, R., Rutter, M., Fairchild, G., Mehta, M. A., Sonuga-Barke, E. J. S., & Team, E. R. A. Y. A. F.-u. (2020). Early childhood deprivation is associated with alterations in adult brain structure despite subsequent environmental enrichment. *Proc Natl Acad Sci U S A, 117*(1), 641–649. https://doi.org/10.1073/pnas.1911264116.
MacLean, W. E., Jr., Jeglum, S. R., Hickey, E. J., & Ament, A. (2023). Head-banging in early childhood: the occurrence of physical injury. *Clin Pediatr (Phila)*, 99228221150693. https://doi.org/10.1177/00099228221150693.
Main, M., & Goldwyn, R. (1994). *Adult Attachment Scoring and Classification Systems*. Berkeley, CA: Department of Psychology, University of California Berkeley.
Main, M., & Solomon, J. (1986). Discovery of a new, insecure-disorganized/disoriented attachment pattern. In T. B. Brazelton & M. Yogman (Eds.), *Affective Development in Infancy* (pp. 95–124). Norwood, NJ: Ablex.
Malloch, S., & Trevarthen, C. (2009). *Communicative Musicality: Exploring the Basis of Human Companionship*. Oxford: Oxford University Press.
Margoles, M. S. (1983). Stress neuromyelopathic pain syndrome (SNPS): report of 333 patients. *J Neurol Orthop Surg, 4*, 317–322.
Marty, M. (1958). Die "allergische Objektbeziehung". In K. Brede (Ed.), *Einführung in die psychosomatische Medizin*. Frankfurt am Main: Syndikat.
Marty, M., & de M'Uzan, M. (1963 [1978]). Das operative Denken ("Pensée operaoire"). *Psyche – Z Psychoanal, 32*, 974–984.
Marty, P. (1991). *Mentalisation et Psychosomatique*. Paris: Laboratoire Delagrange.
Marty, P., & de M'Uzan, M. (1963). La 'pensée opératoire'. *Revue Française de Psychanalyse (suppl), 27*, 1345–1356.
Marty, P., de M'Uzan, M., & David, C. (1963). *L'investigation psychosomatique*. Paris: Presses Universitaires de France.
Marty, P., de M'Uzan, M., & David, C. (1979). Der Fall Dora und der psychosomatische Gesichtspunkt. *Psyche – Z Psychoanal, 33*(09/10).

Matacic, C. (2019). What is love? It depends which language you speak. *Science.* https://doi.org/10.1126/science.aba6465.

Mattila, A. K., Kronholm, E., Jula, A., Salminen, J. K., Koivisto, A. M., Mielonen, R. L., & Joukamaa, M. (2008). Alexithymia and somatization in general population. *Psychosom Med, 70*(6), 716–722. https://doi.org/10.1097/PSY.0b013e31816ffc39.

Maunder, R. G., & Hunter, J. J. (2001). Attachment and psychosomatic medicine: developmental contributions to stress and disease. *Psychosom Med, 63*(4), 556–567. www.ncbi.nlm.nih.gov/pubmed/11485109.

Maunder, R. G., & Hunter, J. J. (2008). Attachment relationships as determinants of physical health. *J Am Acad Psychoanal Dyn Psychiatry, 36*(1), 11–32.

Maunder, R. G., Hunter, J. J., Atkinson, L., Steiner, M., Wazana, A., Fleming, A. S., Moss, E., Gaudreau, H., Meaney, M. J., & Levitan, R. D. (2017). An attachment-based model of the relationship between childhood adversity and somatization in children and adults. *Psychosom Med, 79*(5), 506–513. https://doi.org/10.1097/psy.0000000000000437.

May, U. (2019). Müssen wir unser Bild von Freud verändern? Überlegungen zu Kurt R. Eisslers Interviews im Freud-Archiv der Library of Congress. *Luzifer Amor – Zeitschrift zur Geschichte der Psychoanalyse, 32*(63), 90–100.

McDougall, J. (1974). The psychosoma and the psychoanalytic process. *Int Rev Psychoanal, 1*, 437–460.

McDougall, J. (1995). *The Many Faces of Eros. A Psychoanalytic Exploration of Human Sexuality.* London: Free Association Books.

McDougall, J. (1997). *Die Couch ist kein Prokrustesbett. Zur Psychoanalyse der menschlichen Sexualität.* Stuttgart: Verlag Internationale Psychoanalyse.

McLaughlin, K. A., Sheridan, M. A., & Lambert, H. K. (2014). Childhood adversity and neural development: deprivation and threat as distinct dimensions of early experience. *Neurosci Biobehav Rev, 47*, 578–591. https://doi.org/10.1016/j.neubiorev.2014.10.012.

Meaney, M. J., & Szyf, M. (2005). Environmental programming of stress responses through DNA methylation: life at the interface between a dynamic environment and a fixed genome. *Dialogues Clin Neurosci, 7*(2), 103–123. https://doi.org/10.31887/DCNS.2005.7.2/mmeaney.

Meins, E. (1999). Sensitivity, security and internal working models: bridging the transmission gap. *Attach Hum Dev, 1*(3), 325–342. www.ncbi.nlm.nih.gov/pubmed/11708230.

Meltzoff, A. N. (2007). 'Like me': a foundation for social cognition. *Dev Sci, 10*(1), 126–134. https://doi.org/10.1111/j.1467-7687.2007.00574.x.

Meltzoff, A. N., & Moore, M. K. (1977). Imitation of facial and manual gestures by human neonates. *Science, 198*, 75–78.

Menard, J. L., & Hakvoort, R. M. (2007). Variations of maternal care alter offspring levels of behavioural defensiveness in adulthood: evidence for a threshold model. *Behav Brain Res, 176*(2), 302–313. https://doi.org/S0166-4328(06)00556-0 [pii];10.1016/j.bbr.2006.10.014.

Menninger, K. A. (1934). Polysurgery and polysurgical addiction. *Psychoanal Q, 3*(2), 173–199. https://doi.org/10.1080/21674086.1934.11925205.

Mentzos, S. (2009). *Lehrbuch der Psychodynamik. Die Funktion der Dysfunktionalität psychischer Störungen.* Göttingen: Vandenhoeck & Ruprecht.

Merleau-Ponty, M. (1945 [2012]). *Phenomenology of Perception* (D. Landes, Trans.). London: Routledge.

Merleau-Ponty, M. (1966). *Humanismus und Terror 2.* Frankfurt am Main: Suhrkamp.

Mertens, W. (2019). Wie zuverlässig und wirklichkeitsgetreu sind unsere Erinnerungen? Psychoanalytische Überlegungen zum Gedächtnis aus klassischer und zeitgenössischer Sicht. *Psyche – Z Psychoanal, 73*(12), 974–1001.

Miller, J. G., Vrticka, P., Cui, X., Shrestha, S., Hosseini, S. M. H., Baker, J. M., & Reiss, A. L. (2019). Inter-brain synchrony in mother-child dyads during cooperation: an fNIRS hyperscanning study. *Neuropsychologia, 124*, 117–124. https://doi.org/10.1016/j.neuropsychologia.2018.12.021.

Miller, W. R., & Rollnick, S. (2015 [2013]). *Motivierende Gesprächsführung* (3. Aufl.). Freiburg i.Br.: Lambertus.

Monsen, K., & Monsen, T. J. (2000). Chronic pain and psychodynamic body therapy. *Psychol Psychother, 37*, 257–269. https://doi.org/https://doi.org/10.1037/h0087658.

Moore, S., Kinnear, M., & Freeman, L. (2020). Autistic doctors: overlooked assets to medicine. *Lancet – Psychiatry, 7*, 306–307.

Moran, D. (2017). Intercorporeality and intersubjectivity: a phenomenological exploration of embodiment. In C. Durt, T. Fuchs, & C. Tewes (Eds.), *Embodiment, Enaction, and Culture* (pp. 25–46). Cambridge, MA/London: MIT Press.

Moriguchi, Y., Ohnishi, T., Lane, R. D., Maeda, M., Mori, T., Nemoto, K., Matsuda, H., & Komaki, G. (2006). Impaired self-awareness and theory of mind: an fMRI study of mentalizing in alexithymia. *Neuroimage, 32*(3), 1472–1482. https://doi.org/S1053-8119(06)00491-5 [pii];10.1016/j.neuroimage.2006.04.186.

Morken, K. T. E., Binder, P.-E., Arefjord, N. M., & Karterud, S. W. (2019). Mentalization-based treatment from the patients' perspective – what ingredients do they emphasize? *Front Psychol, 10*. https://doi.org/10.3389/fpsyg.2019.01327.

Nagy, E. (2011). The newborn infant: a missing stage in developmental psychology. *Infant Child Dev, 20*(1), 3–19.

Nashef, A. (2020). Autismus und Autismustherapie in Zeiten von Corona: eine Chance? *Psychopraxis Neuropraxis*, 1–4. https://doi.org/10.1007/s00739-020-00641-9.

Nemiah, J. C., & Sifneos, P. E. (1970). Psychosomatic illness: a problem in communication. *Psychother Psychosom, 18*(1), 154–160. www.ncbi.nlm.nih.gov/pubmed/5520658.

Neumann, E., Sattel, H., Gündel, H., Henningsen, P., & Kruse, J. (2015). Attachment in romantic relationships and somatization. *J Nerv Ment Dis, 203*(2), 101–106. https://doi.org/10.1097/NMD.0000000000000241.

Nickel, K., Maier, S., Endres, D., Joos, A., Maier, V., Tebartz van Elst, L., & Zeeck, A. (2019). Systematic review: overlap between eating, autism spectrum, and attention-deficit/hyperactivity disorder. *Front Psychiatry, 10*, 708. https://doi.org/doi: 10.3389/fpsyt.2019.00708.

Nikendei, C., Mölle, C., Fischer, K., Granov, G., Huber, J., Dinger, U., Herzog, W., Schauenburg, H., & Ehrenthal, J. C. (2020). Persönlichkeitsstruktur und Bindungsstil als Prädiktoren für die erfolgreiche Aufnahme einer ambulanten psychotherapeutischen Behandlung. *Z psychosom Med, 66*, 178–192.

Nimnuan, C., Hotopf, M., & Wessely, S. (2001). Medically unexplained symptoms: an epidemiological study in seven specialities. *J Psychosom Res, 51*(1), 361–367. https://doi.org/S0022-3999(01)00223-9.

Nitsun, M. (1996 [2014]). *The Anti-Group – Destructive Forces in the Group and Their Creative Potential*. London: Routledge.

Nonne, M. (1917). Zweiter Berichterstatter. Achte Jahresversammlung der Gesellschaft Deutscher Nervenärzte am 22. und 23. September 1916. *Dtsch Z Nervenheilkunde, 56*, 37–115.

Nonne, M. (1922). Therapeutische Erfahrungen an den Kriegsneurosen in den Jahren 1914–1918. In O. von Schjering (Hrsg.), *Handbuch der ärztlichen Erfahrungen im Weltkriege 1914/1918* (Vol. 4, pp. 102–121). Leipzig: Johann Ambrosius Barth.

Nummenmaa, L., Glerean, E., Hari, R., & Hietanen, J. K. (2014). Bodily maps of emotions. PNAS – Proceedings of the national academy of sciences of the United States of America, *111*(2), 646–651. https://doi.org/1321664111 [pii];10.1073/pnas.1321664111.

Ogden, P., & Goldstein, B. (2019). Sensorimotor psychotherapy from a distance engaging the body, creating presence, and building relationship in videoconferencing. In H. Weinberg & A. Rolnik (Eds.), *Theory and Practice of Online Therapy: Internet-delivered Interventions for Individuals, Groups, Families, and Organizations* (pp. 47–65). London: Taylor & Francis. Kindle-Version.

Ogden, T. (1988). On the dialectical structure of experience: some clinical and theoretical implications. *Contemp Psychoanal, 23*, 17–45.

Ogden, T. (1989). On the concept of an autistic-contiguous position. *Int J Psychoanal, 70*, 127–140.

Ogrodniczuk, J. S., Piper, W. E., & Joyce, A. S. (2011). Effect of alexithymia on the process and outcome of psychotherapy: a programmatic review. *Psychiatry Res, 190*(1), 43–48. https://doi.org/10.1016/j.psychres.2010.04.026.

Oppenheim, D., & Koren-Karie, N. (2013). The insightfulness assessment: measuring the internal processes underlying maternal sensitivity. *Attach Hum Dev, 15*(5–6), 545–561. https://doi.org/10.1080/14616734.2013.820901.

Orbach, S. (2003). The John Bowlby memorial lecture 2003 – Part I: there is no such thing as a body. *Br J Psychother, 20*(1), 3–15.

Otto, H. (2014 [2018]). Don't show your emotions! Emotion regulation and attachment in the Cameroonian Nso. In H. Otto & H. Keller (Eds.), *Different Faces of Attachment. Cultural Variations on a Universal Human Need*. Cambridge: Cambridge University Press.

Otto, H., & Keller, H. (Eds.). (2014 [2018]). *Different Faces of Attachment – Cultural Variations on a Universal Human Need*. Cambridge: Cambridge University Press.

Panksepp, J. (1998). *Affective Neuroscience. The Foundations of Human and Animal Emotions*. Oxford: Oxford University Press.

Panksepp, J., & Biven, L. (2012). *The Archaeology of Mind. Neuroevolutionary Origins of Human Emotions*. New York and London: W.W. Norton & Company.

Panksepp, J., & Scott, E. L. (2012). Reflections on rough and tumble play, social development, and attention-deficit hyperactivity disorders. In A. L. Meyer & T. P. Gullotta (Eds.), *Physical Activity Across the Lifespan, Issues in Children's and Families' Lives* (pp. 23–40). Springer Science+Business Media.

Paulus, M. P., & Stein, M. B. (2010). Interoception in anxiety and depression. *Brain Struct Funct, 214*(5–6), 451–463. https://doi.org/10.1007/s00429-010-0258-9.

Perepletchikova, F., Treat, T. A., & Kazdin, A. E. (2007). Treatment integrity in psychotherapy research: analysis of the studies and examination of the associated factors. *J Consult Clin Psychol, 75*(6), 829–841. https://doi.org/2007-19013-001 [pii];10.1037/0022–006X.75.6.829.

Pieh, C., Lahmann, C., von Heymann, F., Tritt, K., Loew, T., & Probst, T. (2011). Prävalenz und Komorbidität der somatoformen Störung: eine Multicenter-Studie. *Z Psychosom Med Psychother, 57*, 244–250.

Plassmann, R. (1993). Organwelten: Grundriß einer analytischen Körperpsychologie. *Psyche – Z Psychoanal, 47*, 261–282.

Plassmann, R. (2019a). *Psychotherapie der Emotionen. Die Bedeutung von Emotionen für die Entstehuung und Behandlung von Krankheiten*. Frankfurt am Main: Psychosozial-Verlag.
Plassmann, R. (2019b). Transformative Sprache. Der Anteil der Sprache am Effekt einer Deutung. *Forum der Psychoanalyse*, 35, 5–17.
Podoll, K. (1991). Der Telefonunfall – ein Beitrag zur Geschichte der traumatischen Neurosen. *Fortschr Neurol Psychhiat*, 59, 387–393.
Porter, C., Palmier-Claus, J., Branitsky, A., Mansell, W., Warwick, H., & Varese, F. (2019). Childhood adversity and borderline personality disorder: a meta-analysis. *Acta Psychiatr Scand*, 141(1), 6–20. https://doi.org/10.1111/acps.13118.
Poulsen, A. (1991). Psychodynamic, time-limited group therapy in rheumatic disease – a controlled study with special reference to alexithymia. *Psychother Psychosom*, 56(1–2), 12–23.
Pries, J. (2022). *Adhärenz in psychodynamischer Gruppenpsychotherapie*. Phil. Diss., Universität Witten/Herdecke. Witten.
Pries, J., Niecke, A., Vetter, A., & Schultz-Venrath, U. (2022). More than one way home – student raters' impressions of interventions and group processes in mentalisation based group psychotherapy and group analytic psychotherapy. *Res Psychother: Psychopathol Process Outcome*, 25, 314–326.
Pries, J., Vetter, A., Petrowski, K., & Schultz-Venrath, U. (2019). Expertenumfrage zu Interventionsarten in psychodynamischen Gruppenpsychotherapien – eine Pilotstudie. *Gruppenpsychother Gruppendynamik*, 55, 28–50.
Proust, M. (1964 [1978]). *Auf der Suche nach der verlorenen Zeit*. In *Swanns Welt* (Bd 1). Frankfurt am Main: Suhrkamp.
Purgato, M., Gastaldon, C., Papola, D., van Ommeren, M., Barbui, C., & Tol, W. A. (2018). Psychological therapies for the treatment of mental disorders in low- and middle-income countries affected by humanitarian crises. *Cochrane Database Syst Rev*, 7, CD011849. https://doi.org/10.1002/14651858.CD011849.pub2.
Quinodoz, D. (2002). *Words That Touch. A Psychoanalyst Learns to Speak*. London: Karnac.
Quinodoz, D. (2003). Words that touch. *Int J Psycho-Anal*, 84, 1469–1485.
Reddy, V. N. V. (2008). *How Infants Know Minds*. Cambridge, MA: Harvard University Press.
Reichel-Dolmatoff, E. (1997 [2001]). Vorwort. In K. Gröning (Hrsg.), *Geschminkte Haut. Eine Kulturgeschichte der Körperkunst* (2. Aufl., pp. 12–15). München: Frederking & Thaler Verlag.
Reik, T. (1976 [1948]). *Hören mit dem dritten Ohr. Die innere Erfahrung eines Psychoanalytikers*. Frankfurt am Main: Hoffmann und Campe.
Reuber, M., & Mayor, R. (2012). Recent progress in the understanding and treatment of nonepileptic seizures. *Curr Opin Psychiatry*, 25(3), 244–250. https://doi.org/10.1097/YCO.0b013e3283523db6.
Riedesser, P., & Verderber, A. (1985). *Aufrüstung der Seelen. Militärpsychologie und Militärpsychiatrie in Deutschland und Amerika*. Freiburg i.Br.: Dreisam.
Riem, M. M. E., Doedee, E., Broekhuizen-Dijksman, S. C., & Beijer, E. (2018). Attachment and medically unexplained somatic symptoms: the role of mentalization. *Psychiatry Res*, 268, 108–113. https://doi.org/10.1016/j.psychres.2018.06.056.
Ritsner, M., Ponizovsky, A., Kurs, R., & Modai, I. (2000). Somatization in an immigrant population in Israel: a community survey of prevalence, risk factors, and help-seeking behavior. *Am J Psychiatry*, 157(3), 385–392. https://doi.org/10.1176/appi.ajp.157.3.385.
Rizzolatti, G., & Sinigaglia, C. (2016). The mirror mechanism: a basic principle of brain function. *Nat Rev Neurosci*, 17(12), 757–765. https://doi.org/10.1038/nrn.2016.135.

Robinson, P., & Skarderud, F. (2019). Eating disorders. In A. W. Bateman & P. Fonagy (Eds.), *Handbook of Mentalizing in Mental Health Practice* (pp. 369–386). Washington, DC: American Psychiatric Association Publishing.

Robinson, P., Skarderud, F., & Sommerfeldt, B. (2018). *Hunger: Mentalization-Based Treatments for Eating Disorders*. Cham: Springer International Publishing.

Roenneberg, C., Hausteiner-Wiehle, C., & Henningsen, P. (2020). "Funktionelle Körperbeschwerden": Klinisch relevante Leitlinien-Empfehlungen. *Psychiatrie up2date*, *14*, 35–53.

Roenneberg, C., & Henningsen, P. (2016). Management der somatischen Belastungsstörung – Körperbeschwerden und Psyche. *NeuroTransmitter*, *27*(5), 44–49.

Roenneberg, C., Sattel, H., Schaefert, R., Henningsen, P., & Hausteiner-Wiehle, C. (2019). Clinical practice guideline: functional somatic symptoms. *Dtsch Arztebl*, *116*, 553–560.

Rosa, H. (2016). *Resonanz: Eine Soziologie der Weltbeziehung*. Frankfurt am Main: Suhrkamp.

Rosa, H. (2019). *Unverfügbarkeit* (5. Aufl.). Wien, Salzburg: Residenz Verlag.

Rosendahl, S., Sattel, H., & Lahmann, C. (2021). Effectiveness of body psychotherapy. A systematic review and meta-analysis [systematic review]. *Front Psychiatry*, *12*(1486). https://doi.org/10.3389/fpsyt.2021.709798.

Rottländer, P. (2020). *Mentalisieren mit Paaren*. Stuttgart: Klett-Cotta.

Ruesch, J. (1948). The infantile personality. *Psychosom Med*, *10*, 134–144.

Rullmann, M., Preusser, S., & Pleger, B. (2019). Prefrontal and parietal contributions to the perceptual awareness of touch. *Sci Rep*, *9*(16981). https://doi.org/10.1038/s41598-019-53637-w.

Sandler, S. A. (1947). Camptocormia, or the functional bent back. *Psychosom Med*, *9*, 197–204.

Scalabrini, A., Mucci, C., Esposito, R., Damiani, S., & Northoff, G. (2020). Dissociation as a disorder of integration – on the footsteps of Pierre Janet. *Prog Neuropsychopharmacol Biol Psychiatry*, *101*, 109928. https://doi.org/10.1016/j.pnpbp.2020.109928.

Schäfer, R., & Franz, M. (2009). Alexithymie – ein aktuelles Update aus klinischer, neurophysiologischer und entwicklungspsychologischer Sicht. *Z Med Psom*, *55*(4), 328–353.

Scharff, J. M. (2007). Psychoanalyse und inszenierende Interaktion: Gemeinsamkeiten und Unterschiede. In P. Geißler & G. Heisterkamp (Eds.), *Psychoanalyse der Lebensbewegungen. Zum körperlichen Geschehen in der psychoanalytischen Therapie. Ein Lehrbuch* (pp. 83–98). Berlin: Springer.

Scharff, J. M. (2021). *Psychoanalyse und Zwischenleiblichkeit. Klinisch-propädeutisches Seminar*. Frankfurt am Main: Brandes & Apsel.

Schauenburg, H., Dinger, U., & Buchheim, A. (2006). Bindungsmuster von Psychotherapeuten. *Z psychosom Med*, *52*(4), 358–372. https://doi.org/https://doi.org/10.13109/zptm.2006.52.4.358.

Schilder, P. (1923). *Das Körperschema. Ein Beitrag zur Lehre vom Bewusstsein des eigenen Körpers*. Berlin: Springer.

Schilder, P. (1935 [1978]). *The Image and the Appearance of the Human Body – Studies in the Constructive Energies of the Psyche*. New York: International Universities Press.

Schöndienst, M. (2002). Von einer sprachtheoretischen Idee zu einer klinisch-linguistischen Methode. Einleitende Überlegungen. *Psychother. Soz*, *4*(4), 253–270.

Schöndienst, M. (2017). Zur differenzialdiagnostischen und -therapeutischen Bedeutung diskursiver Stile bei dissoziativen versus epileptischen Patienten. In A. Eckhardt-Henn &

C. Spitzer (Eds.), *Dissoziative Bewusstseinsstörungen. Grundlagen – Klinik – Therapie* (pp. 293–309). Stuttgart: Schattauer.
Schore, A. N. (2007). *Affektregulation und die Reorganisation des Selbst*. Stuttgart: Klett-Cotta.
Schreiber-Willnow, K., & Seidler, K. (2005). Katamnestische Stabilität des Körpererlebens nach stationärer Gruppenbehandlung mit Konzentrativer Bewegungstherapie. *PPmP – Psychosomatik Psychotherapie Medizinische Psychologie, 55*(8), 370–377. https://doi.org/10.1055/s-2005-866877.
Schultz-Venrath, U. (1992 [1995]). *Ernst Simmels Psychoanalytische Klinik 'Sanatorium Schloß Tegel GmbH' (1927–1931) – Beitrag zur Wissenschaftsgeschichte einer psychoanalytischen Psychosomatik Universität Witten/Herdecke 1992. Deutsche Hochschulschriften 2081, Mikroedition*. Egelsbach, Frankfurt am Main and Washington: Hänsel-Hohenhausen.
Schultz-Venrath, U. (2021). *Mentalisieren des Körpers*. Stuttgart: Klett-Cotta.
Schultz-Venrath, U. (2022). Mentalizing Shame, Shamelessness and Fremdscham (Shame by Proxy) in Groups. In O. Badouk Epstein (Ed.), *Shame Matters: Attachment and Relational Perspectives for Psychotherapists* (pp. 90–113). London and New York: Routledge, Taylor & Francis. https://doi.org/10.4324/9781003175612-7.
Schultz-Venrath, U. (2023). Traumatic experiences – restoring mentalizing in group psychotherapies. In C. Calarasanu, U. Schultz-Venrath, & H. Messner (Eds.), *A Psychoanalytic Exploration of Social Trauma – The Inner Worlds of Outer Realities* (pp. 165–182). London: Routledge.
Schultz-Venrath, U., & Felsberger, H. (2016). *Mentalisieren in Gruppen*. Stuttgart: Klett-Cotta.
Schultz-Venrath, U., & Hermanns, L. M. (2019). Ernst Simmel oder die Psycho-Klinik der Zukunft. In A. Geisthövel & B. Hitzer (Eds.), *Auf der Suche nach einer anderen Medizin – Psychosomatik im 20. Jahrhundert* (pp. 124–132). Frankfurt am Main: Suhrkamp Taschenbuch Wissenschaft.
Schultz-Venrath, U., & Masuhr, K. F. (1993). Psychogene und nichtepileptische Anfälle. In G. Nissen (Hrsg.), *Anfallskrankheiten aus interdisziplinärer Sicht* (pp. 151–163). Bern, Stuttgart and Wien: Hans Huber.
Schur, M. (1955). Comments on the metapsychology of somatization. *Psychoanal Study Child, 10*, 119–164.
Schur, M. (1972). *Sigmund Freud. Leben und Sterben*. Frankfurt am Main: Suhrkamp.
Schwarzer, N.-H., Nolte, T., Fonagy, P., & Gingelmaier, S. (2021). Self-rated mentalizing vmediates the relationship between stress and coping in a non-clinical sample. *Psychol Rep*, 1–21. https://doi.org/10.1177/0033294121994846.
Segal, H. (1957). Notes on symbol formation. *Int J Psychoanal, 38*, 391–397.
Seiffge-Krenke, I. (2014). Identität im Wandel und therapeutische Herausforderungen. *Forum Psychoanal, 30*(1), 85–108.
Shah, P., Hall, R., Catmur, C., & Bird, G. (2016). Alexithymia, not autism, is associated with impaired interoception. *Cortex, 81*, 215–220. https://doi.org/10.1016/j.cortex.2016.03.021.
Shai, D., & Belsky, J. (2011). When words just won't do: introducing parental embodied mentalizing. *Child Dev Perspect, 5*, 173–180.
Shai, D., & Belsky, J. (2017). Parental embodied mentalizing: how the nonverbal dance between parents and infants predicts children's socio-emotional functioning. *Attach Hum Dev, 19*(2), 191–219. https://doi.org/10.1080/14616734.2016.1255653.

Shai, D., Dollberg, D., & Szepsenwol, O. (2017). The importance of parental verbal and embodied mentalizing in shaping parental experiences of stress and coparenting. *Infant Behav Dev*, *49*, 87–96. https://doi.org/10.1016/j.infbeh.2017.08.003.

Shai, D., & Fonagy, P. (2014). Beyond words: parental Embodied Mentalizing and the Parent Infant Dance. In M. Mikulincer & P. R. Shaver (Eds.), *Mechanisms of Social Connections: From Brain to Group* (pp. 185–203). Washington, DC: American Psychological Association.

Shai, D., Laor Black, A., Spencer, R., Sleed, M., Baradon, T., Nolte, T., & Fonagy, P. (2022). Trust me! Parental embodied mentalizing predicts infant cognitive and language development in longitudinal follow-up. *Front Psychol* https://doi.org/10.3389/fpsyg.2022.867134.

Shankman, S. A., Gorka, S. M., Katz, A. C., Klein, D. N., Markowitz, J. C., Arnow, B. A., Manber, R., Rothbaum, B. O., Thase, M. E., Schatzberg, A. F., Keller, M. B., Trivedi, M. H., & Kocsis, J. H. (2017). Side effects to antidepressant treatment in patients with depression and comorbid panic disorder. *J Clin Psychiatry*, *78*(4), 433–440. https://doi.org/10.4088/JCP.15m10370.

Shephard, B. (2000). *A War of Nerves. Soldiers and Psychiatrists 1914–1994*. Pimlico: Random House.

Shephard, B. (2001). *A War of Nerves: Soldiers and Psychiatrists in the Twentieth Century*. Cambridge, MA: Harvard University Press.

Sheridan, M. A., & McLaughlin, K. A. (2014). Dimensions of early experience and neural development: deprivation and threat. *Trends Cogn Sci*, *18*(11), 580–585. https://doi.org/10.1016/j.tics.2014.09.001.

Shoenfeld, Y., Shapiro, Y., Drory, Y., Glasevsky, V., Sohar, E., & Kellerman, J. J. (1978). Rehabilitation of patients with NCA (neurocirculatory asthenia) through a short term training program. *Am J Phys Med*, *57*(1), 1–8. www.ncbi.nlm.nih.gov/pubmed/637114.

Shorter, E. (1992). *From Paralysis to Fatigue. A History of Psychosomatic Illness in the Modern Era*. New York: Free Press.

Simmel, E. (1918). *Kriegsneurosen und "Psychisches Trauma". Ihre gegenseitigen Beziehungen dargestellt auf Grund psycho-analytischer, hypnotischer Studien*. Leipzig, München: Otto Nemnich.

Simmel, E. (1944). War neuroses. In S. Lorand (Ed.), *Psychoanalysis Today* (pp. 227–248). New York: International Universities Press.

Skarderud, F., & Fonagy, P. (2012). Eating disorders. In A. W. Bateman & P. Fonagy (Eds.), *Handbook of Mentalizing in Mental Health Practice* (pp. 347–383). Washington, DC: American Psychiatric Publishing, Inc.

Solms, M. (2013a). Das bewusste Es. *Psyche – Z Psychoanal*, *67*, 991–1022.

Solms, M. (2013b). Response to commentaries – the id is not the same as the unconscious . . . and other things. *Neuropsychoanalysis*, *15*(1), 79–85.

Solms, M. (2021). *The Hidden Spring – A Journey to the Source of Consciousness*. New York: Norton & Company.

Solms, M. (2022). The 'hard problem' of consciousness. In J. Mills (Ed.), *Psychoanalysis and the Mind-Body Problem* (pp. 153–185). Milton Park and New York: Routledge.

Solms, M., & Panksepp, J. (2012). The "id" knows more than the "ego" admits: neuropsychoanalytic and primal consciousness perspectives on the interface between affective and cognitive neuroscience. *Brain Sci*, *2*(2), 147–175. https://doi.org/10.3390/brainsci2020147.

Souques, M. M., & Rosanoff-Saloff, X. (1915). La camptocormie. Incurvation du tronc, consécutive aux traumatismes du dos et des lombes. Considérations morphologiques. *Rev Neurol, 27*, 937–939.

Spangler, G., & Grossmann, K. E. (1993). Biobehavioral organization in securely and insecurely attached infants. *Child Dev, 64*(5), 1439–1450. ttp://www.ncbi.nlm.nih.gov/pubmed/8222882.

Sperry, L., & Carlson, J. (2014). *How Master Therapists Work*. New York and London: Routledge, Taylor & Francis.

Spitz, R., & Wolf, K. (1946). Anaclitic depression – an inquiry into the genesis of psychiatric conditions in early childhood. *Psychoanal Study Child, 2*, 313–342.

Stahn, A., Gunga, H.-C., Kohlberg, E., Gallinat, J., Dinges, D. F., & Kühn, S. (2019). Brain changes in response to long antarctic expeditions. *N Engl J Med, 381*, 2273–2275. https://doi.org/DOI: 10.1056/NEJMc1904905.

Staun, L. (2017). *Mentalisieren bei Depressionen*. Stuttgart: Klett-Cotta.

Staun, L., & Schultz-Venrath, U. (2023). Mentalisierungsbasierte dynamische Administration. Zur Förderung epistemischen Vertrauens in psychodynamischen Gruppentherapien. *Ärztliche Psychotherapie, 18*(2), 97–102. https://doi.org/10.21706/aep-18-2-97.

Stekel, W. (1908). *Nervöse Angstzustände und ihre Behandlung* (4. Aufl.). München: Urban & Schwarzenberg.

Stekel, W. (1924). *Peculiarities of Behaviour* (Vol. 1–2). London: Williams and Norgate.

Sterling, P. (2012). Allostasis: a model of predictive regulation. *Physiol Behav, 106*(1), 5–15. https://doi.org/10.1016/j.physbeh.2011.06.004.

Stern, D. N. (1985 [1992]). *The Interpersonal World of the Infant: A View from Psychoanalysis and Developmental Psychology*. New York: Basic Books.

Stern, D. N. (2004). *The Present Moment in Psychotherapy and Everyday Life*. New York and London: Norton & Company.

Stern, D. N. (2010a). *Forms of Vitality*. Oxford: Oxford University Press.

Stern, D. N. (2010b). *Forms of Vitality: Exploring Dynamic Experience in Psychology and the Arts*. Oxford: Oxford University Press.

Stern, D. N. (2012). *Veränderungsprozesse. Ein integratives Paradigma*. Frankfurt am Main: Brandes & Apsel.

Stern, D. N., Bruschweiler-Stern, N., Lyons-Ruth, K., Morgan, A. C., Nahum, J. P., & Sander, L. W. (2010). *The Boston Change Process Study Group: Change in Psychotherapy. A Unifying Paradigm*. New York and London: Norton & Company.

Storch, M., Cantieni, B., Hüther, G., & Tschacher, W. (2010 [2011]). *Embodiment. Die Wechselwirkung von Körper und Psyche verstehen und nutzen* (2. Aufl.). Bern: Huber.

Storck, T. (2016). *Psychoanalyse und Psychosomatik. Die leiblichen Grundlagen der Psychodynamik*. Stuttgart: Kohlhammer.

Storebo, O. J., Stoffers-Winterling, J. M., Vollm, B. A., Kongerslev, M. T., Mattivi, J. T., Jorgensen, M. S., Faltinsen, E., Todorovac, A., Sales, C. P., Callesen, H. E., Lieb, K., & Simonsen, E. (2020). Psychological therapies for people with borderline personality disorder. *Cochrane Database Syst Rev, 5*, CD012955. https://doi.org/10.1002/14651858.CD012955.pub2.

Sturge-Apple, M. L., Skibo, M. A., Rogosch, F. A., Ignjatovic, Z., & Heinzelman, W. (2011). The impact of allostatic load on maternal sympathovagal functioning in stressful child contexts: implications for problematic parenting. *Dev Psychopathol, 23*(3), 831–844. https://doi.org/S0954579411000332 [pii];10.1017/S0954579411000332.

Subic-Wrana, C., Thomas, W., Huber, M., & Kohle, K. (2001). Levels of emotional awareness scale (LEAS): Die deutsche Version eines neuen Alexithymietests. *Psychotherapeut*, *46*, 176–181. www.ncbi.nlm.nih.gov/pubmed/12420248.

Swiller, H. I. (1988). Alexithymia: treatment utilizing combined individual and group psychotherapy. *Int J Group Psychother*, *38*(1), 47–61. https://doi.org/10.1080/00207284.1988.11491084.

Szekely, L. (1962). Symposium: the psycho-analytic study of thinking. Meaning, meaning schemata, and body schemata in thought. *Int J Psychoanal*, *43*, 297–305. www.ncbi.nlm.nih.gov/pubmed/13979907.

Taubner, S., & Evers, O. (2022). Kann man Super-Shrinks ausbilden? Kompetenzentwicklung in der Psychotherapie. *Psychotherapie*, *67*, 400–407.

Taylor, G. J. (2003). Somatization and conversion – distinct or overlapping constructs? *J Am Acad Psychoanal*, *31*, 487–508.

te Wildt, B. T., & Schultz-Venrath, U. (2004). Magical ideation – defense mechanism or neuropathology? A study with multiple sclerosis patients. *Psychopathology*, *37*(3), 141–144. https://doi.org/10.1159/000078866.

Tebartz van Elst, L. (2016). *Autismus und ADHS: Zwischen Normvariante, Persönlichkeitsstörung und neuropsychiatrischer Krankheit*. Stuttgart: Kohlhammer.

Terasawa, Y., Oba, K., Motomura, Y., Katsunuma, R., Murakami, H., & Moriguchi, Y. (2021). Paradoxical somatic information processing for interoception and anxiety in alexithymia. *Eur J Neurosci*, *54*(11), 8052–8068. https://doi.org/10.1111/ejn.15528.

Theweleit, K. (2009 [1977/1978]). *Männerphantasien 1 + 2*. Frankfurt am Main: Stroemfeld/Piper.

Tomasello, F. (2001). *The Cultural Origins of Human Cognition*. Cambridge, MA: Harvard University Press.

Tomasello, M. (2008). *Origins of Human Communication*. Cambridge, MA and London: MIT Press.

Tomasello, M. (2018). Great apes and human development: a personal history. *Child Dev Perspect*, *12*, 189–193.

Tomasello, M. (2019). *Becoming Human. A theory of Ontogeny*. Cambridge, MA: Harvard University Press.

Tomkins, S. (1962). *Affect Imagery Consciousness: Volume I: The Positive Affects*. New York: Springer.

Travell, J., & Rinzler, S. H. (1952). The myofascial genesis of pain. *Postgrad Med*, *11*(5), 425–434. www.ncbi.nlm.nih.gov/pubmed/14920327.

Trevarthen, C. (1979). Communication and cooperation in early infancy: a description of primary intersubjectivity. In M. Bullowa (Ed.), *Before Speech: The Beginning of Interpersonel Communication* (pp. 321–347). Cambridge: Cambridge University Press.

Trevarthen, C. (1993). The self born in intersubjectivity: the psychology of infant communicating. In U. Neisser (Ed.), *The Perceived Self: Ecological and Interpersonal Sources of Knowledge*. Cambridge: Cambridge University Press.

Trevarthen, C., & Aitken, K. J. (2001). Infant intersubjectivity: research, theory, and clinical applications. *J Child Psychol Psychiatry*, *42*(1), 3–48. www.ncbi.nlm.nih.gov/pubmed/11205623.

Trimble, M. R. (1981). *Post-Traumatic Neurosis. From Railway Spine to the Whiplash*. New York: John Wiley & Sons.

Tronick, E. (1982). *Social Interchange in iInfancy. Affect, Cognition, and Communication*. Baltimore: University Park Press.

Tronick, E. (2007). *The Neurobehavioral and Social-Emotional Development of Infants and Children*. New York and London: Norton.

Tronick, E. Z., & Cohn, J. (1989). Infant mother face-to-face interaction: age and gender differences in coordination and miscoordination. *Child Development, 59*, 85–92.

Tschuschke, V., Baumbach, N., Rembold, S. M. E., Horn, E., & Tress, W. (2020). Zur Bedeutung der Gruppenleitung für therapeutische Prozesse in der Gruppe – Ergebnisse einer empirischen Studie mit somatoformen Störungsbildern. *Gruppenpsychother Gruppendynamik, 56*, 105–132.

Turkle, S. (2018). Empathy machines: forgetting the body. In V. Tsolas & C. Anzieu-Premmereur (Eds.), *A Psychoanalytic Exploration of the Body in Today's World. On the Body* (pp. 17–27). London: Routledge.

Tustin, F. (1993). On psychogenic autism. *Psychoanal Inq, 13*, 34–41.

Urbanek, M., Harvey, M., McGowan, J., & Agrawal, N. (2014). Regulation of emotions in psychogenic nonepileptic seizures. *Epilepsy Behav, 37*, 110–115. https://doi.org/10.1016/j.yebeh.2014.06.004.

Vacharkulksemsuk, T., & Fredrickson, B. L. (2012). Strangers in sync: achieving embodied rapport through shared movements. *J Exp Soc Psychol, 48*(1), 399–402. https://doi.org/10.1016/j.jesp.2011.07.015.

van der Kolk, B. A. (1994). The body keeps the score: memory and the evolving psychobiology of posttraumatic stress. *Harv Rev Psychiatry, 1*(5), 253–265. www.ncbi.nlm.nih.gov/pubmed/9384857.

van der Kolk, B. A. (1996). The body keeps the score. Approaches to the psychobiology of post traumatic stress disorder. In B. A. Van der Kolk, A. C. McFarlane, & L. Weisaeth (Eds.), *Traumatic Stress. The Effects of Overwhelming Experience on Mind, Body, and Society* (pp. 214–241). New York and London: Guilford.

van der Kolk, B. A. (2014). *The Body Keeps the Score: Mind, Brain and Body in the Transformation of Trauma*. London: Penguin Books.

van der Kolk, B. A. (2016). *Verkörperter Schrecken. Traumaspuren in Gehirn, Geist und Körper und wie man sie heilen kann* (2. Aufl.). Lichtenau: Probst Verlag.

Vanheule, S., Desmet, M., Verhaeghe, P., & Bogaerts, S. (2007). Alexithymic depression: evidence for a depression subtype? *Psychother Psychosom, 76*(5), 315–316. https://doi.org/10.1159/000104710.

Varela, F., Thompson, E., & Rosch, E. (1991 [2016]). *The Embodied Mind*. Cambridge, MA and London: MIT.

Verhaeghe, P., Vanheule, S., & De Rick, A. (2007). Actual neurosis as the underlying psychic structure of panic disorder, somatization, and somatoform disorder: an integration of Freudian and attachment perspectives. *Psychoanal Q, 76*, 1317–1350. WOS:000251178400015.

Verner, G., Epel, E., Lahti-Pulkkinen, M., Kajantie, E., Buss, C., Lin, J., Blackburn, E., Raikkonen, K., Wadhwa, P. D., & Entringer, S. (2020). Maternal psychological resilience during pregnancy and newborn telomere length: a prospective study. *Am J Psychiatry*, appiajp202019101003. https://doi.org/10.1176/appi.ajp.2020.19101003.

Vogeley, K. (2017). Two social brains: neural mechanisms of intersubjectivity. *Phil Trans R Soc B, 372*. https://doi.org/http://dx.doi.org/10.1098/rstb.2016.0245.

Volz-Boers, U. (2009). Körperempfindungen des Analytikers als Zugang zu perinataler Traumatisierung. In M. E. Ardjomandi (Ed.), *Jahrbuch für Gruppenanalyse und ihre Anwendungen – Wohin mit der Gruppenanalyse?* (Vol. 14–2008, pp. 159–169). Heidelberg: Mattes Verlag.

Volz-Boers, U. (2016). Resonanz im Körper des Analytikers. Das Konzept der sensorisch-intuitiven Haltung. In S. Walz-Pawlita, B. Unruh, & B. Janta (Eds.), *Körper-Sprachen* (pp. 141–152). Gießen: Psychosozial-Verlag.

von Weizsäcker, V. (1926). Arzt und Kranker. *Die Kreatur*, *1*, 69–86.

von Weizsäcker, V. (1940). *Der Gestaltkreis (Theorie der Einheit von Wahrnehmen und Bewegen)*. Leipzig: Thieme.

Waller, C. (2018). Umgang mit Emotionen und Störungen der Kommunikation. In J. Jünger (Hrsg.), *Ärztliche Kommunikation. Praxisbuch zum Masterplan Medizinstudium 2020* (pp. 261–266). Stuttgart: Schattauer.

Waller, E., & Scheidt, C. E. (2002). Somatoforme Störungen und Bindungstheorie. *Psychotherapeut*, *47*, 157–164. https://doi.org/DOI 10.1007/s00278-002-0226-9.

Waller, E., & Scheidt, C. E. (2006). Somatoform disorders as disorders of affect regulation: a development perspective. *Int Rev Psychiatry*, *18*(1), 13–24.

Waller, E., & Scheidt, C. E. (2008). Somatoforme Störungen und Bindungstheorie. In B. Strauß (Hrsg.), *Bindung und Psychopathologie* (pp. 144–187). Stuttgart: Klett-Cotta.

Wampold, B. E. (2015). How important are the common factors in psychotherapy? An update. *World Psychiatry*, *14*(3), 270–277. https://doi.org/10.1002/wps.20238.

Weinberg, H. (2021). Online group psychotherapy: challenges and possibilities during COVID-19 – a practice review. https://doi.org/10.1037/gdn0000140.

Weinberg, H., & Rolnik, A. (2020). *Theory and Practice of Online Therapy: Internet-delivered Interventions for Individuals, Groups, Families, and Organizations*. London: Routledge, Taylor & Francis.

Weir, E., Allison, C., Warrier, V., & Baron-Cohen, S. (2020). Increased prevalence of non-communicable physical health conditions among autistic adults. *Autism*, 1–14. https://doi.org/10.1177/1362361320953652.

Wichmann, B. (1934). Das vegetative Syndrom und seine Behandlung. *Dtsch med Wschr*, *60*, 1500–1504.

Williams, J. H., Whiten, A., Suddendorf, T., & Perrett, D. I. (2001). Imitation, mirror neurons and autism. *Neurosci Biobehav Rev*, *25*(4), 287–295. www.ncbi.nlm.nih.gov/pubmed/11445135.

Willis, J., & Todorov, A. (2006). First impressions: making up your mind after a 100-ms exposure to a face. *Psychol Sci*, *17*, 592–598.

Wimmer, H., & Perner, J. (1983). Beliefs about beliefs: representation and constraining function of wrong beliefs in young children's understanding of deception. *Cognition*, *13*, 103–128.

Winberg, J. (2005). Mother and newborn baby: mutual regulation of physiology and behavior – a selective review. *Dev Psychobiol*, *47*(3), 217–229. https://doi.org/10.1002/dev.20094.

Winnicott, D. W. (1949 [2014]). Mind in its relation to the psyche-soma. In D. W. Winnicott (Ed.), *Through Pediatrics to Psycho-Analysis: Collected Papers D.W. Winnicott*. (pp. 243–254). Routledge, Taylor & Francis.

Winnicott, D. W. (1952 [1958]). Anxiety associated with insecurity. In D. W. Winnicott (Ed.), *Collected Papers: Through Paediatrics to Psycho-Analysis* (pp. 97–100). London: Hogarth.

Winnicott, D. W. (1958). First year of life – modern views on the emotional development in the first year of life. *The Medical Press*, *239*, 228–231, 289–291.

Winnicott, D. W. (1960). The theory of the parent-infant relationship. *Int J Psychoanal*, *41*, 585–595.

Winnicott, D. W. (1965). Ego distortion in terms of true and alse self (1960). *Int Psychoanal Lib*, *64*, 140–152.

Winnicott, D. W. (1971). *Playing and Reality*. London: Penguin Books.
Wiseman, H., & Reuber, M. (2015). New insights into psychogenic nonepileptic seizures 2011–2014. *Seizure, 29*, 69–80. https://doi.org/10.1016/j.seizure.2015.03.008.
Wittchen, H. U., & Jacobi, F. (2005). Size and burden of mental disorders in Europe – a critical review and appraisal of 27 studies. *Eur Neuropsychopharmacol, 15*(4), 357–376. https://doi.org/S0924-977X(05)00075-1 [pii];10.1016/j.euroneuro.2005.04.012.
Wittchen, H. U., Jacobi, F., Rehm, J., Gustavsson, A., Svensson, M., Jonsson, B., Olesen, J., Allgulander, C., Alonso, J., Faravelli, C., Fratiglioni, L., Jennum, P., Lieb, R., Maercker, A., van Os, J., Preisig, M., Salvador-Carulla, L., Simon, R., & Steinhausen, H. C. (2011). The size and burden of mental disorders and other disorders of the brain in Europe 2010. *Eur Neuropsychopharmacol, 21*(9), 655–679. https://doi.org/10.1016/j.euroneuro.2011.07.018.
Wolff, J., Auber, G., Schober, T., Schwär, F., Hoffmann, K., Metzger, M., Heinzmann, A., Krüger, M., Normann, C., Gitsch, G., Südkamp, N., Reinhard, T., & Berger, T. (2017). Arbeitszeitverteilung von Ärzten in einem deutschen Universitätsklinikum. *Dtsch Arztebl Int, 117*(42), 705–117. https://doi.org/10.3238/arztebl.2017.0705.
Wöller, W., & Kruse, J. (Eds.). (2018). *Tiefenpsychologisch fundierte Psychotherapie*. Stuttgart: Schattauer.
Wu, H., Liu, X., Hagan, C. C., & Mobbs, D. (2020). Mentalizing during social inter-Action: a four component model. *Cortex, 126*, 242–252. https://doi.org/10.1016/j.cortex.2019.12.031.
Yunus, M. B. (1983). Fibromyalgia syndrome: a need for uniform classification. *J Rheumatol, 10*(6), 841–844. www.ncbi.nlm.nih.gov/pubmed/6582267.
Zahavi, D. (2007). Self and other: the limits of narrative understanding. In D. D. Hutto (Ed.), *Narrative and Understanding Persons. Royal Institute of Philosophy. Supplement 60* (pp. 179–201). Cambridge: Cambridge University Press.
Zahavi, D. (2010). Complexities of self. *Autism, 14*(5), 547–551. https://doi.org/10.1177/1362361310370040.
Zahavi, D., & Rochat, P. (2015). Empathy not equal sharing: perspectives from phenomenology and developmental psychology. *Conscious Cogn, 36*, 543–553. https://doi.org/10.1016/j.concog.2015.05.008.
Zevalkink, J., Verheugt-Pleiter, A., & Fonagy, P. (2012). Mentalization-informed child psychoanalytic psychotherapy. In A. W. Bateman & P. Fonagy (Eds.), *Handbook of Mentalizing in Mental Health Practice* (pp. 129–158). Washington, DC: American Psychiatric Publishing.
Zevalkink, J., Verheugt-Pleiter, A., & Fonagy, P. (2015). Mentalisierungsorientierte psychoanalytische Kinderpsychotherapie. In A. W. Bateman & P. Fonagy (Hrsg.), *Handbuch Mentalisieren* (pp. 159–190). Gießen: Psychosozial-Verlag.
Zipfel, S. (2018). 200 years of psychosomatic medicine – and still more timely than ever. *Front Psychiatry*. https://doi.org/https://doi.org/10.3389/fpsyt.2018.00674.

Index

Note: Page numbers in *italics* indicate a figure and page numbers in **bold** indicate a table on the corresponding page. Page numbers followed by "n" with numbers refer to notes.

Abraham, Karl 104
"akust." (acoustic) *vs.* acoustic-sensory interaction experience 75
actual neuroses 76–81, 85
adaptation (transformation) 7, 39, 84
adults: adult attachment style 35; attention and memory faculties 27; borderline personality disorder 143; conversion and dissociative disorders 143; extreme emotional deprivation 12; feeling anger 13; male ASD adults 94; mental disorders, sexually abused 8; mimicry and facial expressions 112; nonverbal affective system 14
affects/affective 8; agnosia 91; attunement processes 129; bodily experiences 6; contagion 102; drive system 18; focused inquiry 64; physical symptoms 99; regulation **57**, 85
Ainsworth, Mary 31
Aisenstein, Marilia 66
Alexander, Franz 3, 29, 75, 81, 85, 86
Alexis Zorbas 80
alexithymia 90–94
alloparenting methods 37
allostasis 39, **39**, 118; "allostatic load" 39
American Civil War 103
anamnesis technique 60, 64, 65, 66; associative anamnesis 62
anger 17; expression of 123; feeding stimuli 28; mirroring sexual excitement 19; physiological change 3; regulate relationships 14; rigidity and feelings of 47

animated body 43, 44
Anna Freud Centre (London) website 157
antisemitism 105
antisocial personality disorders 5, 45
anxiety disorders 3, 34, 52, 60, 99, 103; anxiety neurosis 76; pseudo-neurological complaints *78*; psychophysiological theory of 76
Anzieu, Didier 21, 26, 113, 114
Aron, Lewis 77
"atmosphere"/ "shared affect" 147
attachment: behavior 12, 33; deactivation 118, 122; relationships 32, 37; representation 11, 32, 33, *36*, 58, 162; security 34, 114, 117; styles and behaviors 9, 34, **35**, *36*, 125; traumatic relationships 96
attachment theory 37, 115
attention regulation **57**
Auster, Paul 35
autism spectrum condition (ASC) 146
autism spectrum disorder (ASD) 31, 48, 64, 71, 73, 90, 112
autistic-contiguous organization 134
automatic regulatory system 107
automatic (implicit) *vs.* controlled (explicit) 127
autonomic body 86, 108
autonomic nervous system 81, 83, 85

balance (vestibular sense) 10
Barsky, Arthur 50
basis affect systems 15
Bateman, Anthony W. 43, 45, 117, 143
behavioral systems 1, 106, 110, 129

Belsky, Jay 23, 116
Bernhard, Thomas 119
biochemical etiology 79
biologistic reductionism 101
bio-psycho-social model 4, 11, 95
Birksted-Breen, Dana 126
Biven, Lucy 17, 18
blood cell disease 125
Bodily Distress Disorders (BDD) 97
body 8, 43; attachment concept 41; complaint syndromes 60, 100; cultural embeddedness of 46; dissatisfaction 105; dysmorphic disorders 132, 135; empathy 125; equivalence mode 139–141; feelings 150; inner body 108; intercourse 107; language 1, 81; memory traces 60; in mentalization model 40, **57**; in online video therapies 70; outer body 108; perceptions 2; personality disorders 45; Platonic second-world theory of 120; pretend mode 141–142; proto-mental constitution 150; in psychoanalysis 6; psychoanalytic problem 132; psychotherapy 41; sensations 75; and somatic symptom disorders 54; symptoms 30, 43; teleological mode 138–139; *see also individual entries*
body-having mode 131–132
body-image 9, 106, 107, 111; intercourse 134; nucleus 84; transfer mechanism 107
body-mind therapeutic approaches 6, 98
body mirrors 11
body-mode 103, 120, 124; age of intercorporeality 121; clinical examples 133–138; definition of 131, **133**; as earliest mode 131; embodied mentalizing 117; function of 134; as mass phenomenon 102; mentalization 129; teleological mode 132
body-oriented special therapies/body-related therapies 149, 151
body-related signals 65
body scheme 9, 106
body self (corporality) 15, 38, 43, 111; on body-mode 73; development of 10, 15, 76; intersubjective developmental conditions 113; matrix-like network 38; phantasmatic drive-body 43; psychosis patients 93
"bodyworld" 44
borderline personality disorders 4, 26, 139, 143: concept 19; experiences 111
Bowlby, John 31, 37, 41
brain: affective self, development of 8; brain-man 74; brainstem mechanisms 108; communication 27; emotional brain 118; gyrus dentatus 13; interbrain synchrony 110; mechanisms 107; outer body and inner body 108; oxytocin level 12; prenatal development 61; primary process 15; secondary process 15; special skin-to-brain 8; structural-functional dynamics 127; synaptic and dendritic connections 12; tactile sensations 8–9; temporal-spatial structure of 83; tertiary process 15
brainstem mechanisms 108
breathing therapy 149
Brentano, Franz 13, 44
Brown, Dennis Geoffrey 3, 9
Bruch, Hilde 133
Bucci, Wilma 15
buggy technology (in online sessions) 72

Campbell, C. 41, 55
camptocormia 59, 103
CARE (loving caretaking behavior) **17**, 17–18
caregivers 23, 33, 111–112, 130
Cartesian body-soul and drive dualism 43, 75
c-fibers 8
child/childhood: affective expressions 37; bodily interactions 38; childish emotions 10; cultural ideal 38; emotional and sexual abuse 12; internal bodily 35; internal mental states 119; negative emotional expressions 23; neurotoxic cortisol system 39; psyche 28; rigidity and anxiety 39
child–parent(s) interaction 32
chronic fatigue syndrome (CFS) 101
chronic stress disorders 84
chronic vomiting 54
Ciaunica, Anna 22, 117
"classical" psychosomatic disorders 85
Cochrane meta-analysis 143
cognitive-behavioral therapy (CBT) 143

cognitive developmental model 29, 94, 105
cognitive (explicit) mentalization 5, 42
cognitive neurosciences 17, 120
cognitive psychology 4, 27
Cole, Eleanor J. 146
common feeling *(sensus communis)* 9
common-sense model 70
communication 27; problem of 91; technology 72
community 38, 79
compartment mentalization symptoms 82
complex traumatic development with somatization *12*
concentrative movement therapy 149
conscious mental states 2, 30, 82
conspiracy theories/conspiracy beliefs 55, 141
contingent attachment style 37; *see also* attachment theory
contrary-move interactions 128, 152
conversion: concept of 80, 81, 86; disorder 54; and dissociative disorders 143; hysteria 81; model 76–77; *vs.* organ neuroses 54; *vs.* vegetative neuroses 54
coping strategy 103
Corning, James Leonard 2–3
corporeality 120, 133
countertransference concept 125, 126
Covid-19 pandemic 9, 55, 70
credulity 55
Cremerius, Johannes 64
cultural system, body as part of 42
culture-bound syndromes 61
"culture of forgetting" 71

Da Costa, Jacob Medes 103; syndrome 103
Damasio, Antonio R. 14, 16, 18, 107
dance therapy 149
Darwin, Charles R. 16, 129, 130
dementalization 9, 31, 92
Dennett, Daniel C. 43
depersonalization 5, 68
desomatization idea 81, 108
Deutsch, Felix 40, 62, 75, 81
developmental psychology 14, 16, 27, 120; erogenous zones model 6–7; object constancy 94; pre-mentalizing modes 120; primary intersubjectivity 121; psychic activity 141; self-object differentiation 94; structure notion 122; WEIRD psychology 37
Diagnostic and Statistical Manual of Mental Disorders (DSM-5) 95, 97, 98
diagnostic dilemma 95
diagnostic expression 54
dialectical-behavioral (DBT) 143
Diez Grieser, Maria Teresa 10, 57, 131
dimensions of mentalization 126–128; *contrary move* employment 148, 154; psychoeducational modules 157; sensory 153; unconscious 158
disembodiment concept 71, 72
dissociation concept 82
dissociative disorders 84, 101
DNA methylation pattern 33
doctor/therapist–patient relationship 51, *51*, 53
dorsal medial prefrontal cortex (dmPFC) 146
dorsolateral prefrontal cortex (DLPFC) 13
Down syndrome 112
drive: affect-drive system 18–19; attachment as drive 37; Cartesian body-soul and drive dualism, inability of psychoanalytical theory to resolve 75; competitive drive in "Type A behavior" 43; drive model, interaction between body/soul 77; Freud, drive as border between mental and somatic 6; "phantasmatic drive-body" 43; Pierre Marty, first mentalization concepts based on Freud's drive concept 88–90; Stern, "core self" 14; teleological model and drive quality 139
dyadic attachment 105
dynamic balance, of four dimensions 127
disembodiment/dysembodiment 7, 71, 72

eating disorders 48, 133, 154
Eckhardt-Henn, Annegret 84
"effort syndrome" *see* "da Costa syndrome"
ego 18, 74, 76, 106, 108
Eitingon model 163
Ekman, Paul 17
Elias, Leah J. 8
"embodied interactions" 44, 64, 74–75
embodied mentalizing/mentalization 10, 41, 117–122; definition of 106–107
embodied mind, paradigm of 106

embodied resonance 93–94
"embodied self" 113–114; *vs.* embodiment 116
embodiment, concept of 113–114
emerging adulthood 29
emotion/emotional 14, 16, 60, 67, 125; avoidance culture 92; awareness 94, 156; cognitive development 94; definition of 15; dysregulation 4; empathetic affect mirroring of 23; engagement 71; focused therapy 152; literature 15; mental and psychosomatic disorders 3; mentalization 5; physical state 26; physiological change 3; somatic feedback 12
emotional deprivation, early **12**, 12–13, 92, 137
empathy/empathic 10; ability 51; failure 68; machines 71; perception 44; principle 64; relationships 31, 53, 68; validation 58; via neural synchrony 110
Engel, George L. 81, 85, 86
epileptology 118
epistemic mistrust 130, 135, 141, 146, 153, 158–159
epistemic trust 25, *34*, 34, 56, 58–59, 65, 105, 135
equivalence mode 30, 49, 55, 83, 118, 131; and the body 139–141; characteristics of **140**; definition of 140
"Ethics in Psychotherapy" 67
evidence-based therapy 100
evolutionary adaptability 40
explicit mentalizing **57**
The Expression of Emotions in Humans and Animals (Darwin) 16
exteroception 2, **152**
eye-tracking methods 42

face-to-face interaction 37
facial expressions: mothers', mimicking in infants 5, 109, 112–113; for microtracking in mentalizing 64; patients with borderline personality/ somatization disorders 145; in relationship with therapist 72, 144
Falk, Peter 73
fatigue 15, 43, 56, 60; *see also* chronic fatigue syndrome (CFS)
FEAR (separation distress) **17**, 17–18

fear 3, 4, 16, 24, 150, 155
feelings 1, 16, 20, 41, 64, 67, 91
Feldman, Ruth 110
Felsberger, Helga 156
Fenichel, Otto 81
Ferenczi, Sándor 75, 104
fibromyalgia syndrome (FMS) 54
fibromyalgia treatment 98
"flashlight" method 158
Fliess, Wilhelm 76
Fonagy, Peter 2, 10, 29, 41, 43, 45, 84, 117
Fotopoulou, Aikaterini 22, 40, 41, 117, 129
Foulkes, Siegmund H. 121, 157
Freud, Sigmund 5, 18, 43, 62, 64, 75, 86, 99, 146; actual neurosis 81; anxiety neurosis 80; anxiety-related symptoms 79; bodily processes 76; carcinomatous disease 76; concept of conversion 80; conversion hysteria 81; drive concept 88; ego development 18; embodied interactions 74; erogenous zones model 5–6; metaphor 65; phases theory 13; psychosomatic concepts 75; psychosomatic phenomena 77; psychosomatic relationships 75
Friston, Karl J. 111
Fromm-Reichmann, Frieda 140
Fuchs, Thomas 120
functional body complaints (FBC) 53, 95, 97, 100
functional somatic disorders 96; functional syndromes 98
functional relaxation therapy 149

Gaddini, Eugenio 115, 122
Garma, Angel 81
Gedo, John E. 81
generic language 58
Gergely, György 22, 25
Gestalt Circle 118
Global Psychopathology Severity Index 55
Glover, Edward 81
Green, André 53
Greenberg, Leslie S. 152
Groddeck, Georg 75, 81
Grosse Wiesmann, Charlotte 42
group psychotherapy 84
group therapies, mentalizing in, for SSD patients 156–161
Gubb, Karen 30, 90
guilt 17, 20, 88, 130, 156

"haemorrhagica histrionica"/ "neurologica diabolica" 135
Handbook of Mentalizing in Mental Health Practice (Bateman and Fonagy) 41, 45
happiness 4, **17**
Hausteiner-Wiehle, Constanze 136
healthcare system 52; economic pressures in 56; relationship disorder 50
health-promoting process 105
heart rate (HR) 109
heart-rate variability (HRV) 109
Hecker, Ewald 79
"hedonic tone" 14
Heidelberg School 118
Henningsen, Peter 65, 101
Hoffmann, Sven Olaf 84
holding function 71, 73
"homemade" conversational disorders 69
homeostasis 10, 39, *39*, 118
homunculus 74, 108
Hungerer, Sven 136
Husserl, Edmund 43, 44, 119, 120
hyperactivity 39, 92
hyperembodiment 127
hyperkinesia 24
hypothalamic-pituitary-adrenal cortex (HPA) axis 12, 96, 128n1
hysteria concept 81
hysterical paralysis 85

identity development 105
illness anxiety disorder 97
imaginative activity 7, 30
immature cortex 61
immune system 10
inbuilt emotional learning mechanisms 15
incompatible idea 77, 80, 81
individual stressors 39
infants: contingency relations 26; cultural ideal of 38; embodied mentalizing 117; mother–infant relationship 110; motor systems 23; nonverbal kinesthetic mode 23; parents foster epistemic trust 25; respiratory sinus arrhythmia 109; still-face episode 109; in temperament and behavior 34
inferior frontal gyrus (IFG) 146
insecure-ambivalent attachment 116
insecure-avoidant attachment styles 33, 35
Insightfulness Assessment 116
instinct *see* drive

instrument-based examinations 68
integration 28; alexithymic patients 159; of body and mind 29; body and psyche 112; mental functions 82; mentalization model 45; physical examination 62; visual and tactile stimuli 93
integrative diagnostic approach 84
intensity 11, 20, 34, 138, 156
intentionality 13, 42–44, 65, 77; concept of 43; notion of 120
"interbody" experience 121
interbrain synchronies 110
intercorporeality 44, 71, 121, 124
intercultural exchange lack 31
intermediate corporeality 133
internal working model (IWM) 31
interoception 2
The Interpretation of Dreams (Freud) 43
intersubjectivity/intersubjective 22, 121; context 9; exchange 3; psychoanalysis 121; relationship 43; self-concept 14
The Invention of Solitude (Auster) 35
irritable heart syndrome 103

jactations 24
Janet, Pierre 82
Janz, Dieter 4
Jensen, Thomas Wiben 145
joint attention/ joint intentionality 65

Kazantzakis, Nikos 80
Kestenberg, Judith S. 116
kindling model 118
kinesthesia 116
Kobylinska-Dehe, Ewa 43
Krystal, Henry 92

Lane, Richard D. 94
language: anamnesis technique 65; body *vs.* spoken 1; development of 2, 131; generic language 58; nonverbal language 114, 116; organ language 80; protolanguage 86; somatic language 63; verbal language 63, 145; vivid emotional expressions 23
language theory 65
left orbitofrontal cortex (OFC) 13
Lehtonen, Johannes 38
Leikert, Sebastian 10, 15, 74, 87, 135, 145
Leithner-Dziubas, Katharina 146

Lemma, Alessandra 6
Level of Emotional Awareness-Scale (LEAS) 94
Levy, Jonathan 110
life regulation, neuroscientific concept 14
"like-me" assumption 111
Lind, Annemette Bondo 91
linguistic methods 3
lockdown-induced online therapy 7
Loewald, Hans W. 77
Logical Investigations (Husserl) 43
Lombardi, Riccardo 145
long-term therapy 124
love 16, 46, 106
LOVE **17**, 17–18
luminary killer syndrome 51
LUST (sexual pleasure) **17**, 17–18
Luyten, Patrick 34, 84
Lyme disease 68

magical thinking/overmentalizing 54–55, 140
Main, Mary 31
malignant shame **20**, 130
Marty, Pierre 30, 87, 88, 91
mass hysterias 102
maternal activities/attitudes/behavior 12, 28
maternal attachment 146
Maternal Mind-Mindedness 116
maternal sensitivity 33–34, 37, 109, 114, 117
May, Ulrike 64
McDougall, Joyce 81, 86, 140
Meaney, Michael J. 33
Medically Unexplained (Physical) Symptoms (MU(P)S) 97
Meltzoff, Andrew N. 111, 112
memory: autonomic body memory 86; formation 87; symbol 77; systems 130–131; traces 6, 60, 100
mental apparatus 75, 77, 88
mental birth 122
mental disorders 4, 8, 38, 53, 99
mental health 11, 18, 47, 55
"Mentalisation et Psychosomatique" (Marty) 88
mentalization 2–3, 4, 21, 90; ability 41; anamnesis **63**; concept of 45, 89; definition of 43, 156; development of 105; dimensions of 126, *127*; disorders 4, 47, 78, 100; dynamic administration 159; early-childhood developmental stages 57; psychotherapy 137; theory 19

mentalization-based dynamic administration (MDA) 159
mentalization-based group psychotherapy (MBT-G) 143
mentalization-based therapy (MBT), 72, 143; interactions 155–156; MBT-G treatment goals **158**; processual approach **154**; psychotherapists 162–164; somatization disorders 144; SSD patients 156–158; therapeutic attitude and interactions **148–149**
mentalization model 4, 7, 9, 14, 29, 32, 41, 49, 55, 62, 103, 116, 129; development of 90; embodied mentalizing 118; facial expressions and voice 64; intercorporeality 44; intersubjective psychoanalysis 121; observational diagnoses 147; pioneer of 87; psychosomatic symptoms 57; relational psychoanalysis 121
mentalization-promoting technique 58, 66
mental representations 27
mental states: child's internal mental states 119; conscious and unconscious 2; higher-order psychological concepts 22; individual's awareness of 45; and insecure attachment styles 55; intentional mental states 118; somatic markers for 15–16
Mentzos, Stavros 17
Merleau-Ponty, Maurice 44, 113, 120–121, 129
Middle Ages 13
middle-class psychology 37
mimicry 7, 18, 23, 108, 112, 137
mirror-image psycho-bias 101
mirroring processes 133
mirroring sexual excitement 19
mirror neuron system (MNS) 103, 112, 113
mismatch experiences 110
misogyny 105
mistrust 55
modern post-traumatic disorders 102
Moore, M. Keith 112
mother-child interactions 11, 65
mother–child interactions 22, 23
mother–child relationship 110, 125, 134
motivation 18, 77
motivational interview 69
mRNA vaccination 55

202 Index

Müller, Roland 10, 57, 131
Munchausen syndrome 135
Murphy, William F. 62
mutual physical resonance 7
de M'Uzan, Michel 91
myalgic encephalomyelitis (ME) 101

narcissistic personality disorder 69
negative childhood experiences *12*
negative mismatch experience 110
neighborly love 16
Nemiah, John C. 91
nervous system 10–11
neural development, dimensions of *12*
neural mentalization system (MENT) 113
neural system 108, 112
neurasthenic symptoms 80
neurobiological affect systems 17
neurobiological reductionism 43
neurocognitive development 32
neurologica diabolica 135
neurosciences 4
neurotypical healthy individuals 94
nonepileptic seizure 137
nonspecific functional bodily complaints 52
nonverbal interactions 64
nonverbal perspective 42
NURSE scheme 62, **63**

object constancy 94
observational diagnoses 147
obsessive compulsion disorder (OCD) 103, 104n3
Ogden, Thomas 24, 134
olfactory system 27
online video therapies 70
operative thinking *(pensée opératoire)* 30, 91
optimal parenting 37
organ neuroses 75, 81
organ-object imagery 116
otoneurological health disorders 102
Otto, Hiltrud 37
oxytocin system 12, 106

pain (nociception) 10, 11, 13, 43, 60
pain neurosis 76
PANIC (separation distress) **17**, 17–18
panic disorder 11, 100
Panksepp, Jaak 15, 17, 18, 48n3
panpsychism 54, 75

paralysis: psychogenic blindness 85; seizure-like weakness and fatigue 60
parasympathetic activation 85
parasympathetic autonomic nervous system 81
parental embodied mentalizing (PEM) 23, 25, 29, 114, 116
Parental Reflective Functioning 116
Paris Psychosomatic School 87, 91
paroxysmal headache 136
pathological narcissism 70
patients: attentiveness 65; with body symptoms 149; with dissociative seizures 66; feelings and emotions 67; individual linguistic characteristics of 65; motivational interview 69; narcissistic personality disorder 69; with personality disorders 145; psychogenic nonepileptic seizures 136; psychological self 145; psychological state 96; with psychosomatoses 30; semi-structured interview of 91; with somatic symptom disorders 128; with somatoform disorders 68, 140, 144; with somatoform stress disorders 145; subjective theory of illness 146; synchronous movement 67
pension neurotics 104
personality disorders 30, 43, 45
personality profiles 30
phantasmatic drive-body 43
phases theory 13
phenomenological philosophy 44
philosophical approach 7
phobic attack vertigo 99
physical-mental state 153
physical pathomechanism 98
physical stress disorders 98
physical symptoms 7, 78
physical well-being 21
physician, self-conception 65
physiological-bodily sensations 120
physiological expressions 3
physiological vocabulary 9
"pilot experience" 72
placebo-nocebo research 144
PLAY (JOY) (loving caretaking behavior) **17**, 17–18
polypragmatic treatment concept 4
posterior parietal lobe 8

post-traumatic stress disorders 84, 102, 103
predisposing factors 96
prefrontal cortex 8
pregenital sexuality 140
pre-mentalizing body-mode 10, 94, 130–131, *131*; equivalence mode 83; of implicit-automatic dimension 139
pre- and perinatal traumatizations 61, 123
preoedipal developmental disorders 86
preoperational thinking 55
pretend mode 118, 141–142; characteristics of **141**; definition of **133**
primarily stress-regulatory disorders 95
primary affect system taxonomy **17**
primary attachment relationship 26
primary caregiver(s) 8
primary intersubjectivity 121
primary processes 15, 18
primitive tactile-proprioceptive perception system 28
procedural memory 5
property theory 120
proprioception 2, 10, 25, 93, **152**
"prostheses" 47
"proto-conversational" contingency structure 22
protolanguage 36, 86
proto-mental constitution 150
proto-self, primordial feelings of 16
Proust, Marcel 118
"pruning" **12**, 123
pseudo-independence 35
psyche 5, 11, 77, 119; *see also individual entries*
psychoanalysis 29; body and soul in 6; body *vs.* body-self 43; concept of 14, 29, 82; context 64, 132; intersubjective psychoanalysis 121; mental functions in 6; mentalization-based anamnesis 64; modern psychoanalysis 114; psychosomatics 5, 86; regression model 86; relational psychoanalysis 87, 121; theory of 75; treatment 86; *see also individual entries*
psychodynamic: artifactual disorders 137; behavioral psychotherapies 162; body-therapeutic elements 104; child and adolescent psychiatry 31; concepts 82; interpretation 84; jactations 24; literature 140; mentalizing interventions 163; object constancy 94; psychosexuality 18
psychoeducational preparatory group 160
psychogenic: autism 112; blindness 85; disorders 67; infections 103; mass illnesses 102
psychogenic nonepileptic seizures (PNES) 136
psychological separation process 122
psychomotor (focal-complex) seizures 136
psychophysiological regulation 35
psychophysiology 50
psychosexual development 5, 133
psychosexuality 19
psychosis 48
"The Psychosoma and the Group" (Brown) 3
psychosomatic-holistic approach 100
psychosomatics 3, 29, 90, 124; bio-psycho-social model of 4; disorders 4, 38, 50; illness 47; medicine 3, 4, 5, 54, 55; patients 66; symptoms 87, **87**, 124
Psychosomatique et Mentalization (Marty) 30
psychosomatosis 30
psychotherapeutic scene 13
psychotherapeutic training 6, 68, 99, 154, 163
psychotherapeutic treatment 29, 31, 45, 62, 99
psychotherapy 9, 41, 50; acting-out and typical problem behaviors 153; difficult patients 41; group psychotherapy 84, 159–160; and mentalization models 40; online video psychotherapy 71; physical countertransference 6; professionalization of 163; psychosomatic medicine 55; sensorimotor psychotherapy 150; somatic symptom disorders 50; and therapeutic relationships 70; transfer-focused psychotherapy 143; via WhatsApp message 148

racism 105
RAGE **17**, 17–18;
"railway spine" syndrome 102
Rangell, Leo 81
Raynaud's disease 86
real-life interaction analysis 145

Reflective Function Scale (RFS) 146
refugee asylum-seekers 57
relationship-oriented therapy 52
representation theory 31
resistance to psychotherapy 153
resomatization 81
respiratory sinus arrhythmia (RSA) 109
rheumatoid arthritis 101
rhythmic neurophysiological processes 38
rhythmic swaying movements 24
Rizzolatti, Giacomo 146
Robinson, Paul 133
Rolnik, Arnon 72
Romanian orphans 12, 92

Scharff, Jörg 15, 164
Schilder, Paul 106, 111, 134, 142
Schmale, Arthur M. 85, 86
Schöndienst, Martin 65
Schultz-Venrath, Ulrich 131, 156
Schur, Max 81
Schwartz, Gary E. 94
secondary process 15
SEEKING (general motivational and exploratory system) **17**, 17–18
Segal, Hanna 141
seizure-like anxiety disorders 65
self-destructive behavior 33
self-efficacy (feedback) 7
self-embodiment 93
self-evidencing 111
self-experience 163
self-harming sexual practices 125
self-injurious behavior 46
self-object differentiation 94
sensorimotor psychotherapy 150
sensory/sensual: behavior 89; competencies 10; experiences 1, 134; motor body 108; perception 111; perceptual system 85; physical perceptions 1; self 10; stimuli 27
sexual drives, nonsatisfaction of 80
sexual receptivity 8
Shai, Dana 23, 116
shame 129, 130; dimensions of **20**; intentionality of 130
shared presentation system 112
shell shock symptoms 103
Sifneos, Peter E. 91
Simmel, Ernst 75
simulation theory 2
Sjögren's syndrome 101

Skarderud, Finn 10, 133
skin-based phenomena 46
skin conductance (SC) 109
"Skin-Ego" idea 21, 113, 114, 134
Smadja, Claude 66
social: assessment system 113; belongingness 12; biofeedback 24, 25; class problems 12; culture 121; emotional response capacity 17, 32; evolutionary communicative model *34*; exclusion 124; interactions 32; reference system 129; self-regulation 154; sense 42; structures 2; support 12
social and physical distancing 9
sociocultural context 122
sociocultural factors 105
sociocultural mass phenomenon 102
"soldier's heart syndrome" *see* "da Costa syndrome"
Solms, Mark 15, 108
somatic diseases: psychic aspects of 86; and psychosomatic disorders 12; somatic accommodation 101
somatic etiology 70
somatic narration method 145
somatic stress disorder (SSD) 95, 97, 151
somatic symptom disorders (SSD) 3, 4, 5, 33, 35, 48, 50, 69, 91, 144; body-having and body-being modes 131; diagnostic perspective 53; group therapies for 156–161; MBT-G treatment goals for **158**; MBT psychoeducation 157; as organic diseases 55; physician–patient interaction *51*; symptoms of 61; traumatic experiences 61; vulnerability model for *36*
somatization 43, 80, 81; concept 78; disorders 3, 84
somatoform diagnoses 79
somatoform (psychogenic) pain 60
somatoform stress disorders 68, 102, 145; concept and meaning of 85; mentalization, dimensions of 126; symptoms 95
somatophilia 78
somatophilic alibi diagnoses 99, 100
somatopsychic etiology 95
somatosensory cortex 8
soul: processual version of 44; in psychoanalysis 6; soul blindness 91

Sperling, Melitta 81
spoken language 1, 64
status epilepticus 138
status pseudoepilepticus (SPE) 136
Stekel, Wilhelm 80, 81
Stern, Daniel 14, 15, 26, 44
still-face experiment 109
Strange Situation Test 32
stress-modulating systems 96
stress system 12
Subic-Wrana, Claudia 94
superior temporal sulcus (STS) 110
surgery addiction 132
Swiller, Hillel I. 160
"symbiotic" communication 121
symbolic activity 92
symptomatology 52, 59, 64, 139
symptom clusters 84
synchrony: biological, between mother and child 106; desynchrony 106; phenomenon, between infant and primary other 109–113
Szekely, Lajos 6
Szyf, Moshe 33

"tacked-on" fibromyalgia syndrome 101
Takotsubo syndrome 100
"tangential associations" 30
Target, Mary 117
"technical neutrality" 68
teleological mode 55, 118, 132, 138–139; characteristics of **139**; definitions of **133**
telephone phobia 102
telephone therapy 73
temperature (thermoreception) 10
theory of mind (TOM) 27, 48
therapeutic relationship 3
time-grid structure 128
time pathologies 115
touching (sub)culture 9
touch (affection) 7, 8–9, 21, 24, 26, 93–94, 117
touched, therapists by patients 153
traditional "either-or" approaches 96
training analysis/therapy 6
transfer-focused psychotherapy (TFP) 143
transitional phenomena 24
trauma neglect in diagnostic categories 95, 98
traumatic neuroses 102
trauma research 29

trauma as a transdiagnostic affect-regulation disorder 82–87
traumatic emptiness 47
traumatic experiences 123–124, 139; alexithymia/autism spectrum disorder (ASD) 90–95; early 61, 96, 136, 151; narrating through metaphors 60; resomatization 9
Tronick, Ed 109, 110
trust 12, 160
Tsakiris, Manos 40, 41, 129
"Type A behavior" 43

unavailability 7
uncertain-anxious attachment style 35
unconscious mental states 2, 14, 16, 20, 51, 63–65, 107–108, 132, 136
Unoka, Zsolt 22
unrealistic treatment expectations 50

Valentin, Karl 49
van der Kolk, Bessel 84
Varela, Francisco J. 118
vegetative dystonia 99, vegetative neuroses 81, 85
video-based initial interviews 164
video-online therapies 71
violence 105
visual deprivation, early 32, 92
virtual body-to-body communication 72
virtual communication 71
vitality, types of 44, 108–109
Volz-Boers, Ulla 15
vomiting neurosis 54
von Weizsäcker, Viktor 4, 118

Watson, John S. 25
Weinberg, Haim 72
WEIRD (white, educated, industrialized, rich, democratic) psychology 37
Weiss, Edward 5
Western culture 16–17; sensitive responsiveness 37
"whiplash injury" 102
"white relationship" (empty relationship) 30
Wichmann, Bernd 99
Winnicott, Donald W. 11, 21, 71, 116, 119, 155
World War I 54, 102, 103
World War II 102

Zahavi, D. 22

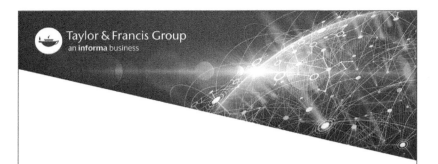

Taylor & Francis eBooks

www.taylorfrancis.com

A single destination for eBooks from Taylor & Francis with increased functionality and an improved user experience to meet the needs of our customers.

90,000+ eBooks of award-winning academic content in Humanities, Social Science, Science, Technology, Engineering, and Medical written by a global network of editors and authors.

TAYLOR & FRANCIS EBOOKS OFFERS:

A streamlined experience for our library customers

A single point of discovery for all of our eBook content

Improved search and discovery of content at both book and chapter level

REQUEST A FREE TRIAL
support@taylorfrancis.com